MANAGING UNCERTAINTY IN ORGANIZATIONAL COMMUNICATION

MANAGING UNCERTAINTY
IN ORGANIZATIONAL
COMMUNICATION

Michael W. Kramer
University of Missouri-Columbia

2004

LAWRENCE ERLBAUM ASSOCIATES, PUBLISHERS
Mahwah, New Jersey   London

Copyright © 2004 by Lawrence Erlbaum Associates, Inc.
All rights reserved. No part of this book may be reproduced in any
form, by photostat, microfilm, retrieval system, or any other means,
without prior written permission of the publisher.

Lawrence Erlbaum Associates, Inc., Publishers
10 Industrial Avenue
Mahwah, NJ 07430

Cover design by Sean Sciarrone

Library of Congress Cataloging-in-Publication Data

Kramer, Michael W.
    Managing uncertainty in organizational communication / Michael W.
    Kramer.
        p. cm. — (LEA's communication series)
    Includes bibliographical references and index.
    ISBN 0-8058-4920-3 (alk. Paper)
        1. Communication in organizations. 2. Uncertainty (Information the-
    ory)   I. Title.   II. Series.

HD30.3.K7 2004
658.4′5—dc21   2003061663
                                                            CIP

Books published by Lawrence Erlbaum Associates are printed on acid-free
paper, and their bindings are chosen for strength and durability.

Printed in the United States of America
10 9 8 7 6 5 4 3 2 1

To students

Contents

Preface

My sense of prefaces and acknowledgments in books is that we respond to them like we do to many of the Academy Award acceptance speeches. We usually consider them too long and frequently ignore them as a result. Therefore, I will be brief.

I began the process of developing this model of managing uncertainty by scribbling some notes on the back of a conference paper (notes that I still have) while being inattentive to another presenter. I am not sure what inspired me; it was not the other presenter. Some credit for my initial thoughts should go to Petty and Cacioppo (1981) for their elaboration likelihood model of persuasion. In the same way that they argue that there is more than one path to persuasion, I felt that there is also more than one way that people manage uncertainty. Bob McPhee's announcement of the Arizona State University Organizational Communication Prize Lecture Conference motivated me to turn those brief notes into a manuscript. This eventually led to the development of a tentative model of motivation to reduce uncertainty that I presented and that was later published (Kramer, 1999). Positive response to it led me to pursue writing this volume.

The model that is presented in chapter 4 represents some of the many ways that people respond to uncertainty in their lives. It attempts to demonstrate some of the complexity of issues involved in organizational communication. The model should be viewed as a model in progress that will need to be changed as new research and insights build on it. The studies I conducted as part of this volume have already modified the model. It is my hope that it will assist readers in understanding and researching this important topic more thoroughly so that additional changes can be suggested.

ACKNOWLEDGMENTS

I will not attempt to thank all of the people who encouraged me to write this or influenced my thinking about the topic. Instead I will focus on a few key individuals. Certainly my department chair, Pam Benoit, provided me with a great deal of support to begin the project and also to complete it, including reading drafts of early chapters of the manuscript. Fred Jablin, my PhD advisor, not only helped me learn to become a researcher and scholar, but also gave specific suggestions about the early model that helped me develop it further and transform it into a book-length manuscript. My father, Howard Kramer, not only helped me develop into the person that I am (my mother Valerie Kramer helped here, too), but also proofread some of the chapters before I submitted the manuscript for approval. Charles Berger responded encouragingly to my ideas even though I criticize some of his work; I hope I respond as graciously to criticism of the work I present here when it inevitably comes. John Couper carefully read the earlier article and gave me some ideas that have been incorporated into this manuscript. A chance conversation with Anne Nicotera at a conference led me to Lawrence Erlbaum Associates, Publishers, and to Linda Bathgate as an editor. It has been a pleasure to work with Linda and the rest of the LEA staff throughout the process. And of course, Carla, my wife, allowed me the time and encouraged me to complete the writing process and listened to me discuss my ideas and research. Without her support, it would have been impossible.

Some individuals include thanking God for their talents and blessings in their Academy Award acceptance speeches. If you know me well, that goes without saying.

CHAPTER ONE

Introduction and Rationale

It was with a great deal of uncertainty that people all over the world faced the beginning of the millennium a number of years ago. Would computers fail, causing worldwide disasters due to the Y2K bug? Would there be water and food shortages? Would utilities fail to function, leaving millions without electricity or heat? Would international air-traffic systems fail, causing air-traffic controllers to be unable to assist pilots who were in the air? Would terrorists seize the moment to create chaos through acts of violence?

The city of Seattle scaled back or cancelled many of its planned celebrations due to fear that terrorists might enter the United States from Canada and disrupt their celebrations. However, most major cities around the world went ahead with their celebrations as planned although with tighter security than for most previous New Year's celebrations. Reports circulated that in New York the manhole covers were welded shut around Times Square to prevent terrorists from attacking the crowd from the sewers.

Some individuals, fearing that life as we know it would come to an end, responded with a bunker mentality; they stockpiled food, water, seeds, and weapons in secure locations. Some withdrew much or all of their money from financial institutions. And yet, although a few people responded in what can now be accurately judged as extreme and unnecessary ways, the vast majority of Americans did little or nothing to prepare. A Gallup poll reported in *U.S. News and World Report* indicated that 55% of Americans planned to do nothing special; the remaining 45% planned to do at least one thing, such as stockpile food or water (Cannon & Cohen, 1999).

Like most people, I personally planned to do practically nothing special in preparation for the new millennium. I did change the dates on my Windows operating systems from showing two-digit years to four-digit years; this was supposed to make my computers Y2K (for Year 2000 or 2K) compliant. I probably made an extra effort to make sure the cupboards and refrigerator were not bare, although we usually have enough food on hand to last a couple of weeks, except for a few staples like bread and milk. Previous experience had taught me that people sometimes plundered grocery stores in anticipation of winter storms, resulting in spot shortages of certain perishable goods. Although such shortages were unnecessary, they were real if you wanted to buy bread and the only items on the shelf were the expensive, novelty breads that your children would not eat. I was satisfied that I was more than prepared.

When I stopped in at my regular grocery store for milk, eggs, and a movie late in the evening on December 30, 1999, and found that they were out of milk, I began to wonder if I had made the right choice. I considered making a run to another store in town, but decided to wait until the next day because we still had enough milk for a couple of days. I decided I would wait until the next day to consider panicking. I was quite relieved when I returned the movie the next day (December 31, 1999) to find that the milk shortage was temporary. The shelves were well stocked with milk and everything else I needed. I proceeded to bring in the New Year and New Millennium without any further preparation.

Across the world, the New Millennium was brought in with great fanfare and no significant problems. The celebration planned in our community came off without a hitch except for a few fireworks that went in a more horizontal than vertical direction.

Why did people respond so differently to the same situation? Why did the uncertainty of the new millennium cause some people to seek out information and carefully prepare for the worst-case scenario, while failing to motivate others to attend to even the information they stumbled across in their passive viewing of the media? Some bought seeds, wooden stoves, and water storage tanks while others failed to understand the nature of the Y2K bug. One news report indicated that at least one individual would not speak on the phone on January 1, 2000, until friends convinced her that she could not get sick from the Y2K bug by answering the phone. She thought the Y2K bug was a flu-like disease that could somehow be transferred over phone lines.

Although we do not routinely face the dawning of the new millennium and the fear of a Y2K bug, we do face uncertainty on a daily basis. "A primary challenge of human being is living in the present with the awareness of an uncertain future" (Eisenberg, 2001, p. 534). We live in an "age of uncertainty." Uncertainty seems to be increasing as the rate of change escalates due to the growing complexity and interrelatedness of our world brought on in part by technological advances (Merry, 1995). There is a great deal of uncertainty in our individual lives. Will we be able to meet our financial obligations? Will our friendships develop and last? Will we be able to continue in our jobs as long as we would like? Will our children grow up and make good choices? There is an equal or greater amount of uncertainty concerning broader social, economic, and political issues. What will the stock market do? Will there be lasting peace in the Middle East? Is global warming occurring? Will energy supplies last? Like the difference in responses to the Y2K uncertainties, we respond to daily uncertainties in a variety of ways. Some individuals simply minimize or ignore as many uncertainties as possible. Others concern themselves only with those uncertainties that directly impact them as individuals. A few take active roles in examining the broader issues that create uncertainty for our society.

Given the uncertainty of our lives and times, it is not surprising that communication scholars and social scientists have been studying the concept of uncertainty. Despite the broad range of uncertainties we can experience, much of the research has focused on uncertainty in initial interactions between strangers in interpersonal contexts. Examining initial interactions between strangers has provided significant insight into how people manage the uncertainty reduction process; however, Berger (1993) notes that there is a need to examine uncertainty reduction beyond the individual level to organizational levels, as well. Individuals in organizations and organizations as collections of individuals face a range of uncertainties. Individuals face uncertainties concerning the appropriate way to function in their organizational roles and maintain relationships. Collectively, organizational decision makers face uncertainty as they determine which new products or long-range goals to adopt.

In response to these concerns, this book focuses on how people manage the various uncertainty-producing situations they face in their organizational lives. As individual organizational members, we face uncertainty when we begin working. What is my actual job? How do I do my job effectively? Whom can I count on as a friend or coworker? Not only as newcomers do we face uncertainty; we face uncertainty throughout our organizational lives. We change positions, receive promotions, gain and lose coworkers and supervisors. Such changes produce uncertainty, as we must adapt to new people and situations. Other experiences of uncertainty occur at the group level of experience. Changes such as acquisitions, new management teams, downsizing, or growth produce uncertainty for groups of people in organizations. Other changes impact the uncertainty of the entire organization. How does our competition's new product affect our own product line? How does the growth in the global economy impact our company?

The uncertainties we experience influence our behaviors in general and our communication in particular. For example, in 1987, in order to manage uncertainty concerning their financial futures, Americans spent an estimated $100 million seeking financial advice, while the United States government spent roughly an equal amount on intelligence gathering in an attempt to gather information to manage the uncertainties of foreign governments (Berger, 1987). These amounts have no doubt increased significantly since then and continue to increase every year. Similarly, the Y2K uncertainties motivated some people to seek information and behave in atypical patterns, although they failed to motivate others. All of this communication and action designed to gather information in order to gain control and advantage over others seems primarily motivated by a desire to manage the uncertainties we experience as individuals or as members of organizations.

Uncertainty reduction as a formal theory of communication has been around for over 25 years, although its conceptual basis has a much longer history. For example, Shannon and Weaver (1949) conceptualized information as the reduction of uncertainty in their mathematical theory of communication. Uncertainty reduction as a formal communication theory attempts to explain human communication behaviors in uncertain situations. As originally conceptualized by Berger and Calabrese (1975), uncertainty reduction theory (URT) focused on explaining the individual or interpersonal communication processes. As such, URT has been applied to many dyadic situations from initial interactions (e.g., Douglas, 1990) to doctor–patient interactions (e.g., Williams & Meredith, 1984). However, one of the great contributions of URT is its heuristic value in directing attention at uncertainty in a wide variety of settings (Goldsmith, 2001). As a result of this, the URT perspective has been applied to individuals as participants of groups (e.g., Booth-Butterfield, Booth-Butterfield, & Koester, 1988) and organizations (e.g. Miller & Jablin, 1991). The influence of uncertainty in political campaigns has even been examined (Kennamer & Chaffee, 1982).

This book focuses on broadening our understanding of how people manage uncertainty in those more communal settings of groups and organizations rather than dyadic or mass communication settings. Such a focus seems warranted given the significant part of each day that most adults spend in organizational settings as employees or volunteers. Uncertainty is a fundamental human experience that must be managed through communication (Goldsmith, 2001). Given that average adults spend more time in group and organizational settings than in any other activity with the likely exception of sleeping, how they manage uncertainty in those settings is of considerable importance.

A thorough examination of how people manage uncertainty will need to go beyond URT as initially conceptualized. Part of the problem with URT as proposed by Berger and Calabrese (1975) is that it fails to account for the rather disparate responses different individuals may have to the same situations. It fails to explain, for example, why some individuals seek out all the information they can and stockpile supplies while others barely pay attention to a barrage of messages and do nothing even though they are faced with the same uncertainties about Y2K. URT also fails to account for the different communication behaviors the same individual may enact as a result of two apparently similar experiences of uncertainty. Two personal examples illustrate the point here.

Some time ago, while serving as a member of the campus Institutional Review Board (IRB), I received two mailings within a matter of hours. One was directed specifically at members of the IRB. It indicated that at our next meeting I was to be the "primary presenter" of one of the proposals. There had never been a "primary presenter" at previous IRB meetings. As a result, I experienced uncertainty; there was no clear indication of what that role was. At roughly the same time, I received a campuswide mailing stating that all faculty who intended to do research involving human subjects were being required to attend a human subjects training session. This also caused uncertainty because as a member of the IRB, I had recently gone through training for serving on the board, but not for doing research. It was not clear if these two were the same or different. I considered seeking information concerning both of these matters. If I had responded in the same manner by seeking information for both situations, then my behaviors would have been consistent with URT: the experience of uncertainty would have motivated me to seek information to reduce my uncertainty. However, I managed my uncertainty and communicated quite differently in the two similar situations.

After thinking about the first situation, I decided that assigning primary presenters was probably a way to make our meetings more efficient. The presenter would very carefully read the particular proposal in preparation for the meeting. At the meeting that person would emphasize any problem areas and the whole board could then make any additional recommendations based on their readings of the proposal. This made sense to me; I was satisfied with my explanation and did not request any information. I would have gone to the meeting prepared to do that and would have paid close attention during the early part of the meeting to see if the other primary presenters behaved in the way I expected. I would have made adjustments based on what I observed. As long as I read the proposal carefully, I could manage my uncertainty. Although I had managed my uncertainty to my satisfaction, apparently one of my colleagues on the board experienced enough uncertainty to ask about the primary reviewer role, because about 2 days later, just before the meeting, I received another memo from the IRB compliance officer explaining the presenter role. The explanation was exactly what I had expected. The memo confirmed that I had reduced uncertainty correctly on my own without seeking information.

The issue of training continued to bother me. I felt that being trained as a member of the IRB *should* count as research training, but I was not convinced that it *did* count. I was particularly concerned because our IRB had been extremely cautious lately because a number of universities had temporarily lost their ability to use human subjects for research due to IRB problems. This extra caution could mean that training to do research and training as an IRB member were two different activities because they were probably covered by different IRB regulations. The more I considered these issues the less certain I was about my need for training. I finally sent an e-mail to the compliance officer. She informed me that I needed to attend the training.

As these two examples illustrate, although in both cases I experienced uncertainty as a member of my organization, I managed the uncertainty in two very different manners. In the first situation, I searched my own thoughts and developed an explanation that reduced uncertainty without seeking any additional information. Even though I was generally satisfied with my conclusion, I continued to monitor for some information to confirm my assumptions. That information eventually came. In the second situation, I was unable to reduce uncertainty sufficiently on my own, and so I sought additional information. As originally conceptualized or later modified, URT fails to explain the complexity of my behaviors in these two situations.

As initially proposed, URT seemed to have a variety of these types of problems. Given these kinds of concerns, it was not surprising that there were numerous studies conducted since 1976 to test URT. The flurry of scholarship in the late 1980s both attacked and defended the theory. Some researchers sought to make adjustments to the theory whereas others offered alternative theories, while basically discarding URT. Still others found support for various aspects of the theory. Overall, the research suggests the need to reconsider URT. Berger (1986) wrote, "Scientific theories are constructed to be modified or discarded rather than accepted as dogma" (p. 34). It is in the spirit of such inquiry that the remainder of this book is written.

In addition to conceptual issues, another area of concern with most research on uncertainty reduction is that it illustrates just one level of uncertainty an individual may experience as a member of a group or organization: the individual level of experience or analysis. This level of analysis focuses on uncertainty encountered in interpersonal interactions with peers, supervisors, subordinates, customers, and clients as part of our organizational experiences. It includes studies of newcomers and transferees personally experiencing uncertainty as they adapt to new jobs (Kramer, 1994). Although these individual experiences with uncertainty are important, other experiences with uncertainty are more communal experiences.

A second level of analysis needs to examine group experiences of uncertainty. As a group assigned to a task force to revise policies, we may collectively be uncertain as to the extent of our responsibilities and power. When we are assigned a new department head, we collectively experience uncertainty about our new supervisor. Uncertainty reduction in these situations involves a group process of communication.

A third level of analysis concerns organizational experiences with uncertainty. An unstable environment creates uncertainty that impacts organizational strategy. Although the individuals ultimately are involved in making decisions, the uncertainty created or reduced has organizationwide implications on individuals throughout the organization and beyond. For example, an entire organization is influenced by the uncertainty created when a disaster like the Exxon Valdez oil spill occurs. The Challenger and Columbia space shuttle disasters created uncertainty not only within NASA, but also for numerous organizations involved in the construction of space shuttles, as well as government agencies involved in funding the program and the general public. Initially, there was uncertainty about the loss of life in the explosions, followed by uncertainty about the causes of the crashes, and about the continuation of the space program, among other issues. Given the large numbers of people impacted by the uncertainty of such events, reducing uncertainty involves more than the individual interaction concerns of most previous research. It involves decision makers at all levels of the organization and has implications for various internal and external organizational audiences.

With this in mind, this volume is designed to accomplish a number of goals. The first goal is to examine the major research conducted using URT, particularly in the communication field, but including research in other related social science fields. The second goal is to propose a reconceptualization of URT that applies it more specifically to organizational settings while addressing some of the problems identified in previous research. This includes proposing a new model for a theory of managing uncertainty (TMU). The proposed model focuses on explicating the multiple methods people can use for managing uncertainty including cognitive processes that do not involve information seeking, as well as various direct and indirect communication behaviors for gaining information. The model also examines how multiple motives explain the presence or absence of communication behaviors designed to seek information. The third goal is to present some initial findings from three new studies that confirm the new TMU model.

To accomplish these goals, the book is organized in the following pattern. First, it presents URT theory as conceptualized by Berger and Calabrese (1975) and further developed in Berger's subsequent writings. A review of most of the significant research at the individual or dyadic level of analysis follows. The criticisms of URT are explicated, as well. Next, research that explicitly or implicitly uses URT at group and organizational level is presented. Then, based on previous research, a reconceptualization of URT is presented as a theory of managing uncertainty (TMU). After developing this new framework, some new research supportive of TMU is presented. In an effort to broaden the application of TMU, qualitative, quantitative, and textual analyses are each used. Finally, implications and recommendations for future research are presented.

As I began this project, I faced a great deal of uncertainty about the process and the chance for successful completion. At times, I consulted those around me. I dismissed some information, but was motivated by other information to make changes. At other times, I worked on my own despite uncertainties. I was managing uncertainty using many of the principles discussed in the following chapters. It is my hope that the resulting effort will reduce uncertainty for you, the reader, concerning the management of uncertainty in your organizational and personal life while motivating you and others to do research that can increase our understanding of human communication in organizational settings.

CHAPTER TWO

Uncertainty Reduction Theory in Interpersonal Contexts

As initially proposed by Berger and Calabrese (1975), uncertainty reduction principles were applied to interpersonal contexts. This chapter examines the theory as it was initially developed and then later expanded. It then examines the interpersonal research based on the theory. Finally, it examines some of the criticisms leveled against URT in the interpersonal contexts. In the process, it provides a review of much of the significant body of literature on URT in the interpersonal context, while suggesting the need to make some changes in the theory.

DEFINING UNCERTAINTY AND CERTAINTY

Definitions of uncertainty in interpersonal contexts have been fairly consistent among various scholars. Definitions generally focus on lack of information related to an inability to predict some future behavior or outcome. For example, there is uncertainty in a situation to the degree that we lack knowledge concerning others and ourselves in a given situation (Berger & Calabrese, 1975). This lack of knowledge can be due to the complexity of the issues, the quality of available information, the probabilities of various outcomes, or the structure of the information (Babrow, Kasch, & Ford, 1998). The more freedom of choices or alternatives in a situation, the more uncertain it is due to the greater difficulty involved in determining the appropriate action to take (Shannon & Weaver, 1949). Uncertainty exists to the degree to which we are unable to render the environment predictable (Berger & Bradac, 1982), or to the degree to which we have difficulty in formulating probability judgments about various actions (Ford, Babrow, & Stohl, 1996). Uncertainty is related to the inability to predict or explain (Salem & Williams, 1984).

We may experience uncertainty about self, others, the relationship to others, or contextual features (Brashers, 2001). These types of uncertainty may exist for a variety of reasons. For example, we may experience uncertainty due to a lack of information, due to the complexity of the information, due to questions about the quality of the information, due to an inability to structure the infor-mation in a meaningful way, or due to the inability to associate information with other information (Babrow, 2001b). Equally attractive alternatives, and valuing information differently can also create uncertainty (Brashers, 2001). So we may feel we are unable to make predictions about a new acquaintance because we know nothing about the person, have received contradictory information, ques-tion the accuracy of the information we receive, cannot sort out the important information from the unimportant, or cannot determine how this person com-pares to others we already know.

Overall, regardless of the cause of the uncertainty, the general conceptual defi-nitions indicate that uncertainty involves a lack of specific types of information for making decisions or predictions. So, for example, I may not have the informa-tion I need to predict how a new peer at work will respond to a sarcastic remark about our organization. Due to my lack of information about this new coworker, I experience uncertainty or have difficulty deciding whether the individual will perceive such a comment positively as a good-natured, humorous remark that builds peer relationships, or negatively as an inappropriate criticism of my own or-ganization. Given the multitude of choices of things I could say, I may settle on mildly poking fun at my organization and watch the reaction it produces so that I can attempt to determine the appropriate level of sarcasm for future interactions. The information I gain helps me decide how to behave in future reactions and helps me to choose appropriate behaviors the next time we interact.

In contrast to uncertainty, certainty exists to the degree that available informa-tion makes the situation predictable for and about others and ourselves. Another way of saying this would be to consider the process of reducing uncertainty as the process of seeking and discovering meaning in a situation that was previously un-certain (Mokros & Aakhus, 2002). Although a predictable situation is a certain one, it is probably more appropriate to consider certainty as a somewhat idealized and unobtainable state. Certainty is elusive; uncertainties may continue unre-solved for years and may actually be beneficial for cognitive development and mo-tivation (Acredolo & O'Connor, 1991). Complete predictability is an illusion (Bradac, 2001). Further, complete certainty, if possible, is probably undesirable. There is a tension between the need for certainty and predictability to create com-fort and the need for uncertainty and novelty to prevent boredom (Baxter & Montgomery, 1996). To continue the previous example, after several interactions in which this new peer replies with quick, witty, sarcastic remarks, I become cer-tain that my use of sarcasm is appreciated and appropriate in most instances with this person. However, even after months or years of interactions, I may still not be sure if sarcasm is appropriate for certain topics, such as religion because it is a deeply personal topic, or in certain settings, such as when a spouse is present who may have different reactions to sarcasm. I become relatively certain about my use of sarcasm when I am alone with this person for most topics, but continue to expe-rience some uncertainty in my interactions with this person on other topics or in other settings. Our relationship becomes rather stagnant as we avoid those topics and settings. Then the peer surprises me with a sarcastic remark about a new topic. The novelty of this remark creates some uncertainty for me, but it is welcomed as it creates a renewed interest in understanding our relationship.

Whereas the previous definitions seem to focus on uncertainty and certainty as if they exist in the situation apart from the individuals involved, uncertainty is dependent on the perspective of the individuals (Babrow et al., 1998). Two individuals in the same situation may not experience the same degree of uncertainty. A group of employees may all receive the same strongly worded memo telling them to be sure to turn in their monthly reports on time. For some employees this is nothing more than a routine, friendly reminder that creates no uncertainty. They virtually ignore the memo and turn in their reports as they typically would. A number of insecure employees may become particularly concerned if they have turned in their reports late the previous month and will possibly suffer the consequences. They may wonder if the supervisor is cracking down on general procedural problems in the department. They experience a great deal of uncertainty as they consider how to respond to the memo. It is the individual's perspective, more than the situation, which creates the level of uncertainty.

INITIAL CONCEPTUALIZATIONS OF URT

Although the concept of uncertainty reduction predated their work, Berger and Calabrese (1975) formulated the basic tenets of uncertainty reduction theory (URT) as a communication theory. It is frequently overlooked that they expressed optimism that URT could be used to examine communication throughout the development of interpersonal relationships. They saw URT as applicable to the entry (initial), personal (developed), and exit (termination) phases of relationships. They simply chose to focus on initial interaction between strangers as a starting point. After explicating seven axioms and 21 theorems for initial interactions, or the entry phase of relationships, they briefly discussed possible implications of URT for the personal and exit phases of relationships. Even though Berger (1987) later wrote that this initial explication of URT contained some propositions that were eventually shown to be of dubious validity, the major tenets have remained consistent (See Table 2.1).

At the core of URT is the idea that individuals experience uncertainty in situations when they are unable to predict the behaviors of others, unable to choose appropriate behaviors for themselves, and/or unable to provide explanations for the behaviors of themselves or others (Berger, 1975). The central proposition of URT is Axiom 3, which states that high levels of uncertainty cause increases in information seeking and that as uncertainty decreases, information seeking declines. This suggests that because strangers meeting for the first time experience high levels of uncertainty concerning each other, they will engage in information-seeking behaviors to reduce uncertainty.

TABLE 2.1

The Seven Axioms of Uncertainty Reduction Theory
by Berger and Calabrese (1975)

Number	Axiom
1.	Given the high level of uncertainty present at the onset of the entry phase, as the amount of verbal communication between strangers increases, the level of uncertainty for each interactant in the relationships will decrease. As uncertainty is further reduced, the amount of verbal communication will increase.
2.	As nonverbal affiliative expressiveness increases, uncertainty levels will decrease in an initial interaction situation. In addition, decreases in uncertainty level will cause increases in nonverbal affiliative expressiveness.
3.	High levels of uncertainty cause increases in information-seeking behavior. As uncertainty levels decline, information-seeking behavior decreases.
4.	High levels of uncertainty in a relationship cause decreases in the intimacy level of communication content. Low levels of uncertainty produce high levels of intimacy.
5.	High levels of uncertainty produce high rates of reciprocity. Low levels of uncertainty produce low reciprocity rates.
6.	Similarities between persons reduce uncertainty, while dissimilarities produce increases in uncertainty.
7.	Increases in uncertainty level produce decreases in liking; decreases in uncertainty level produce increases in liking.

A variety of corollaries related to this central premise were expected. Perceived similarities (Axiom 6) and information seeking (Axiom 1) were hypothesized to reduce uncertainty. Individuals who perceive themselves as similar or who exchange information should experience uncertainty reduction. Reduction in uncertainty was expected to result in increases in nonverbal affiliative expressiveness (Axiom 2), intimacy (Axiom 4), and liking (Axiom 7). An example illustrates how the theory would work in an initial interaction.

If I meet a stranger at work, I experience a great deal of uncertainty initially. I do not know the person's name, let alone her background, interests, or beliefs. Beyond expecting her to follow the most basic politeness norms of our society, I have limited knowledge of her as an individual and have trouble predicting how she will behave or how I should behave in response. As a result, I begin asking questions to reduce my uncertainty. Through information seeking, I learn her name and gradually discover that we share interests in the same type of research and have children about the same age. These similarities increase my liking for the person. As a result, I move closer and talk more intently. Through further discussion with her, I further reduce my uncertainty and increase my liking. Such a scenario demonstrates each of the major axioms of URT.

Berger and Calabrese (1975) cite a wide variety of research to support the development of their theory. A general test of these axioms and the accompanying theorems through structural equation modeling indicated general and robust support for URT, although some of the specific paths were not related as hypothesized in each of the three cultural groups (American, Japanese, and Korean) in the study (Gudykunst, Yang, & Nishida, 1985). Such research confirms the basic premises of URT.

FURTHER DEVELOPMENT AND ELABORATION

The original URT was attractive to researchers because its simplicity made it easy to examine and test, but also made it incapable of modeling complex and unusual situations (Bradac, 2001). Recognizing these limitations, Berger and others have further developed URT in the years since its initial explication. Berger (1979) added three important aspects to URT. First, he recognized that there were different levels or types of uncertainty. *Cognitive uncertainty* involves understanding and being able to make predictions about the other person's motives and behaviors in general. Cognitive uncertainty occurs when I cannot tell whether my new supervisor is typically friendly or grouchy or whether my new coworker likes to finish jobs early or likes the pressure of finishing at the last minute. *Behavioral (linguistic) uncertainty* concerns predictability of specific actions under certain circumstances. Behavioral uncertainty occurs if I am unsure whether the new supervisor is likely to have private conversations with me after the first departmental meeting or whether the new coworker is going to ask to join me for lunch on the first day of work.

At times cognitive and behavioral uncertainties vary together. When two coworkers experience their first major conflict after working together for several months, neither party may be able to predict how the other one will react, or know how to begin to communicate concerning the incident. They experience high levels of both cognitive and behavioral uncertainty.

At other times, cognitive uncertainty is separate from behavioral uncertainty. The common script that is used in an interaction between two people meeting for the first time may not contain much behavioral uncertainty because the scripts provide for patterned behaviors for such interactions (Douglas, 1984). The conversation will predictably begin with a basic greeting, exchange of demographic information, and then move to more specific areas of common interest. The lack of behavioral uncertainty does not mean that the participants do not experience cognitive uncertainty, in that they are unable to predict how the other individual might behave in a less constrained environment. For example, I probably experience little behavioral uncertainty when I meet a coworker for the first time. I can be relatively certain that he will shake hands, at least if I offer, and expect that we will exchange background information. However, I may experience a great deal of cognitive uncertainty because I do not know whether we have the same work ethic or whether he will be someone I can count on for assistance.

In addition to types of uncertainty, Berger (1979) also recognized three different communication strategies for reducing uncertainty—passive, active, and interactive. *Passive* or reactive searches may involve observing the target of uncertainty in solitary or group situations. Passive searches include making social comparisons with others, perhaps by observing the target in interactions with other known individuals. I might notice a new coworker interacting with a trusted peer and make some comparisons based on that observation. Another passive strategy involves searching disinhibited situations in order to understand the individual better; these are situations in which there are few norms or constraints so that the target must exhibit his or her personal traits rather than those predicated by the situation. For example, eating lunch with peers has fewer constraints than a formal meeting. Observing the new coworker at lunch may provide more information than a meeting with a client as a result. *Active* searches involve requesting information about the target of uncertainty from other third parties or actively structuring situations so that observable interaction can occur. For example, to understand my new coworker, I might ask my trusted peer about his or her impressions. Alternatively, I might convince the peer to ask the new coworker a tough question while I listen to the interaction from the next cubicle. In both of these approaches, I actively seek information, but without directly speaking to new coworker. *Interactive* searches most often involve direct interrogation of the target of uncertainty. Here, I may simply approach the new coworker and ask for information about which I am uncertain. However, social norms in many settings limit the number of questions that can be asked. As a result, self-disclosure with the expectation of reciprocal self-disclosure or attempts at deception detection can be interactive strategies. I may tell a new coworker what I recall about my first month on the job in the hope that he or she will reciprocate with his or her thoughts about the new job. I may modestly downplay a compliment the newcomer has given me and make a judgment concerning its honesty based on the response or lack of response.

The third major addition Berger (1979) made to URT was to recognize that not all situations create the same concern for uncertainty reduction. Even though levels of uncertainty might be comparable across situations, a number of factors may influence whether individuals are concerned about gaining the knowledge needed to reduce uncertainty. In particular, Berger (1979) indicates that incentives, deviation, and anticipation of future interactions influence or motivate concern for uncertainty. For example, uncertainty concerning a supervisor who provides rewards (incentives) would be more motivating than the same level of uncertainty about a colleague in another department. I would want to reduce my uncertainty about the supervisor due to the possible raises or better schedule that she can choose to provide me, while it would not be as motivating to reduce uncertainty about a colleague in another department because he has no direct influence over such matters. Similarly, there would be little motivation to provide cognitive or explanatory certainty about a staff member who appears to follow most social norms in comparison to one who regularly violates routine social behavior. I would assume that a staff member who behaves within the social norms has normal or typical motivations. I would want an explanation for someone who regularly breaks the social norms of my department in order to understand the motives behind the behaviors. Finally, uncertainty about a stranger on a plane would be less likely to cause concern than the same level of uncertainty concerning a new coworker. Because I do not anticipation future interactions with the stranger on the plane, I am not concerned about understanding him or her. Because I will be working with the coworker for the foreseeable future, I am motivated to reduce uncertainty about him or her in order to make future interactions more understandable and predictable.

In building the theory further, Berger and Bradac (1982) delineated three levels of knowledge that individuals may have about themselves, other people, or their relationship to each other instead of just cognitive and behavioral uncertainty. The three levels are: (a) descriptive, being able to reliably identify the person; (b) predictive, being able to predict behaviors; and (c) explanatory, being able to explain the reasons for the actions. They note that it is not always important to reduce uncertainty in all three areas in order to manage uncertainty; predictive certainty without explanatory certainty may sufficiently reduce uncertainty to allow for interaction to continue. For example, knowing that a phone solicitor is going to follow the standard script (predictive or behavioral certainty) allows for interaction to continue even though descriptive and explanatory (cognitive) certainties are not present. I am not concerned with being able to identify the phone solicitor as an individual or with understanding his or her motive for taking the job.

Douglas (1990) builds a similar idea that there are different types of uncertainty by suggesting that uncertainty may be domain specific and so the consequences of uncertainty may vary according to the domain or topic. Reduction of uncertainty in one or some domains may be sufficient for communication interaction; reduction of uncertainty in all areas is not necessary. For example, two coworkers from different departments may reduce their uncertainty in one or two areas, such as learning that they both have teenagers and understanding how their jobs relate to each other. They may have lengthy conversations on these two subjects as a result. Their uncertainties about their attitudes toward their supervisors, religion, and politics could remain quite high, but those areas of uncertainty may never be explored. They may periodically interact over an extended period of time about their teenagers and their interrelated work without ever exploring these other areas of uncertainty.

Berger and Bradac (1982) also recognized that cognitive scripts or schemata function to reduce uncertainty in many situations. Scripts are routine actions or coherent sequences of events that are learned through processing social information gained through communication (Salancik & Pfeffer, 1978). These scripts allow individuals to respond and behave without actively processing or thinking (Langer, 1978). These mindless routines are enacted in response to certain environmental cues (Cantor, Mischel, & Schwartz, 1982). Many social interactions are based on enacting these mindless scripts, such as interacting with a cashier at a checkout counter or performing a greeting ritual with an intimate friend. Scripts are an efficient way of managing uncertainty in interactions by providing behavioral routines based on very minimal cues or information even though they may be based on incorrect information or assumptions (Berger & Bradac, 1982). These routines reduce uncertainty by creating predictable behaviors. We do not experience much uncertainty with a cashier. We expect to be asked "Paper or plastic?" and "Do you want your milk in a bag?" We respond mindlessly, as does the cashier. We do not experience uncertainty because of the behavioral pattern is scripted and our relationship predictable. Even though I do not know much about the cashier's background, interests, or attitudes, uncertainty is managed efficiently in the situation due to the script.

More recently, Gudykunst (1995) clarified an important aspect about the role of motivation in uncertainty reduction. He suggested that individuals have minimum and maximum thresholds for motivation to reduce uncertainty. For a situation to motivate information seeking, the level of uncertainty must be greater than an individual's threshold for uncertainty. This suggests that routine interactions with clerks at stores or with people we do not anticipate interacting with in the future are unlikely to create enough uncertainty to motivate information seeking. At the maximum level, it suggests that too much uncertainty may also de-motivate information seeking. If it seems like it will take too much effort to seek information or that the information needed to reduce uncertainty is not available, an individual may also not seek information. For example, if an employee is convinced that no one will know the answer to a question about policy, he or she may not seek any information because it would be futile. This indicates that only situations that produce uncertainty between the minimum and maximum thresholds motivate information seeking as initially conceptualized by URT.

REVIEW OF UNCERTAINTY RESEARCH
IN INTERPERSONAL CONTEXTS

It was something of an understatement when Berger (1987) concluded that research has demonstrated that URT applies to interpersonal situations beyond initial interactions and to contexts other than interpersonal. Principles of uncertainty reduction have been used to examine interpersonal communication, group interactions, communication in organizational contexts, and even mass communication. Results from this body of research have not provided unequivocal support for URT. Rather, the results have demonstrated that some principles of URT seem to operate in certain situations, but not in others. The following review of interpersonal communication contexts begins by examining representative research that is generally consistent with URT before we turn to research that specifically disputes claims of URT.

Various research studies indicate that the basic principles of URT occur in interpersonal or dyadic contexts. These have taken a variety of methodological approaches from studying behavioral data, such as verbal indicators of URT, to examining self-report measures in interpersonal relationships. Three broad areas of research include vocalized indicators, interpersonal relationships, and interpersonal interactions in intercultural settings.

Vocalized Indicators

A number of studies have examined vocalized indicators of uncertainty. In a typical study of this type, Lalljee and Cook (1973) examined the frequency of filled pauses (e.g., ah, um), speech disturbances (e.g., sentence changes, repetitions), and fluency (rate of speech) during initial interactions. Their results showed a marked decrease in filled pauses and increases in fluency after 3 minutes, but no change in speech disturbances. They interpret these results as indicating that decreases in uncertainty result in improved linguistic decision making. In other words, as the situation becomes more predictable over time, the result is smoother, more fluent speech during initial interactions.

In another study of verbal indicators of URT, Sherblom and Van Rheenen (1984) examined increases in linguistic diversity and verbal immediacy as indicators of uncertainty reduction. They hypothesized that increases in linguistic diversity as demonstrated by use of more varied word choice and use of longer, unique words indicated uncertainty reduction. In addition, they hypothesized that an increase in using main verbs rather than auxiliary verbs indicated less qualifying statements; fewer past or future tense verbs indicated a more immediate temporal focus; and fewer possibility verbs (e.g., should, could, may) as qualifiers indicated more verbal immediacy. Each of these would be indicative of uncertainty reduction. Results from analyzing radio talk-show interviews supported most of these relationships except for the case of the possibility verbs. For example, the host and interviewees used more diverse and unique vocabulary and more present tense verbs over time in the interviews.

Building on this work, Haleta (1996) extended previous research by examining the impact of teachers ' use of verbal indicators of uncertainty on the receiver or audience of the message. She found that students who reacted to potential instructors who hesitated and used filled pauses experienced more uncertainty about the instructors and rated them lower on dynamism, status, and credibility than instructors who used more certain or powerful speech. Students described the teachers using the less powerful speech as uncertain of what they were doing and disorganized; they expressed concern over whether they were being given useful or accurate information by the teacher. This suggests that displaying the communication behaviors associated with uncertainty has an impact on the uncertainty levels of the receivers of those messages.

This research suggests that we would expect the following types of behaviors in an interaction between a job recruiter interviewing applicants for the first time and an applicant going to a first interview. Because this is a new context and a new interaction partner, both experience high uncertainty in the setting. After the initial greeting, due to the high uncertainty both parties hesitate and use vocal fillers as they begin talking. The interviewer might start a question, but stop, add qualifiers to the question, and then eventually switch to a different question before ever giving the applicant a chance to respond. The applicant probably hesitates in answering, perhaps speaking with many qualifiers so as not overstate any point. As the interview continues they both become more certain about each other. The interviewer becomes more relaxed, and speaks more fluently about what the company is currently like. The applicant also responds more smoothly in relaying current plans and ambitions. An observer hearing the first part of the interview might rate both participants as not particularly competent or knowledgeable, whereas an observer hearing only the second part might rate them both much higher. If the participants focus on first impressions (primacy), they may rate each other rather poorly. If instead they focus on the end of the interview (recency), they may give each other much higher ratings.

This example illustrates what the research on vocal indicators has demonstrated. The research provides evidence of behavioral indicators of uncertainty in communication. This research indicates that changes in uncertainty produce vocalized differences in communication. In addition, message receivers perceive these vocalized behaviors as indicators of uncertainty. As such, this research provides foundational support that some characteristics of uncertainty reduction are observable at the verbal level of communication.

Interpersonal Relationships

Research into interpersonal relationships has followed a pattern consistent with the original notion of Berger and Calabrese (1975) that URT applies to entry, personal, and exit phases of relationships. Much of the research has focused on initial interactions. A variety of research has also examined URT in the more developed, personal phases of relationships. There has only been cursory concern for uncertainty reduction in exit phases of relationships. Taking a slightly different tack, researchers have also examined how personality characteristics or variables influence uncertainty reduction processes.

Initial Interactions. A variety of research has examined URT in initial, dyadic interactions. Typical of studies examining uncertainty reduction in initial interactions is research that examines patterns of questioning behavior. Kellerman (1991) demonstrated that there are typical patterns, which she called memory organization packets, that individuals follow in initial interactions. She found that these patterns are relatively invariant across interactions despite different conversational goals; the patterns are routine and yet adaptive. Generally, individuals ask many demographic questions in the initial minutes of conversations before moving to more opinion and personality questions later in the conversation (Rubin, 1979). Rather than being superfluous questions, the demographic questions enable interaction partners to begin to make predictions about their partners so that questions of opinions and values can follow. Consistent with URT, the pattern of questions is associated with uncertainty, and uncertainty is reduced as information is exchanged in response to questions over time (Wheeless & Williamson, 1992). In addition, perceived attitude similarity is associated with reduced uncertainty in interpersonal relationships (Prisbell & Andersen, 1980). Although the data do not indicate causal relationships, the results suggest a cyclical process in which information exchange increases perceptions of attitude similarity, which in turn increases information exchange.

Douglas also has examined URT in initial interactions. He found substantial support for URT in comparisons of 2-, 4-, and 6-minute conversations (Douglas, 1990). In particular, he found that information requests or inquiry decreased over time and self-disclosure increased over time. He suggests that this may indicate that individuals become information givers over time instead of information seekers. This interaction may be critical in understanding the uncertainty reduction process as an interactive process because both parties in an initial interaction experience uncertainty.

Taken together, this work suggests that individuals have flexible scripts, what Kellerman (1991) calls memory organization packets, which cause participants to follow fairly predictable patterns of communication in initial interactions. These scripts or packets reduce uncertainty about the process of communicating in initial interactions. By following these scripts, individuals gain information that reduces their uncertainty about other people in initial interactions.

Personal Relationships. Other research in interpersonal relationships has focused on uncertainty-reducing behaviors in relationships beyond the initial interactions, such as during the personal phase of relationships in the development of romantic relationships. In more personal relationships, individuals can experience relational uncertainty including self-uncertainty (unable to predict their own attitudes and behaviors), partner uncertainty (unable to predict their partners' attitudes and behaviors), or relationship uncertainty (unable to predict the development or status of the relationship; Solomon & Knobloch, 2001). These three are related such that partner uncertainty predicts self-uncertainty, which predicts relationship uncertainty (Knobloch, Solomon, & Cruz, 2001). Unexpected events that are appraised as significant and important to relationships result in temporary increases in uncertainty, especially in developing relationships as opposed to more intimate relationships (Knobloch & Solomon, 2002b). Consistent with URT, relational uncertainty is related to negative outcomes such as conflict and jealousy in relationships and as intimacy in relationships increase, relationship uncertainty decreases (Solomon & Knobloch, 2001).

Given these various events and types of relation uncertainty, individuals use a variety of direct and indirect methods to gain information to manage their uncertainty such as conversing with the person, talking to others about the person, and secret tests or spying, such as watching a partner interact with another physically attractive acquaintance (Knobloch & Solomon, 2002a). Indicative of receiving information from third parties, Parks and Adelman (1983) found that students involved in romantic relationships who reported more communication and support from their partners' network of friends and relatives experienced less uncertainty, regardless of the length of time they had dated or known each other. Those with less third party communication and support felt more uncertain and were more likely to break off the relationship after 3 months. Emmers and Canary (1996) found that in romantic relationships both men and women predominantly used interactive strategies in attempts to repair relationships to reduce uncertainty. Use of passive strategies was associated with failure to repair relationships. They speculate that interactive strategies are necessary to repair intimate or romantic relationships. However, the passive or active strategies do reduce uncertainty and may be adequate in less developed relationships. An interesting additional finding of their study was that some men (13%) and women (10%) responded to the uncertainty by simply accepting it without making any effort to gain information through passive, active, or interactive strategies. This suggests that either the level of uncertainty was not sufficient to motivate information-seeking behaviors or that the individuals were able to reduce uncertainty without seeking any information.

In comparing types of developed relationships, Baxter and Wilmot (1984) found that individuals involved in platonic relationships, romantic relationships, or relationships in transition between those types used a range of strategies in order to gain information to reduce uncertainty. As expected by URT, these strategies included direct inquiry and asking third parties. Partners also used various tests to reduce uncertainty. These tests suggest that individuals actively structure situations to see how their partners would respond (Berger, 1979). Partners might experiment with intimate touch, or test their partners by leaving them unsupervised with a friend to determine if they were trustworthy. Baxter and Wilmot (1984) concluded that because open discussion of the state of the relationship is often a taboo subject, individuals relied heavily on these "secret tests" as indirect methods of gaining information to reduce uncertainty. Such research demonstrates that communication through passive and active searches (third parties) are often as important a source for reducing uncertainty as direct (interactive) communication (Berger, 1979).

In an effort to compare entry to developed phases of relationships, Ayres (1979) compared information exchanges in encounters between either strangers or friends. Contrary to what URT would predict in such a comparison, there was no difference in the *number* of questions asked by strangers or friends and during both types of interactions; there was a general decrease in questions during 30-minute conversations. However, there were differences in the *types* of questions and responses in the two types of encounters. Strangers tended to focus on descriptive questions and responses, whereas friends used more evaluative questions and responses. Ayres suggests that these results are more consistent with social penetration theory (Altman & Taylor, 1973) than with uncertainty reduction principles. The same frequency of questions is asked of both strangers and friends, but the depth or intimacy of the questions varies depending on the relationship development or intimacy.

An alternative interpretation of the results that is consistent with URT is that the pattern of gradual question reduction is typical of many encounters regardless of the relationship development or intimacy. When individuals have been separated for a period of time, they ask questions to reduce uncertainty that has developed during their separation, but the nature of those questions is different from those asked in initial interactions because they focus on different types of uncertainty. Strangers tend to focus on reducing descriptive uncertainties by gaining factual information about a stranger, whereas friends focus on reducing cognitive uncertainties by gaining evaluative information of an acquaintance for whom descriptive uncertainties have already been reduced. For example, a supervisor may ask a new subordinate a series of questions during an initial interaction to get to know the person, with the number of questions decreasing during the conversation. The same supervisor will also ask a series of questions of a long-term employee in order to get an update on a project or to check up on a personal issue, but the number of questions will gradually decrease as the uncertainty about those issues is reduced. In both cases the patterns would be consistent with URT. The difference in depth of questions would be consistent with the results of the study by Ayres (1979).

Computer-Mediated Settings. A number of researchers have used URT to compare interpersonal relationship development in computer-mediated communication (CMC) versus face-to-face (FtF) interactions. In summarizing much of this research, Ramirez, Walther, Burgoon, and Sunnafrank (2002) draw a number of conclusions. They note that the early research in this area concluded that people in CMC have a tendency to become more task oriented, impersonal, and even hostile (e.g., flaming or writing very negative remarks) because of the medium being used, but that contemporary researchers instead believe that individuals engage in "strategic cognitive deliberations and communication behaviors to compensate for the media limitations" (Ramirez et al., 2002, p. 215). Likewise, Walther (1994) found that many of the differences in communication in CMC versus FtF groups were associated with anticipation of future interaction, not the communication medium. When CMC users anticipated future interactions with their partners, their communication to reduce uncertainty was quite similar to FtF partners.

The means of communication to reduce uncertainty differs some in CMC versus FtF conditions. Most early research noted the lack of nonverbal cues in CMC compared to FtF settings for gaining information about others (Walther, 1994). In addition, Tidwell and Walther (2002) argue that some of the information-seeking strategies readily available in FtF interactions are not available in CMC, especially passive strategies like observation and active strategies like asking third parties, although interactive strategies such as direct inquiry are the same in both settings. However, in certain CMC settings there are some unique passive and active strategies available to participants for gaining information about others. For example, in CMC groups (rather than dyads), a user may "lurk" on a listserve or in a chat room (i.e., be present but not participate); this allows them to passively observe the target person 's communication. Some groups have archives, which may be searched to obtain past posting from an individual, thereby gaining historical observational information not available in FtF interactions. CMC users may contact others for their impressions of the target, or may receive unsolicited CC (carbon copy or courtesy copies) or BCC (blind CC) where the target party does not know they received the message. These allow for gaining information through indirect, third-party methods.

Despite some of these unique characteristics of the medium, the results of research on initial interactions in CMC have generally been consistent with the previous research on initial face-to-face interactions. Pratt, Wisemen, Cody, and Wendt (1999) examined e-mail messages between pairs of intergenerational e-pals, pairs of elderly individuals interacting with young adolescents. Consistent with other research, they found that initial messages were more polite in tone and contained the most questions. The questions initially were more focused on demographic information, but later included more varied types of questions. Tidwell and Walther (2002) found that CMC participants tended to be more direct and interactive in seeking information about a partner, whereas FtF participants tended to include more peripheral questions and self-disclosures. Although CMC participants were given more time to get to know each other than FtF because of the differences in medium (typing versus speaking), in the end CMC participants actually were more confident about their knowledge of their partners than FtF participants, suggesting that they were more successful in reducing their uncertainty. Overall, the research suggests that computer-mediated communication and face-to-face communication are quite similar in terms of uncertainty reduction principles and outcomes.

Personality Variables.   Researchers have examined the influence of the number of personality variables or characteristics on uncertainty reduction in interpersonal relationships. A pair of studies examined the influence of communication apprehension (anxiety concerning producing communication) and receiver apprehension (anxiety concerning receiving communication) on uncertainty reduction. Wheeless and Williamson (1992) and Schumacher and

Wheeless (1997) found that both types of apprehension were associated with increases in uncertainty. However, whereas communication apprehension was associated with increases in information-seeking behaviors, receiver apprehension was associated with decreases in seeking information.

The potential influence of self-monitoring on uncertainty reduction in interpersonal relationships has also been examined. Self-monitoring is a personality variable that influences information seeking in general. High self-monitors look for external cues from the environment or their interaction partners to determine appropriate behaviors in a given situation, whereas low self-monitors rely on internal cues (Synder, 1974). This results in differences in information-seeking behaviors in general. High self-monitors seek more information about interaction partners than low self-monitors prior to interacting with them (Elliott, 1979). Higher self-monitors also initiate more conversations than lower self-monitors (Ickes & Barnes, 1977). High self-monitors consider informal situations as more valuable for gaining information about partners because the context has less influence on their behaviors, whereas low self-monitors prefer formal situations, although both prefer social to solitary settings (Berger & Douglas, 1981). As a result of differences in information seeking, high self-monitors are more likely to be confident about making attributions and more likely to display nonverbal expressiveness than low self-monitors (Gudykundst & Nishida, 1984).

Building on his other research, Douglas (1991) examined individual differences in levels of what he termed *global uncertainty*. Global uncertainty is a general lack of knowledge of how to interact with others rather than uncertainty about interacting with a specific individual. He concluded that global uncertainty influences communication during initial interactions because those high in global uncertainty often avoid interactions and are unskilled at communicating when they must interact. Further research indicated that high global uncertainty was associated with uncertainty about an interaction partner (Douglas, 1994). The results also demonstrated that even though high global uncertainty was associated with the greatest reductions of uncertainty, due to their high initial levels of uncertainty those with high global uncertainty were still poor at making attributions about their partners compared to those with lower global uncertainty.

Although most of the studies reported have not specifically addressed gender differences in uncertainty reduction behaviors, those that have specifically addressed the issue report mixed results. In an examination of gender differences Sanders, Wiseman, and Matz (1990) compared the use of self-disclosure by oneself and one 's partner, use of interrogation, use of nonverbal immediacy, and attributional confidence for male and female students recalling conversations with same-sex dyadic partner. There were similarities and differences. For example, self-disclosure was similar on religious views, ambitions and goals, choice of career, things that make one furious, health concerns, illnesses, and physical fitness efforts. Women disclosed more on their sensitive feelings, work/school problems, and views on parenting; by contrast, men disclosed more on personal accomplishments and sexual morality. These and differences in the use of interrogation, nonverbal immediacy, and attributional confidence led the authors to conclude that men disclose more impersonal topics while women discuss more personal ones.

Turner (1990) examined gender differences related to unexpected increase in uncertainty in marriages. She found no real difference in the way women and men experienced uncertainty or communicated after the increase in uncertainty, although the results suggested that women were more likely to discuss the situation with a third party. Other research on URT has reported no main effects as a result of gender differences (Gudykunst & Hammer, 1988). Together, the results suggest that there may be some gender differences related to uncertainty and uncertainty reduction processes, but their importance is unclear given the similarities in other behaviors and the number of studies that found no differences.

An extended example illustrates many of the major findings related to dyadic interactions. Two new employees from different departments meet on their first day of work. During their initial interactions they ask demographic and background questions of each other to reduce their uncertainty. The questions trail off as the conversation focuses in on areas of common interest and they find out they know some of the same individuals. When they meet during the next days and weeks, they begin conversations with frequent questions about the work experience since their last interaction, but the number of questions again fades as they find other common experiences to discuss. Because one is a bit apprehensive about communicating and tends to avoid conversation and the other is a high self-monitor who seeks out information frequently, they continue to be uncertain about each other because of their personal differences. The high self-monitor may ask other coworkers about the high-apprehensive individual or simply try to observe other interactions at lunch to see if personality differences explain some of the differences in behavior.

As the example demonstrates, the research in dyadic situations generally has found that certain patterns of behavior are consistent with URT in initial interactions. Normally there are decreases in the use of direct inquiry over time during a conversation and increases in certainty about interaction partners. Questions tend to concern demographic questions in initial interactions, but focus on more attitudinal and value issues in later communication. In addition, principles of URT occur in relationships beyond initial interactions. Depending on the nature of the relationship, different strategies are used to gain information. Finally, certain personality characteristics, such as apprehension and self-monitoring, global uncertainty, and gender, influence uncertainty reduction processes.

Intercultural and Interethnic Interactions

There is an extensive body of research by Gudykunst and his colleagues that has specifically examined URT in interpersonal communication in intercultural or interethnic contexts. Although most of this research is not based on actual interactions, it provides some insight into how URT may work in intercultural settings.

In intercultural settings, people from different cultures experience uncertainty about each other and attempt to create a third culture of shared meaning through interaction (Baldwin & Hunt, 2002). This body of research provides the most thorough testing of URT and its modifications, although the results provide mixed support for the theory according to Sunnafrank (1989).

High-context cultures rely on contextual or setting cues, such as time, place, status, and ritual, to provide information concerning an interaction. Gudykunst (1983) found that high-context (Asian) and low-context (U.S.) individuals report differences in their approaches to uncertainty reduction. High-context individuals are more cautious, display fewer nonverbal behaviors, make more assumptions about attitudes, and ask more background questions than low-context individuals. In a further examination, Gudykunst and Nishida (1984) found a multivariate effect for communication in inter- (between) and intra- (within) cultural communication. Individuals from a high-context culture (Japan) expressed higher attributional confidence, less intent to self-disclose or interrogate, and displayed less nonverbal expressiveness than those from low-context cultures (United States). However, they conclude that cultural similarities reduced uncertainty. Gudykunst, Nishida, Koike, and Shiino (1986) conclude that although URT is applicable across cultures, it may work differently in high-context cultures compared to the way it works in low-context cultures. Individuals in high-context cultures are more concerned with certainty about whether an interaction partner follows cultural norms, whereas individuals in low-context cultures may be more concerned about making accurate attributions about the individual's motives. These appear to be cultural differences concerning the relative importance of behavioral uncertainty versus explanatory or cognitive uncertainty.

Other cultural differences have been examined in addition to those associated with high versus low context. Gudykundst, Nishida, and Schmidt (1989) compared perceptions of members of a collectivist society (Japan) to members of an individualistic society (United States). They found that ingroup/outgroup status (member of same or different cultural groups) had important implications for uncertainty reduction in a collectivist society when compared with an individualistic society like that of the United States. Specifically, for Japanese students, ingroup status was associated with more shared networks and less self-disclosure, but ingroup status had no impact on uncertainty reduction for U.S. students. In addition, there were significant results for a positive versus a negative evaluation of the relationship for both cultures. A positive evaluation was associated with more self-disclosure, interrogation, perceived similarity, attraction, nonverbal affiliative expressiveness, shared networks, as well as attributional confidence, a specific measure of certainty.

Cultural differences also influenced a number of relationships in a study comparing friends and acquaintances in culturally similar and dissimilar dyads (Gudykundst, 1985). Cultural similarity was associated with more shared communication networks but less attraction than cultural dissimilarity. Self-disclosure and attributional confidence were higher for culturally dissimilar *acquaintances* than for culturally similar acquaintances, but lower for culturally dissimilar *friends* than culturally similar friends. Overall, Gudykunst found modest support for URT in that uncertainty about attributions was associated with requests for information.

An examination by Gudykundst, Chua, and Gray (1987) of the influence of relationship type on uncertainty reduction also demonstrated the influence of intercultural contexts. They found that intercultural differences resulted in significant differences across relationship types. As relationships became more intimate, differences decreased, attribution confidence increased, and self-disclosure increased. Overall, this suggests that cultural stereotypes influence the uncertainty reduction process in intercultural interactions initially, but that as interactions continue, the stereotypes disappear and the uncertainty reduction process changes.

An examination of communication between Japanese Americans and Caucasians living in Hawaii by Gudykundst, Sodetani, and Sonoda (1987) found a number of interethnic differences. Specifically, they concluded that Caucasians were more assertive, asking more questions and displaying more nonverbal affiliation than did the Japanese Americans. Overall, the authors indicated that their results support many of the axioms and theorems of URT, but also provide only partial support or no support for others. In further examination of interethnic communication, Gudykundst and Hammer (1988) reported two main findings. First, if the group membership was evaluated positively, this led to the use of uncertainty reduction processes. In addition, when an individual was viewed as a typical member of an ethnic group, rather than atypical, uncertainty was reduced as indicated by an increase in confidence in making attributions about the partner. This suggests that stereotypical attributes were ascribed to members who were viewed as typical of their group.

According to this research, a meeting between two international businessmen, an American and Japanese, would follow a pattern something like this. An American man, as a member of a low-context and individualistic society, would be more aggressive, ask more questions, and self-disclose more. His focus would be on becoming certain about the likely actions of his partner. A Japanese man, as a member of a high-context and collectivist society, would be more reserved and be more focused on whether his partner was following common social norms. If both individuals viewed the other as typical members of their cultural group, they would be fairly confident about their ability to make attributions about the other's behaviors. To the degree that they felt the partner was atypical, they would be less certain.

Overall, the work by Gudykundst and his colleagues suggests that URT is applicable in intercultural and interethnic settings, but that some of the behaviors and outcomes may differ from those predicted by URT due to the context. The research clearly indicates that there are cultural differences in the way communication is used to manage uncertainty (Brashers, Goldsmith, & Hsieh, 2002). Most of this research assumes that national boundaries indicate culture (Baldwin & Hunt, 2002). It would be valuable to use alternative conceptualizations of culture in future research. In addition, examination of actual interactions rather than imaginary ones can provide additional insight into this important area of research. In addition, Goldsmith (2001) suggests that some of the behavioral differences and outcomes may be related to how different cultures or communities define and understand uncertainty. Examination of the meaning of uncertainty in different speech communities may provide additional insight into the affective and behavioral responses to uncertainty across cultures. Given the growth in the global economy and increase in international business, the examination of URT in intercultural and international settings can provide useful information for improving communication in these contexts.

Summary

A wide range of research has examined URT in interpersonal settings, including interpersonal interactions in intercultural settings. Results from this body of research suggest that principles of URT appear to work at times and to some degree. However, these results do not provide unequivocal support for URT. Not only does some research not support URT, but also research by other scholars has clearly demonstrated some problems with URT, and other scholars have attempted to dispute its basic value. For example, Planalp and her colleagues (Planalp & Honeycutt, 1985; Planalp, Rutherford, & Honeycutt, 1988) demonstrated that contrary to Axiom 1, communication sometimes increases uncertainty. Sunnafrank (1986a, 1990) attempted to replace URT with his theory of predicted-outcome value. Based on the research, even Berger (1987) concluded that URT, as initially presented, contains a number of theorems that appear to be of dubious value; at the same time he claims there is support for the theory in general. Having examined research that provides mixed support for URT, the research that specifically criticizes URT is examined next.

CRITICISMS OF UNCERTAINTY REDUCTION THEORY

Even though the previous literature has provided mixed support of URT, a number of scholars have attempted to demonstrate that URT is generally flawed. Although it is important to respond to the substance of those criticisms of URT, it also seems important to point out that some of the criticisms are based on questionable assumptions and methodologies. To begin with, a number of criticisms of URT have failed to recognize some of the developments of the theory since its initial explication by Berger and Calabrese (1975). For example, none of the criticisms examine passive, active, and interactive means of reducing uncertainty simultaneously (Berger, 1979). The design of Sunnafrank's (1990) study only allows for interactive strategies, eliminating the possibility of passive or active approaches to uncertainty reduction. Similarly, none of the research considers different types of uncertainty such as descriptive, predictive, or explanatory uncertainty (Berger & Bradac, 1982). For example, Kellerman and Reynolds' (1990) work on tolerance of ambiguity focuses on explanatory uncertainty (attributional confidence) without recognizing the relative importance of descriptive or predictive uncertainty in some interactions.

In other cases, these criticisms appear to misinterpret or inappropriately characterize URT. For example, Berger (1979) discusses factors that *may* increase concern for uncertainty, such as incentives, deviation, and future interaction. Kellerman (1986) draws conclusions about whether anticipated future interactions *always* increase uncertainty based on interactions between students.

Methodological decisions are also problematic in many instances. Short, artificial or imagined interactions are often used to test the theory. Kellerman (1986) reports that typical initial interactions last approximately 17 minutes when they are allowed to continue until they end naturally. Most of the experimental studies of URT, including her own, end the conversations after 5 minutes. It appears that almost the entire line of research on intercultural communication by Gudykundst and his colleagues is based on imagined interactions and generally fails to include face-to-face interactions.

A complete analysis of problems associated with the criticisms of URT is beyond the scope of this chapter. The substance of the research criticizing URT is presented because, despite the shortcomings in some of the criticisms, it brings up important issues to consider before reconceptualizing URT for organizational settings. By responding to the criticisms, new ideas can be generated to assist in understanding how people manage uncertainty.

Increasing Uncertainty

Initially, Berger and Calabrese (1975) indicated that increases in information would result in decreases in uncertainty (Axiom 1) and increases in intimacy (Axiom 4). Planalp and Honeycutt (1985) found that these patterns did not always occur. Most participants in their study had little trouble recalling situations in which information increased their uncertainty about another individual. A typical example was finding out that the other person in the relationship had deceived them about where he or she was or what he or she was doing. Such a revelation made them uncertain by bringing into question the level of trust in the relationship. Overall, Planalp and Honeycutt categorized the events as finding out about competing relationships, unexplained loss of closeness, sexual behavior, deception, changed personality or values, and betrayed confidences. Not only did such events lead to increases in uncertainty, but also many of these events led to decreases in intimacy or even termination of relationships.

In a follow-up study, Planalp et al. (1988) replicated some of the same findings; they found increases in uncertainty after the events and frequently negative consequences for the relationships. They also found that while uncertainty increased at the time of the event, uncertainty gradually decreased over time after the event. Similarly, Afifi and Burgoon (2000) found that violations of expected behaviors, especially negative violations, increase uncertainty while reducing attractiveness ratings in initial interactions. In particular, in initial interactions if individuals began interacting in a moderately involved manner and then switched to moderate levels of disinterest, observers reported an increase in uncertainty and rated the individual as less socially attractive.

It is important to note that Planalp et al. (1988) found support for other aspects of URT. They found that many respondents (75%) reported that they consulted third parties (their own friends or mutual friends) to discuss their uncertainty or gain advice rather than using direct inquiry. This supports the basic principle of URT that individuals seek information when they experience uncertainty (Axiom 3, Berger & Calabrese, 1975) and suggests that they often use multiple approaches to seeking information (Berger, 1979). Afifi and Burgoon (2000) also found that in most instances, information reduced uncertainty. However, the finding that information can increase uncertainty clearly suggests problems with the initial conceptualization of URT. Information does not always decrease uncertainty (Axiom 1). However, even these findings support some of the additions to the theory that have been addressed since 1975. Berger (1987) indicated that uncertainty reduction is likely to occur based on gaining information in initial interactions between strangers (the purview of the initial axioms and theorems), but recognized that information could have contrary effects over time. The findings that information can have negative effects (increased uncertainty and decreased liking) suggest some of the changes in URT that Berger already has made.

The findings also suggest that further reconceptualization of URT is necessary. Previous research has not considered how information may increase certainty *and* decrease liking. It is quite possible that information gained through interaction could result in increasing certainty concerning unattractive attributes of a person; the result would be a decrease in liking the other person rather than an increase. For example, if I am fairly certain that a particular coworker is not reliable and I discover three more instances where that individual did not do the work as it should have been done, this new information makes me become more certain. At the same time, I evaluate the person even more negatively and increase my dislike for the person. In other words, through communication we sometimes become certain that we dislike someone. Although this was not the focus of their study, Afifi and Burgoon (2000) provide some evidence to support this idea. Their results seem to suggest that consistently negative interaction (rather than positive followed by negative) resulted in lower levels of uncertainty and lower ratings of attractiveness. Overall, the research suggests the importance of recognizing that information can have multiple effects, and information does not always result in decreases in uncertainty and increases in liking. Further examination of how increases in information can result in increases in certainty and negative evaluations needs to be folded into a more complete theory of managing uncertainty.

Predicted Outcome Values

One of the most sustained criticisms of URT comes from a series of articles by Sunnafrank (1986a, 1986b, 1989, 1990). Whereas URT views uncertainty reduction as central to relationships, Sunnafrank (1986a) maintains that outcome-maximization, rather than uncertainty reduction, is the central characteristic of relationships. Uncertainty reduction is simply a tool for determining predicted outcome values (Sunnafrank, 1986b). The predicted outcome value (POV) approach is basically a social exchange approach in which individuals make relationship decisions primarily by calculating cost–benefit ratios and comparing those to alternatives (Altman & Taylor, 1973; Thibaut & Kelley, 1959). The cost–benefit ratio may be calculated on the basis of a variety of exchanges including money, goods, services, information, affect, and status (Foa & Foa, 1980). If the costs outweigh the benefits, the relationship gradually deteriorates and is terminated, but if the benefits outweigh the costs, the relationship develops and improves. From the POV perspective, seeking information to reduce uncertainty is simply a method of determining the cost–benefit ratio of a particular relationship (Sunnafrank, 1989). In developing the POV approach, Sunnafrank (1986a) basically argues that if the POV is positive, communication will generally follow the predictions of URT as initially conceptualized (Berger & Calabrese, 1975). He argues that if the POV is negative, communication will generally move in the opposite direction of the predictions of URT. That is, if the POV is negative there will be less information seeking, less intimate content, and so forth.

Sunnafrank (1990) provided some empirical support for his view by measuring uncertainty, predicted outcome value, and a variety of communication behaviors from students forced into brief initial interactions with strangers. He also reinterpreted the research results of Gudykunst and his colleagues to demonstrate that they are more supportive of POV than of URT (Sunnafrank, 1989). In particular, he noted findings that POV was a significant covariate of outcomes such as self-disclosure, interrogation, and attributional confidence (Gudykundst et al., 1989) as supportive of his perspective.

Grove and Werkman (1991) provide additional support for POV by comparing initial interactions between students and either able-bodied or visibly disabled (in wheelchairs) strangers. Their results indicated that positive evaluations of able-bodied strangers were associated with more information seeking and nonverbal affiliation while negative evaluations of visibly disabled strangers were associated with more filled pauses and less nonverbal awareness. As such, POV provides insight into interpersonal relationships and URT by recognizing that positive and negative evaluations influence information seeking and relationship development. Of course, social exchange theory provides many of the same observations about communication processes (Altman & Taylor, 1973).

These criticisms fail to uncover any fatal flaws in URT, although they do suggest the need for additional changes in URT. As Berger (1986) indicates in his response to Sunnafrank (1986a), POV begins with uncertainty reduction as the process by which predicted outcome value assessments are made. As such, it is difficult to argue that POV is more central to interpersonal relationships than URT. This simply develops into the proverbial question of which came first, the chicken or the egg. Sunnafrank actually argues that uncertainty reduction precedes POV, but that POV is more important. In response, Berger concludes that POV is a subset of the larger uncertainty reduction process.

Sunnafrank 's empirical work, and apparently his conceptualization of URT as well, fails to consider that individuals may seek to reduce uncertainty through passive, active, and interactive strategies (Berger & Bradac, 1982). One possible interpretation of his findings is that if a negative evaluation of the other person is made, an individual will quit using interactive strategies to seek additional information, but may continue to use passive and active strategies such as observation and information seeking from third parties. This suggests the need to examine how the use of various information-seeking strategies may change over time to further develop URT. Positive evaluation may result in interactive information-seeking strategies, whereas negative evaluations may result in alternative approaches. For example, if a new coworker makes a generally negative first impression on me, I probably will not continue to interact with that person to further reduce my uncertainty. However, I may quite actively listen to what others say about the individual in order to determine if my initial impressions were accurate or not.

Finally, and perhaps most importantly, neither Sunnafrank nor Berger (1986) in his direct defense of URT, consider that making a negative predicted outcome value assessment can be considered the completion of the uncertainty reduction process. Douglas (1994) suggests that uncertainty reduction may occur more in critical instances than in a linear process because some information is more critical than others in evaluating a partner. Information gained can result in learning that you wish to continue to interact with a person to find out more or a determination that this is someone you do not wish to interact with in the future. Uncertainty is reduced, not by the absolute amount of information, but when the information is perceived to be adequate for making decisions within the interaction (Clatterbuck, 1979).

In an instance where a positive evaluation of an interaction partner is made, uncertainty reduction continues along the lines of the original theory. The individuals continue to seek information and discuss areas of common interest. Sunnafrank provides conceptual and empirical support for this pattern. In instances where a negative evaluation is made, a critical reduction in uncertainty has already occurred so that the process is complete; there may be no need for additional uncertainty reduction behaviors. Enough descriptive, behavioral, or explanatory knowledge exists for either cognitive and / or behavioral uncertainty to be reduced sufficiently to make decisions about further interaction. This decision makes further information seeking unnecessary and unlikely.

Sunnafrank's empirical results can support this type of interpretation. As such they suggest the need for further elaboration of URT rather than a replacement of it with POV.

Two hypothetical examples that could have occurred in Sunnafrank's (1990) study can illustrate these points. Two students begin interacting. Through the typical demographic-type questions that occur in initial interactions, they discover that they have the same major, live in adjoining dorms, like tennis, and know some of the same people. This would most likely create a positive evaluation of the relationship potential or a positive predicted outcome value. Because they recognize that they could easily have future interactions, the two would continue to use interactive communication to find out additional similarities and perhaps explore possibilities of studying together or playing some tennis. Two other students meet and discover that their majors are completely different (science and art), they live on opposite sides of the campus, one loves sports while the other hates sports, and they have trouble finding anything in common except that they both grew up in the same state. Most likely this would result in a negative evaluation of the relationship potential or a negative predicted outcome value. These students can predict that they will not likely interact in the future and that if they do, those interactions will primarily be polite social exchanges of greetings and abbreviated conversation. As a result, they do little additional information seeking about the other although they recognize each other and continue to take some notice of each other in class through observation.

In both situations the interactions begin with uncertainty reduction. In both instances, interactive strategies are used to reduce uncertainty. In the first case, an interactive strategy of reducing uncertainty continues because there are additional areas of interest to explore. Knowledge of another in one area always opens possibilities of additional uncertainties in yet unexplored areas (Acredolo & O'Connor, 1991). In the second case, after some initial interactive communication, both are satisfied to rely on a passive strategy for further reducing uncertainty. But, most importantly, in the first situation, information seeking continues because of the many areas of uncertainty yet to be explored during the initial conversation. In the second, uncertainty has been reduced to a level where it is no longer an issue. Both parties have descriptive certainty and predictive certainty; they recognize each other and can predict what any future interactions will be like. Even though they may not have explanatory certainty about the other person's motives, predictive certainty is often sufficient for two individuals to function adequately with others (Berger & Bradac, 1982), particularly if they expect to have limited future interactions.

Overall, the work of Sunnafrank indicates that positive and negative evaluation of relationship potential appear to be important motives in managing uncertainty. In addition, during interactions there are ongoing changes in levels of uncertainty that can change information-seeking patterns. Further elaboration of URT can address these issues of changing levels of uncertainty and multiple motives.

Tolerance of Uncertainty

Kellerman and Reynolds (1990) focused on another limitation of URT while criticizing POV at the same time. Building on Berger's (1979) notion that concern about uncertainty varies according to anticipated interactions, deviance, and incentives, they explored how tolerance for uncertainty influences information seeking in uncertain situations. In support of Berger, they did find that anticipation of future interaction was negatively associated with tolerance of uncertainty; those expecting future interaction were apparently more intent on reducing uncertainty than those who were not expecting to interact again. However, there were no such relationships for deviance and incentives. Further, after testing five different models of uncertainty reduction, they conclude that how much you want to know (motivation) is more important than how much you actually know (uncertainty) in predicting information seeking. They suggest that a more parsimonious model of information seeking focuses on *tolerance of uncertainty* rather than uncertainty.

Unfortunately, their test of the theory focuses on interactive or direct information seeking, with only passing consideration of passive strategies (monitoring) and no consideration of active (third party) strategies and focuses on explanatory certainty rather than behavioral or descriptive certainty. These limitations make their specific criticisms of URT difficult to assess. However, overall the work of Kellerman and Reynolds (1990) emphasizes the need to examine how levels of motivation influence uncertainty reduction behaviors, apart from actual levels of uncertainty. People with a high tolerance for uncertainty may need to experience extreme levels of uncertainty before they become motivated to seek information, at least in an interactive manner. Those with a low tolerance for uncertainty may be motivated to seek information from relatively small amounts of uncertainty, although even they may not rely on interactive strategies to reduce uncertainty and instead use passive and third-party strategies. This suggests the need for further elaboration of URT to consider the role of motivation in uncertainty reduction.

SUMMARY

This chapter has examined the previous research on URT in the communication field. After examining the initial theory and its elaboration, a broad range of literature examining interpersonal communication based on URT was examined. Although much of the literature finds support for the basic concepts of URT, a number of criticisms have been advanced. While Cragan and Shields (1998) have concluded that "URT's critics have missed the mark" (p. 146), the criticisms raised do provide evidence that further development of the theory is needed. A more complex understanding of uncertainty reduction is needed to understand human communication in organizational settings.

CHAPTER THREE

Uncertainty in Group
and Organizational Contexts

Research into the role of uncertainty has not been limited to the interpersonal context. Whereas the previous chapter focused on dyadic interactions in nonspecific settings, this chapter focuses on uncertainty as it relates to communication interactions in group and organizational settings. Most of the traditional lines of organizational research concerning its structure and communication patterns are concerned with managing uncertainties (McPhee & Zaug, 2001). However, unlike the interpersonal literature, this research frequently does not explicitly test the axioms and theorems of URT. Rather, it examines the principles of uncertainty in these collective settings with cursory or implicit implications for URT. Like interpersonal scholars, some organizational scholars argue that reducing uncertainty is the primary role of communication in organizations (Farace, Taylor, & Stewart, 1978). New members of a work group face uncertainty in trying to determine the group's norms for productivity and social interaction. A product development committee faces uncertainty in determining how to respond to a competitor's new product and in assessing how this might impact their organization's own production. Organizational decision makers face uncertainty from the national or global economy. Clearly, coping with uncertainty is vital to maintaining organizational viability in adapting to the environment (Duncan, 1972). This chapter reviews a wide range of the research that has explored how people respond to uncertainty in such collective settings.

UNCERTAINTY AND SENSEMAKING

Before reviewing the literature on uncertainty in group and organizational settings, it is important to briefly discuss a related concept, sensemaking. A cursory comparison of the references in articles on uncertainty reduction and sensemaking will reveal very little overlap. For example, Weick (1995) lists 55 key articles on sensemaking in organizations. Few of these are cited with any regularity in the literature on uncertainty in organizations. Similarly, the articles that are frequently cited in organizational research based on URT research are rarely mentioned in the sensemaking literature. While there are a few scholars who draw on both literatures, the lack of overlap between the two areas of research suggests that they are different concepts resulting in separate areas of research.

The degree of overlap that you see between uncertainty reduction and sensemaking is probably an indication of the degree to which you are a "combiner" or a "separator." Combiners tend to see ideas, concepts, or objects as similar and focus on general characteristics that connect them. Separators tend to make fine distinctions between ideas, concepts, or objects and focus on unique characteristics of each.

If you have a tendency to see commonalities between concepts and ideas (a combiner), you will see uncertainty reduction and sensemaking as related to each other or even as the same basic concept. They have a number of characteristics in common. For example, both approaches have to do with how people generate meaning and understanding in their experiences. People understand situations by making sense out of them as a means of coping with the uncertainties present. Both examine how people use symbols to generate information and meaning in situations. Through language and social interaction, people make sense or reduce uncertainties in their organizational lives. Scholars from both areas describe them as processes by which people deal with unexpected situations in their environments that make it difficult to determine the appropriate action or response (Mishel, 1988; Weick & Sutcliffe, 2001). Unexpected events create uncertainty and result in sensemaking activities. For those who see the commonalities in both approaches, it would seem necessary to review both the uncertainty and sensemaking literature for this volume.

If you have a tendency to make distinctions between concepts (a separator), you will see these as two significantly different approaches to understanding organizational experiences. Two significant differences are consistently articulated. Weick (1995) discusses sensemaking as the process that occurs when equivocality is present, that is, when multiple meanings could be assigned to a given situation; sensemaking helps assign meaning to the situation when there are too many plausible meanings and it is a challenge to decide which information to prioritize. In contrast, he describes uncertainty as occurring when there is inadequate information to assign meaning to the situation. This definition of uncertainty is consistent with much of the URT literature, which focuses on individuals' need to gain information to address some unexpected situation that is not known or understood (Berger & Calabrese, 1975).

A second emphasis of sensemaking that has been articulated that makes it potentially different from uncertainty is that sensemaking is typically described as a retrospective process. According to Weick (1995, 2001), sensemaking occurs after the fact as individuals remember back to understand their past lived experience. By considering past information, individuals make sense of their current projects, goals, and experiences. Uncertainty reduction is described much more as a proactive, present tense, process of understanding a situation in which individuals actively seek information to address their lack of information (Berger & Calabrese, 1975). Reducing uncertainty often involves proactive information seeking (Ashford & Black, 1996), although passive forms of receiving information also occur (Kramer, 1993). Sensemaking may not involve any action and may simply involve reconsidering past experiences (Louis, 1980).

In addition to these two differences that have been articulated, a number of other differences seem apparent. Most sensemaking research uses qualitative research methods and is consistent with an interpretive-symbolic or interpretive perspective of communication, whereas most uncertainty research uses quantitative research methods and is consistent with a mechanistic or functional perspective of communication (Fisher, 1978; Krone, Jablin, & Putnam, 1987; Putnam, 1983). This suggests that they have different epistemological assumptions. In addition, Weick (1995) argues that sensemaking is grounded in identity construction, whereas most uncertainty research focuses on understanding others and the external environment. Viewed from a perspective that focuses on distinctions, there would be no reason to review the literature on sensemaking in a book about uncertainty.

Given these similarities and differences, this volume focuses primarily on reviewing the research that explicitly takes an uncertainty approach and does not attempt to review the large body of research that takes a sensemaking approach. However, given my own tendencies toward being a combiner, I do occasionally include articles that have taken a sensemaking approach in developing a revised model of managing uncertainty reduction and so some are included in the review of literature. As a result of this inclusion and the revised model developed in the next chapter, the connection between uncertainty and sensemaking is briefly revisited in the last chapter.

Focusing primarily on research specifically related to uncertainty, the literature on uncertainty in collective settings is divided into three major sections in this chapter. The first section on uncertainty in group settings is quite brief due to the limited amount of research specifically in the area. This is followed by an examination of uncertainty as experienced by individuals in organizational settings. The primary focus of this section is on internal audiences such as organizational newcomers, or individual responses to job transfers, reductions in force (layoffs), and mergers and acquisitions. The section includes a few studies that focus on how members of external audiences, such as the community, respond to uncertainty. The third major section of the chapter examines more collective experience of organizational uncertainty. It frequently focuses on the impact of environmental uncertainty on organizational decision makers.

GROUP CONTEXTS

There is a dearth of research specifically addressing uncertainty in group contexts. Likewise, the literature on information seeking between groups to manage uncertainty is "barren" (Baldwin & Hunt, 2002, p. 280). First, the two research studies that explicitly examine uncertainty in group contexts are discussed. One is an experimental study of undergraduate students meeting for the first time as a group. The second concerns a group or team in an organizational setting, although the organizational context is generally ignored. Despite this paucity of uncertainty research on group settings, the two studies provide some unique insights into uncertainty and uncertainty reduction processes in groups. Then Poole's (1978) conceptual discussion of information seeking in intergroup communication is presented. After examining this scholarship that explicitly discusses uncertainty, a case is made that managing uncertainty is an implicit part of a number of other areas of group research. Two specific examples are examined briefly, models of decision making in groups and group norms.

Primary tension in a group, the social unease or stiffness that accompanies groups initially getting acquainted, is quite similar to uncertainty, according to Booth-Butterfield et al. (1988). They point out that both primary tension and uncertainty in initial interactions between strangers are associated with similar behaviors. Both are associated with longer pauses, lack of interruptions, and low- intimacy topics. Whereas previous research on primary tension has been based on qualitative description, their experimental study focused on observable behaviors during primary tension in groups that differed according to the levels of uncertainty. Specifically, they compared groups that received biographic and demographic information typical of initial interactions to reduce their uncertainty prior to meeting the first time with groups that did not receive this information. The groups that received the introductory information had less silence and qualifiers in their talk and also were less tentative than groups that did not receive the information. Booth-Butterfield et al. interpret this as strong support for the general principles of URT. The results suggest that even minimal reductions in uncertainty assist group members in having more fluent communication. This presumably results in smoother, more productive group interaction.

In the second study, Middleton (1997) provides a unique perspective on uncertainty in an intensive-care medical team. Through a discursive analysis, he examines uncertainty as an intersubjective process. He views uncertainty as a resource in the creation of a shared meaning for teams. By remembering (creating certainty) or forgetting (creating or maintaining uncertainty), individuals contribute to a collective definition of the uncertainty in the current situation. In this way, team members can either reduce uncertainties or create uncertainties. For example, by pointing out (remembering) that the current procedural problem is like a previously addressed one, the uncertainty can be effectively reduced and the appropriate action determined. Failing to connect a current situation to a past one (forgetting) can create uncertainty to allow for a new creative solution to a problem. The important conclusion Middleton draws is that the status of what is certain or uncertain is established and accounted for in the sequential group talk.

This intersubjective process of establishing what is certain and uncertain influences the actions and behaviors of the group.

Middleton (1997) further identifies three general approaches to managing uncertainty through discursive remembering and forgetting. First, by remembering or forgetting past experiences, individuals can create uncertainty about current practice and thereby influence change. Recalling a time when a different procedure was used can create uncertainty about current practice, or forgetting the details of a past event can allow enough uncertainty to try something new. For example, if a group member recalls (remembering) how the intensive-care team dealt with a problem of providing coverage during shift changes in the past using a different approach, this can call into question and create uncertainty about the current procedure. Second, remembering past experiences can establish relationships to current uncertainties. This may lead to changes in the procedure. For example, if a member of the team recalls (remembering) that documenting services in a particular way worked in the past, it can be used to address the documenting problem that is currently being discussed. Third, remembering or forgetting the past can make personal connections to the present so that hypothetical examples can influence uncertainties. For example, by asserting that it is not clear how the team addressed the issue of vaccines previously (forgetting), a team member can suggest a number of hypothetical cases so that a procedure to address all of them can be adopted. Through these various techniques, groups negotiate their shared understanding of the uncertainty in the situation. This negotiation process allows the group to either maintain an old procedure, or change and adjust to new ones.

In a conceptual piece, Poole (1978) more explicitly identifies how work groups seek information to assist them in accomplishing their tasks as they deal with uncertainty. He hypothesizes that work groups experience different levels of uncertainty depending on the availability, uniformity, and interdependence of their information needs. When information is available, uniform, and independent from other groups, groups experience limited uncertainty because they have access to predictable information without having to rely on others. This would mean they have fewer information needs and less motivation to seek information. The more unavailable, unpredictable, and interdependent with other groups, the more the group must develop communication network links to obtain the information they need. Effective groups develop the communication patterns needed given the level of uncertainty in their information environment. This conceptual work by Poole provides some interesting ideas about how uncertainty in group contexts influences information seeking without providing empirical tests of the hypotheses.

While there is a lack of research explicitly examining uncertainty in group contexts, a cursory examination of research in group decision making indicates that the ability to manage uncertainty is an implicit part of many group decision-making processes. Decision-making groups must determine who knows what, how to pool information, how to coordinate action, and how to reconcile differences to reach agreement; they develop "transactive memory" based on the knowledge and expectations of individual members and create processes for storing and retrieving that information at appropriate times based on their level of interdependency (Hollingshead, 2001). In essence, this suggests that group members face uncertainties as they attempt to coordinate and integrate their individual knowledge bases to function effectively as a collective group.

In specifically discussing decision-making processes, Dewey (1910) explained that the reflective thinking process begins when there is a problem, doubt, hesitation, perplexity, or mental difficulty that motivates or challenges an individual to think. These descriptors of motivators to reflective thinking are quite similar to definitions of uncertainty. In addition, Dewey writes that reflective thinking involves the act of searching, hunting, and inquiring to find material that will resolve the doubt or dispose of the perplexity. This process of gathering information is quite similar to information seeking to reduce uncertainty. So while Dewey did not explicitly examine reducing uncertainty, it is apparent that the decision-making processes he explained involve reducing uncertainty through information seeking.

While the process of reflective thinking was initially proposed for individuals, and the steps of reflective thinking were organized differently in the two editions of the book by Dewey (1910, 1933), his general suggestions for decision making have largely been adopted as the prescriptive models of group decision making that have been prevalent in group communication textbooks over the past decades (e.g., Fisher, 1980; Keyton, 1999). The general steps of effective decision making are typically variations on these: (a) the problem is identified and analyzed; (b) criteria for an effective solution are developed; (c) possible solutions are generated; (d) the solutions are evaluated to select the best one; and (e) the solution is implemented and evaluated. According to these prescriptive models, groups are more effective if they follow these steps.

Descriptive models of the characteristics of effective group decision making have often found similar results. For example, Hirokawa and Rost (1992) found that compared to ineffective groups, effective groups exhibit these characteristics: (a) more problem/task analysis and less problem/task analysis-inhibiting communication; (b) slightly more criteria establishing communication and a great deal less criteria inhibiting communication; (c) more communication evaluating the positive qualities of various choices and less communication inhibiting evaluation of the positive qualities; and (d) more communication evaluating the negative qualities of choices and slightly less communication that inhibited the evaluation of negative qualities of choices. The authors conclude that while it is not important that groups go through linear phases of these types of communication, groups that are vigilant in these characteristics are more effective.

The similarities between the prescriptive and descriptive models are rather apparent. What is implicit from this brief examination of both types of models is that the characteristics of effective group decision making involve managing uncertainty effectively. For example, identifying and analyzing the problem facing the group involves reducing uncertainty by clarifying the exact nature of the problem (it is this, but not that) and by collecting information to reduce uncertainty about the actual causes and effects of the problem as part of problem analysis. Establishing criteria involves setting minimum or maximum goals that an effective solution must meet (it must be accomplished in no more than 3 weeks and it must not cost more than so much). This reduces uncertainty about which possible solutions can or cannot be adopted. Considering the positive and negative outcomes of various solutions is designed to help the group reduce uncertainty about the future (this solution will cause these good things to happen, but also will result in this negative outcome). The overall process described by both the prescriptive and descriptive models of decision making is designed to reduce uncertainty about what plan to adopt and how to implement it effectively. Overall, then, decision making models implicitly rely on groups effectively reducing uncertainty to make effective decisions.

Analysis of groups making poor decisions also implies that failure to manage uncertainty results in ineffective decisions. The most notable work in this area by Irving Janis (1972) finds that ineffective groups often do not practice the principles described and prescribed previously that help manage uncertainty. Ineffective groups fail to analyze the problem effectively, inhibit the consideration of alternatives, and fail to consider the possible negative outcomes of their actions, among other fallacies. Calling this failure in group processing *groupthink*, Janis and others have blamed various ineffective high profile disasters on this type of ineffective decision making, from the Bay of Pigs invasion under President Kennedy to the Watergate break-in and cover-up under President Nixon.

In another examination of ineffective decision making, Hirokawa, Gouran, and Martz (1988) point to various problems that led to the Challenger space shuttle disaster. Examining the transcripts of the public hearings, they found evidence that decision makers used vague and ambiguous language and relied on inaccurate information and beliefs. Changes in the decision procedures from postponing launches if there were any safety concerns to postponing only if there was clear evidence of unacceptable danger also created unexpected challenges for the engineers as they made ineffective attempts at persuading others to delay the launch. These various problems each contributed to uncertainty in the situation and led to the incorrect decision to launch the fatal flight.

Each of these analyses indicates that effective decision making would have averted these disasters. Implicit in them is that better management of uncertainty would have resulted in effective decisions. Groupthink can be averted when group members examine issues more thoroughly, consider additional information and options to reduce uncertainty in the situation by having a better understanding of their choices and their impact. Ineffective—indeed, fatal—decisions like the launch of the Challenger can be avoided if communication and procedures are clearer so that participants have accurate information to manage uncertainty as they make decisions. Taken together, the research on effective and ineffective group decision making implies that managing uncertainty is an important part of good decision making.

Another area of group research that implicitly involves managing uncertainty is the study of norms and rules in group settings. A brief examination of the research on norms and rules in groups indicates some of the ways they help manage uncertainty for group members. As rules or norms develop over time, they have three main characteristics, according to Shimanoff (1980). First, they are followable, such that individuals can choose to follow, break, or change them. Next, they are prescriptive of what is obligatory, prohibited, permissible, and preferable, such that deviations from them are evaluated and sanctioned. Finally, they are contextual, such that they apply to certain types of similar situations, but not all situations. Shaw (1981) summarizes a number of other characteristics of group norms: (a) norms do not exist for everything; norms only develop for significant and reoccurring activities; (b) norms may not apply equally to everyone; a particular norm may apply to a person of low status but not to a person of high status; (c) norms vary in the degree to which they are accepted; everyone in a group may accept a particular norm, or a subgroup may not follow the norm; (d) a varying range of deviation may be acceptable so that the consequences for following or breaking the norms may vary; moderate deviations from one norm may have no appreciable consequence, while a minor deviation from another norm may result in serious sanctions, such as exclusion from the group or worse.

Implicit in these discussions of group norms is that norms inherently help group members reduce uncertainty about their group interactions. New or zero-history groups experience high levels of uncertainty because the communication norms for their collective interaction have yet to be established and group members must rely on experiences in similar groups to guesstimate the group norms until they become clear. Newcomers to groups experience uncertainty about the norms of the established group while members of the group experience uncertainty about the behaviors of the newcomers. Through interaction over time, group members gain an understanding of group norms and thereby reduce their uncertainty about appropriate and inappropriate behaviors for themselves and others. As they gain an understanding of the norms, they also understand how to respond to various situations appropriately. They also know how to respond to group members who fail to follow the norms. The process of creating and learning group norms is implicitly an uncertainty management issue. Group members reduce their uncertainty by gaining an understanding of the group norms for appropriate and inappropriate behaviors.

Clearly, more work can be done on uncertainty in group contexts. Previous research demonstrates that uncertainty reduction through information sharing impacts group communication by increasing fluency during initial group interactions. Research also has examined some of the ways that groups participate in creating a shared understanding of the level of uncertainty facing them. Other group research suggests the importance of managing uncertainty for groups making decisions and establishing interaction norms. However, much of this research has only implicitly examined these as uncertainty reduction processes. More research explicitly examining uncertainty management by groups is needed. In addition, because many groups are embedded in organizational contexts, research should also consider the impact of the organizational context on the groups where applicable. For example, Middleton (1997) did not examine how the larger hospital policies and procedures impacted the group processes of managing uncertainty for the intensive-care medical team. The research that explicitly and implicitly examines uncertainty in groups emphasizes the need for additional research on how groups manage uncertainty through their communication interactions.

ORGANIZATIONAL CONTEXTS

Conceptualizations of uncertainty in the organizational context are generally consistent with interpersonal definitions of uncertainty. Uncertainty involves a lack of information for making decisions, not knowing the probable outcomes of a particular decision, or lacking confidence in stating probabilities of outcomes (Duncan, 1972). Uncertainty may involve state uncertainty concerning what is changing in the environment, effect uncertainty concerning whether those changes will impact the organization or its members, or response uncertainty concerning the likely impact of any response to environmental uncertainty (Milliken, 1987). Like the definitions used in interpersonal contexts for examining URT, a lack of predictability is the focus throughout these various definitions.

Uncertainty is prevalent at all levels of organizations, but consistently has different implications at different levels of analysis (Browning, Sitkim, & Sutcliffe, 1999). As a result, uncertainty in organizational contexts has been conceptualized and examined at two or three levels. For example, Heath and Gay (1997) discuss macro uncertainty (between the organization and stakeholders), network uncertainty (between individuals inside and outside the organization), and intra-individual uncertainty (within individual cognitive processes). Others have simplified this to two levels. Uncertainty has been divided into corporate uncertainty involving enterprise level issues of uncertainty, and individual uncertainty involving issues such as uncertainty associated with individual experiences (Driskill & Goldstein, 1986). Similarly, external uncertainty concerns problems with predictability and change in the environment outside the organization, perhaps related to the quality of information available, whereas internal uncertainty concerns employee behaviors and the maintenance of operations and procedures (Farace et al., 1978; Jorgensen & Petelle, 1992).

The division into two levels of analysis coincides with the idea of individual or micro levels of analysis, such as how individuals adjust to changes that create uncertainty for them, and organizational or macro levels of analysis, such as how organizations respond to an unpredictable economy. As a result, this portion of the review is divided into two primary categories, individual and organizational levels of analysis.

INDIVIDUAL LEVEL OF ANALYSIS

At the individual level of analysis, research has primarily focused on how individuals respond to uncertainty in their organizational settings. The assumptions for this body of research are that information adequacy and uncertainty are related and that uncertainty creates negative affective responses but that information and certainty create positive responses. This perspective is consistent with Axiom 7 of URT, which states that there is a negative relationship between uncertainty and liking. In organizational settings, when individuals feel that they are receiving insufficient information, they experience uncertainty and as a result dissatisfaction. Conversely, when they feel they are receiving sufficient information, they experience certainty, and as a result will experience satisfaction and confidence in their organizational roles.

A few studies that explore the general relationship between uncertainty and affective response or satisfaction in organizational settings are considered first. Then, the studies that explore how individuals respond to uncertainty during changes are reported. The two general categories of change that have been examined are employees' responses to individual changes and to organizational changes. In examining individual changes, a significant amount of research has examined how newcomers or job transferees respond to the individual experience of changing jobs. In examining how individuals react to organizational changes, research has examined how employees respond to the uncertainty that results from changes such as reductions in force (layoffs) or mergers and acquisitions.

Uncertainty and Affective Response

The amount or adequacy of internal communication relates to the levels of uncertainty and resulting satisfaction for organizational members. Uncertainty may be experienced concerning a variety of areas such as task (how to do the job), maintenance (organizational progress and goals), and human or personal information (social relations). Uncertainty due to lack of these types of information is predictive of dissatisfaction with supervisors and dissatisfaction with the organization in general (Salem & Williams, 1984). Dissatisfaction is often a precursor to various problems such as low productivity or employee turnover.

Clients/Customers and the Public

The adequacy of external communication with customers or clients is another area where individual reactions to uncertainty have been examined in organizational settings. One area of focus in this research has been on a particular type of client interaction, caregiver–patient interactions. These represent a specific type of individual level of analysis since the interactions typically take place in an organizational setting, although they are often treated as health communication. In these caregiver–patient interactions, information management is a collaborative process in which both patients and caregivers need to manage uncertainty about each other (Brashers et al., 2002). Resolving those uncertainties involves a process of mutual influence (Hines, 2001). Some research in this area has focused primarily on the uncertainty that doctors face as they deal with the medical issues (Fox, 1959, 2000). Other research has focused on how patients experience and manage their uncertainties (Mishel, 1997, 1999).

Uncertainty is inherent in the doctor–patient interaction. Doctors face uncertainties about their personal knowledge about the medical situation, the state of knowledge in the field in general, and their ability to determine if the uncertainty is the result of their own limitations or the limitation of the medical field (Fox, 1959). The rapid increases in new knowledge and technology simply change the nature of the uncertainties by raising new questions and concerns about the diagnosis, treatment, and prognosis of their patients (Fox, 2000). Patients experience uncertainty about a variety of aspects of their situation including the severity of their illness, their short- and long-term prognosis, the specificity of the diagnosis, the management of their treatments, the social support they receive, and their interactions with the medical professionals (Mishel, 1997, 1999). Doctors and patients cope with these uncertainties through active strategies such as seeking additional information to gain a sense of knowledge and control of the situation, as well as by seeking social support from others facing similar situations including sharing a sort of grim humor or gallows humor that might seem inappropriate to those outside the situation (Mischel, 1988; Fox, 1959). While these descriptions of uncertainty in doctor–patient settings provide a general sense of the experience of uncertainty, they offer little insight into the way interactions of doctors and patients help each to manage their uncertainties.

In a specific examination of doctor–patient interactions, Williams and Meredith (1984) compared the information expectant mothers received to the information they needed, and found that they experienced uncertainty primarily concerning what to expect during labor, what to expect at the time of delivery, and breast-feeding. The researchers found that uncertainty reduction or information adequacy (a match between needs and amount received) was associated with doctor–patient satisfaction. As would be expected, first-time mothers experienced greater uncertainty than experienced ones because of their lack of previous experience. One unique finding was that patients reported receiving too much information about the dangers of drinking and smoking, and too many written materials in general from their care providers. This suggests that too much information is perhaps redundant and perceived negatively.

Because there are multiple, interrelated uncertainties in health care interactions, patients experience uncertainty about outcomes (medical, social, psychological), evaluations of outcomes (desirability or undesirability of various options), and the interconnectedness of these uncertainties (Hines, 2001). In an examination of some of the interrelated uncertainties of cardiac patients, Sheer and Cline (1995) examined patients' experiences of uncertainty concerning the nature of their illnesses, their relationship to the doctor, and the medical setting. They found that all types of uncertainty were negatively related to perceptions of information adequacy, but that a medical interview reduced uncertainty. In addition, information adequacy was associated with lower post-interview uncertainty. Their surprising finding was that the desire for more information was unrelated to any measures of uncertainty or information adequacy. Patients wanted more information regardless of their initial level of uncertainty. Sheer and Cline interpret this as an indication that in medical situations, patients have a high need for information regardless of their level of uncertainty. They call this a "ceiling effect" that is probably due to the serious consequence of cardiac problems for the patients. These results demonstrate that desire for information may be unrelated to actual levels of uncertainty. The need for reassurance may be as important as uncertainty levels in determining the desire for more information. Redundant information may provide patients with additional confidence that their knowledge of the situation is adequate.

In examining preferences for communicating given the uncertainty in acute and chronic health care situations, Hines, Badzek, Leslie, and Glover (1998) found that nurses are more comfortable discussing present conditions and treatments, rather than future prognosis, and they prefer discussing issues of the chronically ill rather than end-of-life decisions. These findings suggest that the higher the levels of uncertainty the more uncomfortable the nurses are in discussing the situation with their patients. The previous research would suggest that these would be situations in which patients would be particularly interested in receiving information.

Taken as a whole, the research on caregiver–patient interactions in organizational settings suggests that they are in a situation that has high levels of uncertainty despite increases in medical knowledge and technology. Through interactions, caregivers and patients attempt to manage the uncertainty by gaining and exchanging information and seeking social support. The adequacy of the information exchanged influences patients' satisfaction.

The second type of external interaction that has been examined concerns community members' reactions to public relations communication concerning risks of hazardous facilities. In examining external communication related to risks to the community, Nathan, Heath, and Douglas (1992) found that community members who were less risk tolerant experienced more uncertainty and saw more risk and less benefit in a local smelter plant. However, they suggested that it took uncertainty *and* involvement to motivate information seeking.

Consistent with URT, in another study, Heath, Seshadri, and Lee (1998) found that members of the general public who felt more knowledgeable felt less uncertain about the risks of a chemical plant. In addition, they found that dread was associated with a lack of communication openness and increases in uncertainty. Interestingly, those in close proximity to the plant (less than 5 miles) felt less uncertain and supported the plant more than those living farther away (more than 20 miles) did. This appears to be the result of the company's concerted effort to communicate with members of the surrounding community, resulting in more positive attitudes toward the company in the close communities. The company made little effort to communicate with more distant or latent communities, which resulted in less positive attitudes in the more distant communities.

Taken together, the results examining individuals' reactions to internal and external communication are quite consistent with URT. The research suggests that employees, customers or clients, or members of the community experience uncertainty and dissatisfaction when they perceive that information is not adequately provided. The practical implications of these results seem quite clear. Providing additional information to interested parties such as employees, customers, or stakeholders in the community will generally have a positive impact. Uncertainty will be reduced for these individuals through communication. As uncertainty decreases, satisfaction, liking, or support will increase. These relationships are consistent with Axiom 7 of the original theory (Berger & Calabrese, 1975).

Job Transitions: Newcomers

A significant body of research has used principles of URT to examine the experiences of employees in transition. The focus has primarily been on newcomers entering organizations for the first time, although other research has examined job transferees as they assume new positions in the same organization but at new locations. These job transitions are considered a time of high uncertainty as employees adjust to new settings, expectations, and relationships. Most of this research is based on a socialization or assimilation model.

The assimilation process of joining or becoming a part of an organization is generally defined as consisting of two parts: socialization and individualization (Jablin, 1987). Socialization involves the efforts of organizational members to influence others to learn the appropriate behaviors and fill organizational roles or needs for the benefit of the organization at large. Through socialization, organizational members "learn the ropes" and become competent in their roles (Van Maanen & Schein, 1979). Individualization involves members' efforts to influence the members of the organization to change and adjust to their own individual needs (Jablin, 1987). Through individualization, employees affect change and redefine their roles in the organization.

Much of the research on socialization is based on phase models, which suggest that employees' experiences change over time. In a typical phase model, Jablin (1987) suggests that there are four phases. Anticipatory socialization occurs before individuals officially join an organization, when they are still not members of the organization. The encounter phase involves the first days or months on the job, when members still feel like newcomers. This is the period of highest uncertainty. Metamorphosis begins when members feel that they are no longer newcomers, but full members of the organization. It continues throughout their tenure in the organization even though they may be promoted or change jobs. Finally, exit occurs as members prepare to leave the organization and then separate from it. Rather than precise chronological time periods, these phases are more correctly understood as psychological changes that occur in members as they adjust to their changing roles in organizations. For example, it is more appropriate to consider the encounter phase as completed when individuals are no longer preoccupied with the transitions and instead are focused on maintaining the new situations rather than to consider the phase completed after a specific number of weeks or months on the job (Schlossberg, 1981).

Although the interaction of socialization and individualization creates uncertainty throughout individuals' organizational tenure, members experience particularly high levels of uncertainty as they face transitions. Socialization is particularly strong during boundary passages, such as when individuals join the organization or are promoted, because they involve learning new tasks and developing new relationships (Van Maanen & Schein, 1979). During such changes, members experience behavioral uncertainty concerning what will be rewarded and punished and role evaluation uncertainty concerning whether they can be successful in their new roles (Lester, 1987). Successful passage through organizational entry is related to the ability to reduce uncertainty (Mignerey, Rubin, & Gorden, 1995). Uncertainty is particular high for newcomers. Joining an organization is much like meeting someone for the first time. Uncertainty levels are at least as high for newcomers meeting people in their new organizations as they are for strangers meeting for the first time in other social settings (Lester, 1987).

To illustrate the role of uncertainty and the interaction of socialization and individualization during transitions, consider an example of a new waitress joining a group of seasoned veterans at a local restaurant. The veterans have established patterns for work assignments (who works where and when), for doing various tasks (what procedure is used for dispensing food orders), and even for relationships (who socializes with whom during and after work). Some of these patterns are based on organizational policy, such as procedures for handling customers who use credit cards to pay their bills. Others are just habits that have developed over time, such as two of the veterans who may like to work the same shifts and at adjoining sections of tables. The new waitress is uncertain about all of these issues or topics. Most likely, the veterans will attempt to teach (socialization) the new waitress these various procedures and patterns and she will most likely adopt many of them. At times, she may ask the veterans how to do a job because it is unfamiliar to her, or she may instead ask the manager. At other times, she may simply observe the veterans to get the information she needs rather than ask for help. In addition, based on prior work experience, she may feel that a different pattern for storing supplies would be more efficient for her. She may attempt to make such a change (individualization) either by discussing it with the veterans or by simply doing it differently. In addition, her presence may cause a shift in social relationships as she makes friends with certain individuals to meet her social needs at work.

Throughout this time, she will experience some uncertainty as to which patterns must be followed and which ones she can change. The longer she is in the organization, the more familiar she becomes with the patterns. As a result, she will become more certain of what she must do a certain way and what can be changed. As she develops work and friendship relationships she will most likely become more satisfied with her decision to join and remain in the restaurant. Of course, just when she becomes fairly certain about things, a new employee is hired and the manager announces a new procedure for closing the restaurant at night. She must adjust to these uncertainties as well and continue to try to understand her role in the situation.

This example illustrates many of the areas of research that have been examined concerning newcomers. Due to the importance of uncertainty in the process for newcomers joining organizations, research has examined the types of uncertainty, sources for seeking information to reduce uncertainty, and methods of seeking information to reduce uncertainty. In addition to this, outcomes related to each of these have been examined. Some of the major findings in each of these areas are presented next. Included in this review is research that both explicitly and implicitly uses uncertainty reduction principles to examine the newcomer experience.

Types of Uncertainty.   A number of different types of uncertainty have been differentiated in the research (see Table 3.1). As part of the transition into new jobs, newcomers face uncertainty concerning many issues. They may experience uncertainty about mastering basic job tasks and procedures; building an image or role identity; building relationships with others; constructing a frame of reference to understand the workplace; mapping the relevant players and power relationships; locating themselves in the task and social networks; and learning the local language (Louis, 1982). They experience uncertainty about their tasks, roles, relationships, isolation, and performance and must make sense of their experiences (Nelson & Quick, 1991). In attempting to summarize previous research, Morrison (1995) suggested that there were seven types of information necessary to reduce uncertainty: (a) technical, or task mastery; (b) referent, or requirements and expectations; (c) social, or relationships to others; (d) appraisal, or quality of effort; (e) normative, or organizational culture; (f) organizational information, or structure and procedures; and (g) political, or power distributions. These conceptualizations are consistent with URT, which recognizes that there are different levels or types of uncertainty (Berger, 1979).

Morrison (1993b) found that newcomers' concern for these types of information changed over time; they became less concerned about technical, normative,

TABLE 3.1

Types of Uncertainty for Newcomers

Louis, 1982	Nelson & Quick, 1991	Morrison, 1995	Ostroff & Kozlowski, 1992	Miller & Jablin, 1991
Tasks/ procedures	Tasks	Technical/task	Task	
		Referent		Referent
Image/identity	Roles		Role	
Workplace frame	Make sense of experiences	Culture/normative	Culture/norms	
		Org. information		
Power/players		Political/power		
Task/social networks	Relationships	Relationships	Group	Relational
Local language				
	Isolation			
	Performance	Appraisal		Appraisal

and social information, but more concerned about referent and performance information as their tenure on the job increased. This suggests that newcomers focus on learning the details of their job initially, but as they master many of the tasks, they begin to focus on broader issues such as how they are being evaluated. Based on a slightly different typology, Ostroff and Kozlowski (1992) found that newcomers gained knowledge of their group quickly, but later gained more knowledge of their task and role; they were least certain about the culture and norms of their organizations. Again, this suggests that newcomers become concerned about reducing uncertainty about broader organizational issues only after they have gained an understanding of their immediate work environment.

Miller and Jablin (1991) provided a parsimonious typology of three types of uncertainty that has been used in other research. Members can experience referent uncertainty concerning understanding how to do their job; appraisal uncertainty concerns understanding how well one is performing; relational uncertainty concerns getting along with other members. Based on this typology, Teboul (1994) demonstrated that newcomers experience different levels of these types of uncertainty. He found that newcomers experienced the most referent uncertainty, followed by appraisal uncertainty, and experienced the least amount of relational uncertainty. In a follow-up study, Teboul (1997) found that members of the majority and minority culture experience the same frequency of referent uncertainty, but that minority members experience more frequent relational uncertainty. Overall, the research demonstrates that newcomers experience various types of uncertainty during the transition process of joining organizations.

Sources for Uncertainty Reduction. In addition to types of uncertainty, sources of information for reducing uncertainty for newcomers have also been examined (see Table 3.2). Most researchers have focused on information sources within the organization. For example, Louis, Posner, and Powell (1983) examine peers, supervisors, and senior coworkers as sources of information and found that peers were the most available and helpful sources. Frequency of interaction with such sources is associated with adjustment and uncertainty reduction (Reichers, 1987). Nelson and Quick (1991) found that daily interactions with peers and staff were the most available and most helpful compared with other sources. Morrison (1993b) reported that newcomers prefer supervisors for technical information, but peers for most other types of information and that written materials, compared to other sources, are used infrequently.

TABLE 3.2

Sources of Uncertainty Reduction

Louis, Posner, & Powell, 1983	Nelson & Quick, 1991	Morrison, 1993b	Ostroff & Kozlowski, 1992	Miller & Jablin, 1991	Teboul, 1994
Peers	Peers	Coworkers	Peers	Peers	Coworkers
Supervisors	Supervisors	Supervisors	Supervisors	Supervisors	Supervisors
Senior coworkers			Mentors	Other members	
	Secretary/ staff				
		Subordinates			Subordinates
		Newcomers			
		Impersonal	Manuals	Written materials	
		Outside sources			Friends
					Partner
					Family
				Clients/ customers	
		Watching			
		Trying	Task		

Other researchers have included sources of information for reducing uncertainty both inside and outside the organization. In addition to official sources (including written materials), the immediate role set (including peers and supervisors), other organizational members, and the task itself, Miller and Jablin (1991) theorized that extra-organizational sources such as clients or customers were potential sources of information. To test this notion empirically, Teboul (1994) included friends, romantic partners, and family as extra-organizational sources. He found that the preferred sources for information in order of importance were coworkers, supervisors, friends, romantic partners, family, and subordinates. His follow-up study found slight differences between majority and minority members in their preferences for sources of information (Teboul, 1995). For example, African-Americans valued partners and friends more than majority members did.

Overall, this research indicates that newcomers have a multitude of sources for gaining information for reducing uncertainty. They gain information from the job itself and from people both inside and outside of the organization. Although they can choose to reduce uncertainty through interaction with the source of uncertainty, they use many other indirect sources as well.

Methods of Information Seeking to Reduce Uncertainty.   Research has also examined the methods of information seeking to reduce uncertainty (see Table 3.3). Miller and Jablin (1991) provide a fairly comprehensive list of methods for seeking information to reduce uncertainty. Overt questions are direct requests for information from the target individual. Indirect questions involve hinting or non-interrogative questions like, "Don't you think … ?" Third party requests entail asking some other individual to gain information from or about the target of uncertainty. Testing is the act of violating perceived norms in order to assess the reactions

TABLE 3.3
Methods of Information Seeking to Reduce Uncertainty

Berger, 1979	*Miller & Jablin, 1991*	*Morrison, 1993a, 1995*
Interactive	Overt questions	Inquiry
Active	Indirect questions	
	Third party	
	Testing	
	Disguising	
	Observing	Observation
Passive	Surveillance	Passive, without seeking

and gain understanding. Disguising conversations includes strategies like subtle requests, joking, or self-disclosure with the hope of reciprocity. Observing encompasses carefully attending to gain specific information, whereas surveillance involves general monitoring for the possibility of making sense afterwards.

Based on this typology, Teboul (1994) found that newcomers' order of preference for type of information seeking was overt, surveillance, observation, indirect, third party, disguising, and testing. He found no relationship between type of uncertainty and information-seeking strategy and found very little difference in choice of method for different information sources. In addition to the typology, Morrison (1993a) also examined passive information receiving. Passive information receiving occurs when people voluntarily provide information without a prompt. For example, a peer might just walk up and explain a procedure to a newcomer even though the newcomer never asked for the information. Morrison found that passive information receiving, apart from actively seeking or monitoring for information, was an important predictor of employees' role clarity and task mastery at work.

In a further study, Morrison (1995) examined whether certain types of information were associated with specific methods of information seeking. She reported that appraisal information, technical information, and referent information were rated most useful, followed by political information. However, she found that the methods of seeking information varied according to the type of uncertainty. Inquiry was the preferred method for gaining technical information, but monitoring was preferred for social, appraisal, normative, and political information. Inquiry and monitoring were used equally for referent and organizational information. Morrison also found that passive or unsolicited information was very important in newcomer socialization.

The focus on various methods of information seeking for uncertainty reduction is consistent with URT; faced with uncertainty, newcomers seek information from a variety of sources through a variety of methods. Evidence further suggests that the method of seeking information may be related to the newcomers' background. For example, women entering traditionally male-dominated occupations preferred overt requests as the most valuable method, followed by observation (Holder, 1996). Hispanics, perhaps due to language or cultural differences, use less overt information seeking than majority Whites (Teboul, 1997). Overall, this research indicates that newcomers apparently make use of a variety of approaches to reduce uncertainty. This is consistent with Berger's (1979) notion that there are passive, active, and interactive methods of reducing uncertainty.

Outcomes of Uncertainty Reduction.

URT suggests that information seeking should reduce uncertainty and increase liking. The examination of outcomes from socialization has generally been supportive of these relationships. Consistently, newcomers who receive information to reduce uncertainty are more satisfied, more knowledgeable, and more likely to remain in their organization. Indicative of uncertainty reduction, Morrison (1993a) found that role clarity and task mastery improved with information seeking. Indicative of positive affect, daily interactions with peers and staff were positively related to job satisfaction and intention to stay (Nelson & Quick, 1991) and information seeking was related to job satisfaction, performance, and intention to stay (Morrison, 1993b).

Similar findings are reported in other research. Institutionalized socialization tactics are those that provide formal group training in which the steps and time table for progress are clearly defined (Jones, 1986). Mignerey et al. (1995) found that institutionalized tactics lead to uncertainty reduction. Specifically, they found that the combination of organizations using institutional socialization tactics and employees valuing feedback lead to information and feedback seeking, as well as reductions in role ambiguity. An examination of women entering traditionally male-dominated, blue-collar occupations found that overt, indirect, and third-party information seeking was particularly associated with reductions in role ambiguity and increases in role clarity (Holder, 1996).

Overall, the research on newcomers is consistent with URT. Newcomers experience various types of uncertainty. They use a variety of sources and methods for seeking information to reduce uncertainty. When they gain information, they feel more certain of their task and social roles and become more satisfied with their organizations. Returning to the earlier example of the new waitress, we see that she experienced uncertainty about her role and her social relations. Through communication with her peers and supervisor, she gradually learned the job expectations, as well as areas where she could change those expectations. As she reduced relational uncertainty, she developed friends and became more satisfied and comfortable in her job. Of course, she will experience new uncertainties as workers who leave are replaced with new employees. She will seek information to reduce uncertainty about these newcomers, but at the same time she may serve the role of providing information to these new employees to reduce their uncertainty.

Job Transitions: Transferees

In a vein similar to the previous research on newcomers, a series of articles by Kramer (1993, 1995, 1996, Jablin & Kramer, 1998) has examined transferees' experiences with uncertainty during their job transitions. Transferees take new positions in their current organization, but typically must physically relocate themselves and their families to new communities. Frequently, they are promoted or assume different job responsibilities as part of the job transfer. Kramer's work suggests that transferees are like newcomers in a number of ways. Like newcomers, they can experience uncertainty about their jobs, their performance, and their relationships. Although transferees are already familiar with their organization's general culture, like newcomers, they experience uncertainty about the roles in the new subculture (Kramer, 1993). They gain information that reduces their uncertainty from peers and supervisors (Kramer, 1995, 1996).

Kramer's work suggests that transferees manage their uncertainty differently than newcomers. Actively seeking information is not particularly associated with role clarity and job satisfaction for transferees. Rather, receiving unsolicited information from peers and supervisors and developing close relationships with peers were better predictors of reductions in role ambiguity and increases in satisfaction (Kramer 1995, 1996). Overall, his results suggest that transferees who receive feedback and social support without having to seek it reduce uncertainty and adjust to their new positions more quickly. What is not clear in his research is why some transferees receive this unsolicited information more than others do.

Finally, a few articles have compared how transferees and newcomers manage uncertainty. In a comparison between new and transferred law enforcement officers, Kramer (1994) found that both new and transferred officers increased requests for information as they assumed their new jobs, but then decreased those requests over time as they became more certain of their new roles. However, their experiences were not identical. Transferees developed closer peer relationships than newcomers, and newcomers continued to seek feedback from their peers over time while transferees reduced their requests as they gained experience. In a comparison of new and transferred employees at a retail store, Kramer, Callister, and Turban (1995) found that newcomers reported more information receiving, particularly through monitoring, than transferred employees, but that transferred employees reported more information giving than newcomers. This suggests that transferred employees were serving as sources of information for reducing uncertainty in the newcomers. In addition, transferred employees were more knowledgeable about the organization and their roles than newcomers, but there were no differences in their levels of job satisfaction. Kramer et al. also found that both newcomers and transferred employees who received unsolicited information experienced significant reductions in uncertainty about their role and their organization.

Overall, the research on transferred employees is complementary to the research on newcomers. Even though their experiences are somewhat different from those of newcomers, transferees do experience uncertainty in their new jobs and through communication reduce their uncertainty and respond with more positive affect toward their jobs. Taken together, the research on newcomers and transferees generally supports the principles of URT. However, unlike URT, the results suggest that unsolicited or passive reception of information has a significant impact on reducing uncertainty; it is often at least as important as actively seeking information.

Organizational Change

The previous section concerned individuals' responses to uncertainty created when they experience changes or transitions in their personal work situation. Other research has focused on how individuals respond to broader organizational changes that influence many employees. Some of these studies have examined the impact of sources and types of information. For example, Miller and Monge (1985) examined employees' responses to messages announcing an anticipated organizational innovation that included a change from traditional offices to an open landscape (cubicles). They manipulated the positive and negative information that they provided about the need for the change, the description of the change, or the interpretation of the change. The surprising finding was that any information, even negative information, was perceived as better than no information (control group). However, it was the cumulative effect of information, not information at a particular moment, that reduced stress for employees. This suggests that providing information is an ongoing process, not a one-time event. In a similar vein, Ellis (1992) surveyed nurses involved in a hierarchical restructuring of a hospital. She manipulated social information concerning the positive or negative impact the change would have on the nurses to examine the message impact on their attitude toward the change. She found that social information was particularly important for those experiencing high uncertainty and that a source perceived as credible had a greater positive impact than one perceived as low in credibility.

Another organizational change that creates uncertainty for organizational members is a reduction in work force, or the layoff of employees. Casey, Miller, and Johnson (1997) examined employees' methods of seeking information after a reduction in the work force resulted in increased uncertainty. Employees reporting increases in information deprivation and job insecurity about future employment indicated increases in uncertainty. The researchers found that the employees reduced their use of direct inquiry and relied more heavily on indirect information seeking such as observations, indirect inquiry, testing limits, and even third-party inquiries. Apparently, direct requests to their supervisors were perceived as too risky and so employees relied on these less obtrusive techniques. In another examination of communication during reductions in force, Johnson, Bernhagen, Miller, and Allen (1996) found that information deprivation or lack of information was associated with career uncertainty and a propensity to leave the organization; however, communication support from the manager reduced this negative relationship. In addition to communication, receiving more financial rewards served to reduce career uncertainty. Although rewards are not communication per se, one can argue that the rewards communicated a level of certainty about their future to the employees.

Mergers and acquisitions between organizations are another organizational change that creates uncertainty for employees. Employees often experience uncertainty and anxiety about a wide range of issues including job security, fear of declining status or job prospects, and loss of control over their careers, their autonomy, and their organizational identity (Napier, 1989). They experience uncertainty about what aspects of their organizations' culture will continue and what aspects will change (Buono, Bowditch, & Lewis, 1985). Frequently, they experience shock as they become aware of differences between the cultures of the two merging companies (Bastien, 1992).

The levels of uncertainty are often so severe during mergers and acquisitions that one researcher recommends that all negotiations concerning a potential merger be conducted in secret to minimize uncertainty (Graves, 1981). Of course, such a recommendation fails to consider the impact of information leaks that often occur during negotiations. So in contrast, DiFonzo and Bordia (1998) argue that it is better to release partial information than to experience the anger, low morale, and low productivity that occur when secrecy creates uncertainty that leads to rumors.

Consistent with URT, due to the stress created by uncertainty concerning mergers and acquisitions, employees seek out information from formal sources, as well as informal sources including customers and spouses (Napier, Simmons, & Stratton, 1989). Also supportive of URT, receiving information generally has a positive impact on employees. Directive, realistic, accurate, and timely information assists in reducing uncertainty for employees (Cornett-DeVito & Friedman, 1995). Increases in formal and interpersonal communication helps create certainty and improve employee morale, productivity, and profitability (Bastien, 1987). For example when employees in two banks received reassurances from their CEOs, their job security concerns and uncertainty were reduced (Buono et al., 1985). However, not all results from communication are positive. Kramer, Dougherty, and Pierce (in press) found that while communication during an airline merger reduced uncertainty for pilots in the acquired company and increased their sense of job security, it actually resulted in a decrease in their attitude about the merger as they became dissatisfied with the way the merger impacted their seniority.

In an experiment designed to test the ability to manage employee uncertainty through communication, Schweiger and DeNisi (1991) examined the impact of a planned communication intervention on employees after a merger. One plant received newsletters twice a month, participated in weekly meetings, and had access to a merger hotline while a comparable plant received the treatment typical of the company, simply a formal announcement with no follow-up communication. Results clearly indicated that both plants experienced increases in uncertainty and stress after the merger announcement. The communication intervention resulted in a leveling off of both uncertainty and job satisfaction for employees at the one plant, whereas employees at the other plant with no communication continued to experience increases in uncertainty and decreases in satisfaction. In fact, the differences were significant enough that the organization adopted the communication intervention at the second plant after 3 months rather than continuing the experiment. Clearly, communication impacted employees' uncertainty and affective responses.

Similarly, Napier et al. (1989) found that a monthly merger newsletter and a hotline for asking questions after the merger were beneficial for employees of two banks that merged. However, they concluded that no matter how much communication occurs concerning the merger process, employees are likely to feel that they need more information. Overall, Napier (1989) concludes that the research suggests that an effective communication program can lead to less anxiety and higher satisfaction during mergers and acquisitions.

The results from research examining how individuals manage uncertainty as a result of organizational changes are fairly consistent with URT. Due to a lack of adequate information surrounding organizational changes, organizational members experience uncertainty. The uncertainty frequently leads to dissatisfaction and intentions to leave. Additional communication with organizational supervisors or other members results in uncertainty reduction and more positive feelings toward the organization and intentions to remain in the organization.

ORGANIZATIONAL LEVEL ANALYSIS

Uncertainty as an Organizational Phenomenon

Uncertainty at the external, enterprise, or organizational level of analysis has typically been discussed in terms of environmental uncertainty. Environmental uncertainty is a psychological state, not an objective one, in which the decision makers or managers of an organization feel unable to predict those physical and social factors that influence their organization (Beam, 1996; Jorgensen & Petelle, 1992). The organization's perception of uncertainty is a type of cumulative concept based on individual members' perceptions of uncertainty, although it is not simply an arithmetic summation of individual perceptions (Downey & Slocum, 1975). Both external factors, such as the amount of information available in the environment, and internal factors, such as the structure of the organization, influence this perception (Huber, O'Connell, & Cummings, 1975). Even though this means an organization's uncertainty is based in part on individual perceptions, the joint decision making and communication processes result in a shared or agreed-on perceived environmental uncertainty. It is in the shared perception that it is an organizational-level phenomenon.

The organization's perception of uncertainty is influenced by characteristics of the environment in the sense that environmental characteristics are more likely to invoke certain perceptions than other perceptions; the environment moderates perceived uncertainty (Downey & Slocum, 1975). However, an organization's uncertainty is ultimately a perception that may be unrelated to any objective characteristics of the environment. It is the organizational decision makers' perception and evaluation of the environment that matters rather than objective characteristics of the environment (Child, 1972). For example, the organizational decision makers of a small manufacturing firm may have experienced no problems in the past with their suppliers. Due to this, most likely they will come to agree that their suppliers are reliable and as a result, develop no contingency plans. Alternatively, they may come to agree that a contingency supplier is needed because their suppliers may be facing a number of environmental constraints. A low unemployment rate may create worker shortages for the supplier. In the first case, the perception is of a certain environment, and in the second, the perception is of an uncertain environment. Neither perception of uncertainty is necessarily related to the actual environment that the organization faces. In both cases the decision makers of the organization have an agreed-on level of uncertainty and react according to those perceptions.

Consistent with URT, scholars generally agree that the perception of environmental uncertainty is related to a lack of information. For example, Huber et al. (1975) used an organization simulation and found that as information load increased, uncertainty decreased. Both the content and amount of the information are important. The experience of uncertainty may be caused by a lack of information relevant to the decisions, a lack of knowledge about organizational decisions, or a lack of ability to assign probabilities to various decision options (Duncan, 1973; Farace et al., 1978). That is to say that decision makers may be uncertain about the situation in the environment, the possible actions they could take, or the value of those various actions (Conrath, 1967). For example, decision makers in an international exporting company may not be able to obtain accurate information about the stability of a current foreign government and thus experience uncertainty concerning what actions to take. Even if they have accurate information about the current government, they may not be certain about the various options they have for dealing with that government and its policies. Finally, even with accurate information about the current situation and a clear picture of the options that they have, they may be unable to accurately predict the outcomes of the various choices.

Although certain characteristics of the environment are likely to invoke certain perceptions, it is important to recognize that organizations can actually influence their environments through the choices made by their decision makers (Child, 1972). By making choices about products or services and strategies, organization decision makers select the environment to which they must react. If the decision makers decide to focus on low cost rather than designer clothes, they are selecting a particular environment in which to work while at the same time reducing the importance of other particular environments. In the case of extremely large organizations, decision makers may have the ability to influence their environment by managing their internal processes. For example, at certain times in recent years the members of OPEC (Organization of Petroleum Exporting Countries) have been able to influence their environment by creating demand for their product by under-producing in comparison to the demand. Of course, at other times they have been unable to influence their environment effectively because of over-production. If an efficient alternative to the internal combustion engine is ever developed, OPEC members will lose much of their ability to exert influence on their environment and face an uncertain environment due to changing demands for their product.

The research related to organizational levels of uncertainty has tended to focus either on classifying environmental uncertainty or on examining different patterns that decision makers use when they respond to environmental uncertainty.

Classifying Environmental Uncertainty

Researchers have used a variety of approaches to define the environmental uncertainty that organizational decision makers face. One of the most frequently cited typologies developed by Child (1972) suggests there may be environmental uncertainty due to environmental variability (changes), environmental complexity, or environmental illiberality (hostility). In a similar manner, Huber et al. (1975) say that environments may be uncertain due to turbulence, dynamism, or complexity. Huber and Daft (1987) discuss two of the same characteristics, turbulence and complexity, but consider information load the third component of the environment. To illustrate these concepts, decision makers in new-technology organizations face both a constantly changing environment as today's "state of the art" machines become obsolete in a couple of years or even a few months, and a changing rate of variability as the rate of change seems to be ever increasing. Those in organizations involved in international markets face a complex environment in which they must consider both the regulations at home and for each country in which they choose to compete. Decision makers in an organization facing a hostile takeover experience their own type of environmental uncertainty as they consider accepting the offer, finding alternative suitors, or other alternatives. Microsoft Corporation faced a hostile environment when the U.S. government determined that it was an unfair monopoly and told it to divide the company into parts. In each case, the ability of the organization to respond to the uncertainty of the environment is limited by the amount of information that can be processed from the environment and used effectively within the organization.

Emery (1967) differentiated four types of environments based on competition that organizations faced in the environment. Placid, randomized environments are ones in which the organization has no competition; however, events in the environment occur randomly so that no particular strategy is better than another one. Placid, clustering environments are ones in which the organization has no competition, but an appropriate strategy can improve the situation by identifying the clusters of predictable factors in the environment. In disturbed-reactive environments, the organization must respond to the competition from other systems and attempt to improve its own situation, typically at the expense of the other organization. Turbulent fields are dynamic, changing environments in which the competition and the characteristics of the environment are constantly changing. Although we may consider turbulent fields to be a 21st century phenomenon, Emery noted that these types of turbulent environments were becoming common in 1967.

Duncan (1972) focused on the components of the uncertainty of the environment rather than general descriptors. He noted five components that make up organizations' external environments (customer, suppliers, competitors, socio-political, and technological) and three for the internal environments (personnel, function and staff units, organizational level). These components then vary according to the simple–complex dimension and the static–dynamic dimension. Facing a decision, a decision-making unit may have few or many components to consider, and those components may be stable or constantly changing. Duncan found that uncertainty is highest in complex and dynamic environments and lowest in simple and static environments. In addition, Duncan argues that the static–dynamic dimension is more significant in creating uncertainty than the simple–complex dimension. In support of this, Acharya (1983) reports findings that suggest that public relations practitioners consider perceptions of change to be very important in determining environmental uncertainty, but that perceptions of complexity are not as critical.

The ability to respond appropriately to the environment is influenced by characteristics of the perceived environmental (e.g., its complexity, turbulence, and information load), the structural characteristics of the organization (e.g., mechanistic or organic), and personal characteristics of the individuals involved (e.g., tolerance of ambiguity and cognitive complexity; Huber & Daft, 1987). Because of this, the dynamic process of adjusting appropriately to environmental change and uncertainty is a complex process involving decision makers at many levels of the organization (Miles, Snow, Meyer, & Coleman, 1978). Lawrence and Lorsch (1967) emphasized that the subsystems within organizations need to be responsive to their subenvironments. For example, members of the sales department need to be responsive to the market environment, and members of the research and development department need to be more aware of the science environment. Those in production need to be concerned with the technical-economic environment. The challenge for effective organizations is both to differentiate the subsystems so that each subsystem can focus on its subenvironments and to integrate them so that the larger organizational system is responding to the overall environment. The authors indicate that the more successful organizations obtain both.

Decision Makers' Responses

Decision makers must respond to environmental uncertainty in order to maintain organizational viability. Failure to respond properly can lead to catastrophic results. For example, Weick (1993) examined the uncertainty facing the forest fire fighters in the 1949 Mann Gulch fire in which all but two crew members died in the fire. Alder (1997) examined both the Mann Gulch disaster and the 1994 Storm King Mountain fire in which 14 firefighters were killed. In these situations, the unpredictable fire was only one cause of uncertainty. In the Mann Gulch fire, the leader, Dodge, ordered his men to drop their tools and enter an area where he had set a backfire. Because this had never been done before, the members of the crew experienced uncertainty. They disobeyed the orders and died as a result. In the Storm King Mountain fire, the firefighters involved had never worked together before. An unclear chain of command and a lack of communication led to uncertainty in the face of a changing environment and led to the death of 14 of them.

Most inappropriate responses to environmental uncertainty do not have immediate life-and-death implications for decision makers like the preceding examples. However, the choices of decision makers facing environmental uncertainty do have long-term impacts on the organization and its members, and the more uncertain the environment the more impact the decisions of the upper echelon decision makers have on organizational outcomes (Carpenter & Fredrickson, 2001). Responding appropriately to environmental uncertainty involves information acquisition and information interpretation (Huber & Daft, 1987). Information acquisition includes scanning the environment for information both in specific attempts to solve problems and for more general motives of gaining information and condensing and distributing it to the appropriate sources within the organization at a suitable time, where it must be interpreted to create meanings that assist decision makers in responding to the environment. Given the complexity of managing environmental uncertainty, it is not surprising that a significant amount of research has examined how decision makers respond to the environmental uncertainty.

Research suggests that decision makers manage uncertainty differently depending on whether the decisions are routine (relatively certain situations) or nonroutine (relatively uncertain situations) and whether or not they believe that they have influence over the environment. Duncan (1973) found that effective decision-making units used more flexible processes for dealing with nonroutine decisions due to conditions of high uncertainty, but relied on more structured approaches for routine decisions due to the limited uncertainty. Similarly, effective units used more flexible processes for nonroutine decisions than for routine decisions when they perceived they had little influence on the environment. Specifically, as uncertainty increased, decision units used processes that were less hierarchical, less impersonal, more participatory, less rule oriented, and less role differentiated (Duncan, 1974).

Conrath (1967) reported a similar finding. He found that decision makers spent more time searching for information and considered and evaluated more alternatives in uncertain conditions. In certain conditions they relied on standard procedures rather than on seeking information, whereas in uncertain conditions they relied more on informal communication networks. An examination of bankers found that they were more likely to seek additional information in a volatile, uncertain environment than in more stable conditions (Leblebici & Salancik, 1981). In an examination of newspaper organizations, Beam (1996) found that perceived environmental uncertainty was associated with a marketing research orientation.

A marketing research orientation is really an information-seeking strategy in which, through focus groups, surveys, and other opinion gathering techniques, the organization ascertains the needs and wants of its target audience and then adapts its product accordingly.

Overall, these findings suggest that decision makers seek more information and use more flexible decision making procedures when they experience high uncertainty and believe they have influence on their environment. For routine decisions involving low uncertainty, standard operating procedures are common and effective. This suggests that standard operating procedures are scripts or schemata that allow decision makers to respond without much active processing in conditions of low uncertainty (Berger & Bradac, 1982). When uncertainty is high and they believe they can control aspects of their environment, decision makers seek information. Taken together, these results demonstrate support for the basic premise of URT at the organizational level. As uncertainty increases, information seeking increases (Axiom 3, Berger & Calabrese, 1975).

Other studies have examined how decision makers respond to specific situations of environmental uncertainty. Risk managers, such as industrial hygienists, must attempt to minimize risks for employees and the organization. Heath and Gay (1997) suggest that industrial hygienists use a two-step process to manage this uncertain environment. Uncertainty by itself was only associated with passive monitoring of the media to get a sense of the issues. This monitoring could lead to cognitive involvement, which they defined as determining whether the issues related to the self-interest of the individual or the organization. They found that when industrial hygienists were cognitively involved they actively made communication efforts to gain information, especially from other businesses and the media. They relied on other businesses for technical information to manage the uncertainty in making decisions.

A particularly volatile environment faced the media in Hong Kong during the transition from British to Chinese (communist) government. The media needed to ingratiate themselves enough to China to continue as profitable organizations while not impeding their legitimacy in the capitalist Hong Kong environment (Fung & Lee, 1994). They needed to befriend the government in Beijing without alienating the government in Taiwan or other noncommunist countries. Fung and Lee found that strategies for managing these uncertainties included shifting away from political commentary to focusing on noncontroversial subjects and diversification into property development investments. These strategies seemed designed to assist organizational survival in the face of environmental uncertainty.

Browning et al. (1999) compared how two groups of decision makers in different organizations dealt with uncertainty. In the first organization, engineers and technicians dealt with a production anomaly where products being produced failed quality control tests initially, but passed them a few weeks later. These engineers felt uncertainty about the problem, but were certain about the processes to use to isolate the problem and fix it. In the second organization, parking valets experienced certainty about the goal, which was to increase revenue while reducing fender-benders, but uncertainty about how to go about reaching those goals. Both the engineers and the valets were able to reduce the uncertainty over time. Perhaps ironically, the engineers, who were uncertain as to the nature of the problem, were able to articulate the process they used to reduce uncertainty, while the valets, who were certain about the problem, were unable to give much detail on the process that they used to address the issues.

Most of the previous examples assume an almost deterministic quality of the environment as if decision makers can only choose how to respond to it. Child (1972) recognized that organizations can influence their environments by choosing particular environments in which to function or by exerting resources on the environment. Miles et al. (1978) further developed this concept in their frequently cited typology of four organizational strategies. Defenders manage the environmental change and uncertainty by sealing off a particular part of the domain and responding to it; this creates a stable environment or niche for the organization. Prospectors manage environmental change and uncertainty by constantly exploring it for opportunities; this creates a stable pattern for dealing with the uncertainty. Analyzers develop a core activity, like defenders, but also search for new opportunities, like prospectors. This again creates a stable, consistent pattern for dealing with the environment even though it is a challenge to maintain the balance. Finally, reactors fail to recognize changing environments and avoid dealing with uncertainty by maintaining past approaches as much as possible. This creates an unstable situation until the organization moves to one of the other strategies or fails.

Overall, the review of research on environmental uncertainty is fairly consistent with URT. It suggests that as perceived environmental uncertainty increases, decision makers in organizations become more willing to expend resources on processing and transferring information to reduce uncertainty. Decision makers in high-performing companies in high-uncertainty environments engage in significant amounts of information processing across organizational boundaries to gain understanding of their environment (Farace et al., 1978). Although this research provides general information about how decision makers in organizations respond strategically based on their perceptions of uncertainty in the environment, it provides little information about the actual communication processes they use to develop an understanding of the uncertainty they face, to determine what information they will seek, or to select a strategy to manage the environmental uncertainty.

SUMMARY

This chapter has examined the research that explores how individuals in group and organizational settings manage uncertainty. Much of the research is consistent with URT. Group members are less fluent in their communication when they are uncertain. Organizational members seek information through a variety of means when they face uncertainty due to their own job changes or changes in the organization. Decision makers in organizations seek information to reduce environmental uncertainty. Gaining information generally reduces uncertainty and improves attitudes and actions in response to the uncertain situations.

Although the research is generally supportive of URT, there is a need for reconceptualizing the theory to address results that are inconsistent with the theory. For example, regardless of their levels of uncertainty, some individuals, such as cardiac patients, seek information (Sheer & Cline, 1995). Newcomers and transferees receive important information for reducing their uncertainty for clarifying their roles without seeking it (Kramer et al., 1995). Uncertainty alone does not motivate active information seeking for decision makers such as risk managers; it also takes involvement (Heath & Gay, 1997). The following chapter presents a theory of managing uncertainty to address these concerns.

A Theory of Managing Uncertainty: A New Model

Although the previous chapters have reported research that generally has supported URT and have even to some degree defended URT from its critics, a number of the criticisms of URT suggest a need to reconsider URT. In general, the problems with URT as originally proposed are related to its oversimplified presentation of the communication process by suggesting a direct causal relationship between levels of uncertainty and various outcomes such as information seeking. URT fails to be sensitive to the predisposition that people bring to the process or the complexity of social information (Douglas, 1994). Individuals who are naturally inquisitive or less tolerant of uncertainty respond to uncertainty differently from those who are less inquisitive and more tolerant of uncertainty. Along these lines, the work by Kellerman and Reynolds (1990) indicates the importance of examining how the different motivation levels individuals bring to the interaction influence initial uncertainty reduction behaviors. In addition, when information is exchanged the result is a complex process, not a simple reduction of uncertainty. The work of Sunnafrank (1986a, 1986b, 1990) suggests a complex pattern in which information gained affects subsequent evaluations and levels of uncertainty which in turn influence communication behaviors in different ways. The work of Planalp and her associates (Planalp & Honeycutt, 1985; Planalp et al., 1988) demonstrates that information gained through interaction has a complex influence on subsequent levels of uncertainty that includes decreases or increases in levels of uncertainty and both positive and negative outcomes. These and a number of other issues suggest the need to reconceptualize URT.

Two main concepts in particular are the focus of the perspective on managing uncertainty that is presented in this chapter. First, current understanding of the uncertainty reduction processes recognizes that uncertainty reduction processes and communication processes are not the same. According to Kellerman (1993), "Uncertainty reduction processes are reflected in and influenced by interaction processes although they are neither dependent on nor described by them" (p. 512). Uncertainty reduction can occur apart from interaction and without information seeking. For example, a worker may be experiencing uncertainty about how to perform a particular procedure on the cash register that is rarely used. Before having the chance to seek additional information from a coworker because none are available at the moment, she remembers the procedure (or at least thinks she does), reduces her uncertainty on her own, and thus completes the transaction. Alternatively, communication interaction designed to exchange information can occur without impacting uncertainty. Many of us have probably sought information by consulting an owner's manual or help menu for our computer and found that our uncertainty level remained the same or even increased from consulting information in this way. In light of this understanding, a reconceptualization of URT needs to consider a number of issues.

First, we must consider that uncertainty does not always produce some strategy of information seeking, such as passive monitoring, active consultation of third parties, or interaction with the source of uncertainty. There are times when uncertainty may not result in information seeking. Previous research suggests some of the reasons this occurs. One reason for this is that similar levels of uncertainty do not always create motivation to reduce uncertainty through information seeking. This idea has already been partially developed in the work by Kellerman (1986), which suggests that during initial interactions, individuals have heightened desires to exchange opinions and explanatory information when they anticipate future interactions. As such, a chance meeting of someone and meeting someone who will be part of an ongoing work relationship within organizational settings will not create equal levels of uncertainty or motivate the same levels of information seeking. Similarly, uncertainty about an employee in one's own department is more likely to motivate information seeking than uncertainty about an employee in another department, particularly if the two departments work rather independently of one another.

Another reason uncertainty does not always motivate communication interaction is that uncertainty is not always viewed negatively. An underlying assumption of URT is that the experience of uncertainty is always negative and must be reduced (Babrow, 2001a; Mishel, 1990). An uncertain future may be more desirable than a certain future that is very negative because the uncertainty allows for optimism and hope in the situation (Mishel, 1988). Contrary to URT, previous research suggests that individuals may avoid seeking information to maintain uncertainty in order to avoid confronting a potential negative reality, or they may seek information to create additional uncertainty when a negative appraisal of the situation has been made. Specifically, AIDS (Acquired Immune Deficiency Syndrome) patients often avoid seeking diagnosis for long periods of time to avoid confronting the reality of their illness and may seek additional information or opinions when a situation seemed certain and bleak in order to find hope in uncertainty (Brashers et al., 2000). The same behaviors occur in other situations, as well. If an employee is beginning to believe that the organization is about to face layoffs due to a downturn in the economy, the employee may avoid seeking information in an effort to maintain optimism that no layoffs will occur. If another coworker creates a clear, negative picture of numerous layoffs in the near future, the individual may seek another source of information with a more positive outlook on the situation to create a more uncertain picture of the possible layoffs and thereby relieve some of the concern and stress.

In addition to recognizing that uncertainty management processes are not equivalent to communication interaction, the second major concept that is addressed in this chapter concerns the way multiple motives influence communication interaction and information seeking in interpersonal and organizational settings. Proponents of URT argue that uncertainty reduction is the central motive that determines communication behaviors (Berger, 1986; Berger & Calabrese, 1975; Berger & Bradac, 1982). Opponents, such as Sunnafrank (1986a, 1986b, 1990), argue that predicted outcome value and social exchange principles are the primary determinants of communication. Both approaches fail to consider that alternative motives may simultaneously exist to explain communication behaviors. Even if uncertainty or social exchange principles are primary motives for communication in many situations, they are not necessarily the primary motives in every situation. As Anderson (1996) indicates, URT considers uncertainty reduction as an autonomous determinant of communication behaviors. Similarly, social exchange principles as developed by Sunnafrank place maximizing the outcome value for the interaction as the singular motivator of communication. Communicators often have conflicting goals or motives that they must balance rather than maximizing any particular one (Eisenberg, 1984). The motive of reducing uncertainty must be considered in relationship to other competing and conflicting goals (Goldsmith, 2001). A more complete development of managing uncertainty in a communication theory needs to consider that multiple motives or goals influence communication behaviors.

A personal story illustrates the importance of these two concepts, the ability to manage uncertainty without interaction through internal cognitive processes and the impact of alternative motives on seeking information. I was asked to be a guest teacher in a graduate class at one of the other universities in our state. I experienced uncertainty about a number of things. I had never before attended that university and really did not know what the students in their Masters degree program were like. To address my uncertainty, I considered my previous interaction with former students from that program. I recalled that the majority of the students were part-time, nontraditional students seeking terminal Masters degrees. Based on this information, I did not seek any additional information about the audience. I assumed that they would be much like the students in my own Masters degree program, even though it was in a different city. I assumed they would prefer discussion rather than listening to a lecture and prepared accordingly. My assumptions proved generally to be correct and the presentation and discussion went along much as I expected.

As I was leaving there, I ran into a former undergraduate student from my own university. She welcomed me and told me about her current studies. She asked me about what I was doing. As we conversed, I began to experience more and more uncertainty. Her face was familiar and I could place her in a class with some other faces, but I could not think of her name or when she had graduated. Because she remembered me and we were having an enthusiastic conversation, it seemed like it would be rude to ask her what her name was. She seemed to assume I knew it and I did not want to break that positive image she had of me by saying that I could not remember her name. My desire to maintain a positive image with her was more important to me than reducing my uncertainty about her name.

As this story illustrates, although I experienced uncertainty about both the class and the former student, I managed the uncertainty in two very different manners. In one case, I searched my own thoughts and developed an explanation that reduced uncertainty without any additional information seeking. Because I was able to manage my uncertainty internally, I was not motivated to seek information. The uncertainty reduction process did not involve any information seeking—although I did do some monitoring of the class in order to confirm my assumptions. In the case of the former student, I felt that it was more important to maintain my image as a caring professor than it was to reduce my uncertainty. So even though the level of uncertainty was sufficient to motivate information seeking, the competing motive prevented me from asking her what her name was. As originally conceptualized or later modified, URT fails to explain the complexity of my behaviors in these two situations. In both situations I managed uncertainty, but in neither one did I exhibit communication interaction to manage uncertainty. Predicted outcome value (Sunnafrank, 1986a) is equally incapable of explaining these two different responses. As a result, a reconceptualization of URT is presented.

THE MODEL

Figure 4.1 provides a model to illustrate the theory of managing uncertainty (TMU). This model is a further development of the one initially presented in Kramer (1999). The model contains six major components. One component is the *Experience of Uncertainty*. Some trigger event, perhaps a chance interaction with a new coworker or an unexpected announcement, produces uncertainty. Another component is the *Cognitive Attempts at Uncertainty Reduction*. After experiencing an uncertainty-producing event, individuals may use a variety of internal processes to manage uncertainty without seeking information. A third component is *Motivation to Reduce Uncertainty*. Here, depending on the success of attempts to reduce uncertainty internally, different levels of motivation to seek information are possible. If the cognitive processes addressed the important aspects of uncertainty, there may be little motivation to further reduce uncertainty; if cognitive processes could not address the uncertainty, motivation to further reduce uncer-

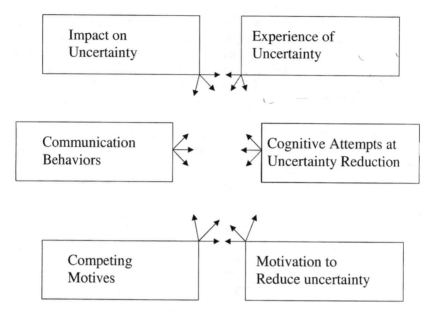

FIG. 4.1.   A model for a theory of managing uncertainty.

tainty would be high. An additional component is *Competing Motives.* Although the individual may be highly motivated to seek information, there may be competing motives that reduce or prevent such behaviors. For example, it may be too embarrassing to ask for needed information. Likewise motivation could be low, but competing motives might provoke information seeking anyway. For example, politeness norms may become a primary motive in asking someone for background information. A fifth component is *Communication Behaviors.* A range of communication behaviors, from passive information seeking to interactive information requests, is possible. The final component is *Impact on Uncertainty.* As a result of the various cognitive and behavioral processes just described, the level of uncertainty in the situation may change. However, this final component may be closely related to the *Experience of Uncertainty* as the process continues in a somewhat cyclical manner.

An unfortunate limitation of two-dimensional models is that they almost always appear to present a simplistic, linear process. Such drawings make it appear that these components occur in a step by step process and that an individual must complete one step before moving on to the next step. Even though authors explicitly explain that their process is not linear as the visual model might suggest, such models are frequently criticized for appearing to be linear. In an attempt to avoid appearing linear, the components of TMU are presented in more of a cyclical pattern in Fig. 4.1. Further, the multiple arrows from each component suggest that the components do not necessarily follow in either a linear or a cyclical pattern. The components should be seen as suggesting more of a rough sequence. Because of its two dimensional representation, the model fails to adequately represent the way that feedback loops influence the process, that simultaneously processing of components may occur, or that components may be omitted in some situations. The managing of uncertainty suggested by the conceptual model actually occurs in a much more fluid and interactive pattern.

For example, when I have gone on on-site job interviews, I have simultaneously attempted to reduce uncertainty by various internal cognitive processes while seeking information by asking questions. At the same time, I try to manage the competing motives of seeking information and appearing competent. Many of these factors occur simultaneously and subconsciously. I may not be aware that I am observing something about an individual's attitude or about the classroom facilities, but later I may draw conclusions based on that information. In light of this, it might be more appropriate to draw even more arrows between the various components of the model. However, because it is difficult to write about simultaneous processes concurrently and for ease of presentation, the model is described next in a simple sequence. Although the model is applicable to individual, group, and organizational experiences of uncertainty, each section begins with a detailed description of the individual level of analysis in organizational settings. Examples at the group and organizational levels of analysis then follow.

THE EXPERIENCE OF UNCERTAINTY

Individual Level of Analysis

As has been noted previously, uncertainty is an individual perception or a perception that is shared among members of a group or organization. Uncertainty is not an objective reality. For example, newcomers may experience uncertainty about how their performance in their training program will influence their initial appointments and salaries. Unbeknownst to them, it may be that all newcomers in the organization actually receive the same initial pay after training regardless of their performance and that their initial appointments have already been determined prior to training based on organizational needs. However, it is the perception of the potential gains and losses that face a newcomer that creates levels of uncertainty, not the actual range of options that exist (Lester, 1987). Thus, the newcomers may experience uncertainty even though the situation is highly determined.

Uncertainty and Ambiguity. Uncertainty can be experienced for a variety of reasons. The experience of uncertainty is often related to different types of ambiguity in the setting. Ambiguity occurs in the interaction of the source, message, and receiver when the events or messages may have multiple interpretations or meanings; it contrasts with clarity where interpretations are limited (Eisenberg, 1984). Ambiguity can be present in a situation for a variety of reasons. There may be ambiguity in a setting because it contains entirely new cues, contains too many different cues, or contains contradictory cues. Budner (1962) described these issues as novelty, complexity, or insolubility. If an employee is assigned a new job duty that no one has ever performed before, there is ambiguity due to the new cues. Many computer manuals and employee handbooks are too complex with too many cues for the typical reader to understand. This makes it difficult for the reader to determine what is important or unimportant. Similarly, ambiguity can lead to uncertainty when there are contradictions in situations due to a mixture of incentives or deviations, and when there are uncertainties concerning whether future interactions will occur (Berger, 1979; Kellerman & Reynolds, 1990). For example, in class one day, a student recalled how one of her managers told her to clean the glass display cases in a particular manner and the other manager told her to clean them in an entirely different manner. She experienced uncertainty because she could interpret the situation in a number of ways. Because one manager deviated from the other and future interactions with both supervisors would likely impact her job evaluations and pay raises, she was not clear how to respond to the contradictory directions. In each of the preceding situations, ambiguity or multiple interpretations of the messages in the situation can lead individuals to experience uncertainty.

Even though the amount and type of ambiguity in a situation influences the experience of uncertainty, it does not determine whether uncertainty is experienced. Cognitive and social factors intervene in shaping the perceived environment rather than simply objective characteristics (Beam, 1996). On one hand, individuals may not perceive uncertainty in a context even though it appears ambiguous to many other people. The individuals may not attend to or notice the ambiguous communication or situation or they may not evaluate the information as ambiguous. For example, a new supervisor may give a set of apparently contradictory cues to a group of subordinates. The supervisor tells them to work until a job is done, but to avoid working overtime. These directives may seem like incompatible goals to many people. There is ambiguity because multiple interpretations are possible. The ambiguity of the cues could cause many of the employees to feel uncertain as to what action to take. However, a particular inattentive employee may never be aware of the discrepancy and another particular individual may not experience uncertainty in this situation due to previous experience. From experience with other supervisors, the person recognizes that getting the job done is the primary directive and that minimizing overtime, not avoiding it completely, is the secondary goal. This employee is certain what to do in this situation regardless of whether the assumptions are accurate. So although the situation appears ambiguous at some observer or objective level, the experience of uncertainty may be quite separate from that for the individuals involved.

On the other hand, individuals may perceive uncertainty in situations that most people would consider unambiguous. For example, a supervisor may tell the office assistant to get the copier machine working correctly. Most people would probably feel that there is little ambiguity in this directive; the assistant should try to fix the copier and call the repair service if necessary. However, a particularly tentative new employee may not be certain how much effort to put into the repair before calling the service and may wonder if the repair service should be allowed to continue regardless of cost. The assistant may eventually ask for clarification on each step of the process as a result, perhaps annoying the supervisor for failing to follow simple directions. What appears as unambiguous to the sender or at some objective or observer level creates a great deal of uncertainty for this particular assistant.

Conceptually this makes ambiguity an environmental, contextual, or message phenomenon and uncertainty a personal, subjective feeling or experience. Consistent with this, Bradac (2001) emphasized that increasing the ambiguity in the language of a message can allow for increases in uncertainty. Such a conceptual distinction is compatible with URT, which has consistently viewed uncertainty as a perceptual response to situations. However, previous research has not always made this type of distinction and has frequently used the two terms interchangeably. For example, Eisenberg (1984) argues that ambiguity must be defined relationally and not as the property of messages. He appears to be arguing that ambiguity occurs in the meaning created in the interaction of the message by the communicators. From the perspective of TMU, it would be more appropriate to call the meaning created through interaction of the person and the situation the certainty or uncertainty perceived for the situation, not the ambiguity in it. In fact, when Eisenberg argues that strategic ambiguity can create unified diversity, he seems to be arguing that a strategically ambiguous statement can create certainty for the audience. With strategic ambiguity, each member of the audience can think they understand the meaning of an ambiguous organizational goal statement without recognizing that they are not actually in agreement. They experience certainty despite or because of an ambiguous message. In addition, by defining clarity in terms of the degree to which the source reduces the number of interpretations of a message, Eisenberg seems to associate clarity (and thereby ambiguity, its opposite) with the source and message rather than receivers. So, even though ambiguity and uncertainty have been used interchangeably and inconsistently in previous literature, for the purposes of this chapter, ambiguity is considered a quality of the message or environment that potentially influences experiences of uncertainty. Uncertainty is the individuals' response or perspective taken on those messages or events.

Overall then, uncertainty is the perception of a situation based in part on the ambiguity in that setting. However, ambiguity does not necessarily result in uncertainty. The experience of uncertainty is influenced by the ambiguity in a situation, but not determined or controlled by it. An individual's cognitive processes can prevent or reduce the likelihood of ever experiencing uncertainty in a given situation.

Scripts or Schemas.

A primary determinant of uncertainty in a situation is whether the individuals have scripts or schemas for the situation. Berger and Bradac (1982) indicated that cognitive scripts or schemas function to reduce uncertainty. Scripts or schemas are routine actions or sequences of behaviors that allow for mindless responses to situations (Cantor et al., 1982). TMU goes further and states that such scripts actually influence the experience of uncertainty. Because uncertainty is a psychological state rather than an objective reality, scripts can actually block or prevent any experience of uncertainty. They are cognitive plans for preventing uncertainty (Bradac, 2001). When we have a script for a situation and events generally follow the script, we typically do not experience uncertainty. For example, one of the simplest and most frequently used scripts in an organizational setting is the simple greeting. Few individuals experience uncertainty when someone says, "Good morning." Although this script is flexible enough to allow for a range of responses, the situation is predictable and most people know how to respond appropriately. The existence of a greeting script actually prevents the experience of uncertainty. In many other routine situations, uncertainty is not experienced because individuals have scripts that help them to understand the goals and procedures for accomplishing those goals. In many such situations, neither party wants to engage in a long conversation to construct reality (Berger, 2000). Scripts allow for efficient communication without experiencing uncertainty. So for example, when interacting with the cashier at the grocery store, neither party experiences much behavioral uncertainty or expects conversation to reduce other types of uncertainty.

Scripts are not limited to simple routines like greeting rituals. Complex scripts in organizational settings assist individuals by preventing the experience of uncertainty for them. For example, phone solicitors have scripts for handling most of the anticipated responses they receive and even for how many refusals it takes before they accept rejection. Teachers have scripts for managing certain inquiries from students about the correctness of a test item. Many organizations have a general script for weekly meetings of middle management. Even though these scripts are more complex and more flexible than the greeting ritual, they serve the same purpose of essentially preventing the experience of uncertainty in many situations because the scripts make the events predictable.

One of the ways that organizational members develop schemas that reduce or prevent the experience of uncertainty is through the socialization process. Downey and Slocum (1975) suggest that the organizational socialization processes influence the experience of uncertainty. Training reduces uncertainty by explaining how to do certain tasks and how to follow the norms of the organizational culture. The socialization process teaches how or when to experience uncertainty by creating scripts that help determine what is routine and what is unexpected and even includes training for proper displays of reactions to uncertainty. For example, if members are socialized to expect little discretion in completing their roles, they most likely experience little uncertainty when they are told to follow standard operating procedure in an ambiguous situation, nor are they likely to express negative responses.

Trigger Events.   It is when an event or communication message does not match an existing script that it triggers the experience of uncertainty for individuals. Certain types of events or messages are more likely to produce uncertainty rather than mindless use of automatic routines or scripts, such as if the form of the message is novel, if the information contained in the message might prove salient for future nonhabitual action, if the situation demands reflection on the meaning of the message, if the content of the message violates expectations, or if the message contains cues suggesting potential bias (Hewes, Graham, Doelger, & Pavitt, 1985). Similarly, Mishel (1988) theorizes that uncertainty is experienced when situations appear random rather than patterned, novel rather than previously experienced, or unexpected rather than expected. Planalp and Honeycutt (1985) identified a number of specific events that create uncertainty in interpersonal relationships. Many of these are applicable in organizational settings as well. For example, finding out that your coworker has lied to you or has passed on confidential information to someone else is most likely a violation of a script. Such revelations create uncertainty by making it unclear how to relate to the coworker in the future.

Again, it is important to remember that it is not the objective characteristics of the communication or event that causes the uncertainty. The experience of uncertainty is perceptual rather than objective and so a violation of a script does not necessarily create uncertainty. Uncertainty is not created by whether the communication actually fits previous scripts or not. Rather it is the perception that the situation is different from the scripts that triggers uncertainty. As a result, an activated interest is also necessary for the experience of uncertainty (Nigg, 1982). If a coworker makes a rude remark about the quality of the reports turned in by the department members, but I assume it refers to the reports turned in by others, I may not experience any uncertainty about my own work. Only if I take an active interest in the comment because I believe the comment applies to me will I perceive it as a criticism of my work, a violation of the script I expected to hear, and thus experience uncertainty. Attending to the message as relevant is a necessary step toward the creation of uncertainty.

Group and Organizational Level of Analysis

Members of groups and organizational decision makers collectively develop their experience of uncertainty. Like at the individual level of analysis, the experience of uncertainty is often based on ambiguity in situations or experiences of new or unexpected communication or events in their external environment.

Agreement on the perceived characteristics of the environment, such as how dynamic or complex it is, influences the collective level of uncertainty (Downey & Slocum, 1975). For example, a new government regulation for food handling for restaurant employees may seem ambiguous due to its complexity and the multiple interpretations possible. Because the regulation affects all members of the group or organization, the collective or shared understanding of the regulation will determine the members' level of uncertainty about the regulation. Through communication interaction the members agree on whether this regulation has created uncertainty for them.

Scripts or schemas can be used to evaluate whether the regulation is novel or consistent with expectations. By either remembering or forgetting how the members have responded to past regulations, the members determine their level of uncertainty (Middleton, 1997). If no one can recall similar regulations in the past, the members may decide that they are quite uncertain as to how to respond to the new food handling regulation. However, their collective behavioral repertoires, broad experiences and abilities, and social expectations may reduce uncertainty (Downey & Slocum, 1975). If someone remembers a similar regulation enacted (and perhaps later discarded) by the Food and Drug Administration several years earlier, the members may decide that they know exactly how to respond to the regulation and not experience uncertainty as a result. Thus, the experience of uncertainty is determined for the group or organizational members in much the same way as it is for an individual. It is their collective agreement on their perception of the situation the determines the uncertainty in the situation.

Summary

Overall, the experience of uncertainty relates to ambiguity in the communication or context. However, because the experience of uncertainty is subjective, the ambiguity or clarity of the situation or message does not determine the level of uncertainty. Individuals or collections of individuals must attend to the communication event and then determine if it generates uncertainty for them. The individuals or collectives may have cognitive scripts or schemas, patterns of routine or expected behaviors for the situation. These scripts and schemas help prevent or preclude the experience of uncertainty. Uncertainty is perceived when the events or communication trigger uncertainty because they fail to follow or fit the cognitive scripts or schemas.

COGNITIVE ATTEMPTS AT UNCERTAINTY REDUCTION

Once uncertainty has been experienced, individuals attempt to manage the uncertainty. Most previous research on URT has assumed that managing uncertainty involves communication interactions. Honeycutt (1993) was one of the first scholars to recognize that various cognitive processes work to reduce uncertainty without communication interaction. Communication is not everything; nor is everything communication (Poole, Seibold, & McPhee, 1985). Whereas URT proposed that the way that people manage uncertainty is to seek information, TMU contends that individuals have other options for reducing uncertainty without seeking information. These various options can be subsumed under the general category of cognitive attempts at uncertainty reduction. These cognitive attempts at reducing uncertainty are somewhat different from the previously discussed scripts and schemas in that while the scripts and schemas work to prevent or preclude the initial experience of uncertainty, the cognitive processes are used to manage the uncertainty once it has already been experienced.

A variety of such approaches can be identified based on previous research. The important aspect of these strategies is that they are internal processes that individuals can use to manage or reduce their uncertainty without interacting or seeking information from others. Similarly, at the group or organizational level, these strategies allow for the reduction of uncertainty without seeking information from external sources. Each of these approaches demonstrates that uncertainty reduction and communication interaction can be separate processes (Kellerman, 1993).

Individual Level of Analysis

Berger (1993) concludes that research provides evidence that individuals often seek to put a minimal amount of effort into processing social information. They prefer shortcuts and quick results when possible. The implications of this for uncertainty reduction are important. It is often possible to reduce uncertainty with minimal effort through cognitive processes rather than more sustained efforts such as seeking information. Although passive approaches to information seeking involve less effort than direct inquiry, cognitive reduction of uncertainty apart from actual communication generally involves even less behavioral effort. A variety of cognitive processes that can be used to reduce uncertainty apart from information seeking can be identified based on previous research. Uncertainty is similar to dissonance or doubt about alternatives (Honeycutt, 1993). As a result, a number of these strategies are largely variations on dissonance reduction; each of them involves changing the evaluation of some component of interest to allow equilibrium to return (Festinger, 1957). As applied here, by changing evaluations of the uncertainty experience, individuals can manage uncertainty (Babrow, 2001b). These reevaluations may even involve perceptual distortions to manage uncertainty (Bradac, 2001). In addition, some of these cognitive processes are associated with particular personality types or characteristics.

Denial of Uncertainty. One way to cognitively reduce uncertainty is for an individual simply to deny its existence after experiencing it. By evaluating the uncertainty as nonexistent, the uncertainty no longer needs to be addressed. Along this line, Heath et al. (1998) cite research that suggests that individuals deny uncertainty when it is too difficult to assess or understand or perhaps creates too much dread or cognitive dissonance. In their study, they found that people living near a nuclear power plant reported less uncertainty than those living farther away from it do. They suggest that this lower level of uncertainty was due to more intense information campaigns by the plant operators in the immediate vicinity of the plant. An alternative explanation would be that these differences are due to denial of uncertainty by those living near the plant. To manage the uncertainty and dissonance that may exist from living near a chemical or nuclear plant, those residents living close may simply deny or ignore any information that creates uncertainty. By denying uncertainty, individuals take a position that they understand their situation or at least understand it adequately, even though they may not. Although denial of uncertainty may not accurately reflect the risk or uncertainty of their situation, it does manage the uncertainty in such a way that it no longer concerns individuals or results in observable communication behaviors.

Tolerance of Uncertainty.   Another way that individuals may manage uncertainty once it is experienced is by developing a tolerance for the uncertainty. Unlike denying the existence of uncertainty, when individuals have a tolerance for uncertainty, they recognize that uncertainty exists, but they choose to tolerate the uncertainty for a variety of reasons. Through a variety of cognitive assessments, individuals increase their ability or likelihood of tolerating uncertainty. They manage their uncertainty by reevaluating the importance of the uncertainty rather than by actually increasing their knowledge or certainty about the situation (Babrow, 2001b).

The concept of tolerance for uncertainty is similar to tolerance of ambiguity although it is probably not synonymous with it. Recall that ambiguity has to do with messages or events that have multiple interpretations. Budner (1962) defines tolerance of ambiguity as the tendency to perceive ambiguous situations as desirable and intolerance of ambiguity as a tendency to perceive them as threatening. Minimally, individuals with a high level of tolerance of ambiguity do not view ambiguity or multiple interpretations as problematic or negative. They may find ambiguity invigorating because it allows for alternative interpretations and approaches rather a singular response. Tolerance of ambiguity results in an appraisal of some communication or event, which has multiple potential interpretations, as positive or neutral without particularly considering the impact of the appraisal as important.

Uncertainty has to do with an individual's inability to assign meaning or predictability to communication or to an event, perhaps due to its ambiguity or other causes. Kellerman and Reynolds (1990) conceptualize tolerance of uncertainty as the amount of concern an individual has over reducing uncertainty. Individuals with high tolerance for uncertainty are less concerned about reducing uncertainty in a situation than those with a low tolerance of uncertainty, who would be anxious to reduce uncertainty. An inability to assign meaning to something does not disturb an individual with a high tolerance for uncertainty for a given situation. In this way, tolerance of uncertainty seems to address a slightly different issue than tolerance of ambiguity. Tolerance of uncertainty focuses on the amount of concern or motivation an individual feels to reduce uncertainty because meaning or predictability cannot be assigned, whereas tolerance of ambiguity involves the acceptance of multiple meanings.

Whereas URT assumes that uncertainty is negative and that the reduction of uncertainty is positive, by including a tolerance for uncertainty, TMU allows for individual appraisals of uncertainty as tolerable so that there is no concern or motivation to reduce uncertainty. People differ in their preferred level of uncertainty. This suggests that tolerance of uncertainty is in part a personality trait that may not vary from situation to situation although it is in part a situational response as an individual tolerates uncertainty about some things, but not others. Although some individuals prefer uncertainty reduction in most situations, others enjoy or tolerate some uncertainty because too much certainty may create boredom and apathy (Baxter & Montgomery, 1996; Farace et al., 1978). Some individuals are better at withholding judgment until they have necessary information or at accepting a lack of closure for a period of time (Acredolo & O'Connor, 1991). Specifically, individuals who are more risk tolerant experience less uncertainty and desire less information (Heath et al., 1998). In addition, receiver apprehensives (individuals who fear misunderstanding or misinterpreting messages) develop an intolerance for messages that are not clear enough to reduce uncertainty (Schumacher & Wheeless, 1997). The importance of tolerance of uncertainty can be illustrated by considering how individuals make career choices. Although many factors influence career choices, career choices are probably partially based on an individual's tolerance for uncertainty. Many individuals never consider a career in theater or oil speculation because the level of uncertainty is above their level of tolerance for uncertainty. Careers in accounting or manufacturing have significantly lower levels of uncertainty by comparison, and thus may be too predictable and certain for other individuals.

At least three factors identified in previous research can be used to help create a tolerance for uncertainty in specific situations. One way to create tolerance of uncertainty is through an assessment of the likelihood of future interactions. In situations in which no future interaction is anticipated, there is no particular need to reduce uncertainty because it can be tolerated temporarily with the expectation that it will not have significant impact in the future. In support of this reasoning, Kellerman (1986) found that when individuals did not anticipate future interactions they had a reduced desire to exchange opinion and explanatory information and exhibited less co-orientation and reciprocity with partners. Similarly, Kiesler, Kiesler, and Pallak (1967) found that individuals who did not anticipate future interactions with partners were less likely to react negatively to interaction norm violations than those anticipating future interactions with their partners. People use the assessment of likelihood of future interactions to create tolerance of uncertainty in many interactions. We meet many individuals, some quite eccentric in our daily lives. They may sit by us in a waiting room, serve us lunch or cash our check or pass us on the street. Despite the uncertainty we experience from these individuals, we generally tolerate it because we consider that our likelihood of future interaction is quite small. However, when individuals are uncertain about whether future interactions are likely to occur or not, they feel a stronger need to seek information and to determine liking of each other (Douglas, 1988).

A second way to create tolerance of uncertainty is by assessing that there is limited potential harm or benefit in a situation. The appraisal of harm or benefit may have much to do with the experience of uncertainty (Brashers et al., 2000). Conrad and Poole (1998) argue that there is a curvilinear relationship between uncertainty and harm or benefit on information seeking. Low levels of uncertainty and either low harm or benefit potential results in limited motivation to seek information. As the levels of uncertainty or evaluations of harm or benefit increase, information seeking increases, until at some point the situation becomes overwhelming and then motivation to reduce uncertainty by seeking information declines. This suggests that an assessment of limited harm or benefit can create a tolerance of uncertainty in a given situation. In essence, we tolerate the uncertainty in situations because we do not expect that they will have any direct impact on us. The assessment of future interactions is probably related to this harm or benefit evaluation. A lack of future interaction would suggest that little harm or benefit would likely come from reducing uncertainty.

I probably use the assessment of harm and benefit to create tolerance for uncertainty in determining my attendance at various meetings on campus, such as campus or college faculty meetings, and meetings related to my role as Director of Graduate Studies. Each semester a number of these meetings are scheduled. I am always uncertain as to the exact nature of these meetings. Sometimes an agenda is distributed in advance, but at other times the meetings are simply on the schedule. I am always uncertain about whether something significant will occur at any particular meeting. Based on previous experience, I have concluded that there is little harm in missing most of these meetings and equally limited benefit for attending them. I tolerate the uncertainty of not knowing what occurred at these meetings as a result. My assessment of harm or benefit does change from time to time. When a particular issue that seems to create the possibility of greater harm or benefit is announced in advance, such as new policies for enrolling international students, I attend such a meeting. When a new committee chair or new administrator is appointed, I feel that both the potential for harm of not attending and the potential benefit from attending increase. These new leaders may take a more aggressive role and become strong advocates for change. This could lead to harm or benefit depending on the changes they desire. As a result I make a point of attending the first meeting or two for the new leaders. Once it becomes apparent that they will primarily be maintaining the status quo, I conclude that the harm and benefit potential is low and my attendance again slips as I tolerate the uncertainty of not attending.

A third strategy for creating tolerance of uncertainty involves segmenting the uncertainty, for example, into descriptive, predictive, and explanatory uncertainty (Berger & Bradac, 1982). As discussed previously, descriptive uncertainty involves reliably identifying the person, predictive uncertainty involves being able to predict behaviors, and explanatory uncertainty involves being able to explain the reasons for the actions. It is not necessary to have certainty in all three areas in order to manage uncertainty. Certainty in two or even just one of these areas may be sufficient to create a tolerance for uncertainty in the other one or two areas. I experience uncertainty when I discover that I have a new mail carrier at work. However, because I have predictive certainty—I know that the mail will still be delivered each day—I do not concern myself with descriptive or explanatory certainty. I can tolerate the uncertainty of not knowing what happened to the old carrier or why the new one chose this job because I can still function quite easily.

TMU suggests that people can use the assessments of likelihood of future interaction, harm or benefit, or segmenting uncertainty to create a tolerance for uncertainty on a regular basis. These strategies may be used singularly or in combination to manage uncertainty in a situation. When we must stand in line to get our license renewed at the department of public safety and we must stand next to an individual with a strong smell due to body odor or excessive perfume, we are faced with uncertainty about many aspects of the individual. At the same time, we know that we are likely to experience limited harm or benefit from our limited interactions and we recognize that we are unlikely to have any future interactions with the individual. In addition, we have predictive certainty (they will wait their turn and pay their bill like the rest of us) and perhaps descriptive certainty (we could identify them if we saw them again, at least in the short term). As a result, we do not concern ourselves with explanatory certainty about the olfactory condition because we do not really need to know why the person is that way.

One personality characteristic, self-monitoring, appears to be closely related to tolerance for uncertainty. Self-monitoring (Snyder, 1974) is a personality variable that influences information seeking in general. Low self-monitors rely on internal cues to determine appropriate behaviors in a given situation, whereas high self-monitors look for external cues from the environment or their interaction partners. This results in different levels of information seeking. Low self-monitors seek less information about an interaction partner than high self-monitors prior to interacting with them (Elliott, 1979). Low self-monitors initiate fewer conversations than high self-monitors (Ickes & Barnes, 1977). Low self-monitors prefer formal situations for gaining information about a partner whereas high self-monitors prefer informal situations because the context has less influence on behaviors (Berger & Douglas, 1981). As a result of differences in information seeking, low self-monitors are less likely to be confident about making attributions and less likely to display nonverbal expressiveness than high self-monitors (Gudykunst & Nishida, 1984). In addition, self-monitors differ in the specific type of information they value when seeking information (Berger & Douglas, 1981).

Overall, this suggests that individuals who are low self-monitors have a higher tolerance for uncertainty than high self-monitors do.

Overall, tolerance for uncertainty is a cognitive process for reducing the experience of uncertainty without seeking information. Uncertainty often only influences part of our experience without causing any general disruption. Only after it expands to exceed our personal level of tolerance of uncertainty by exceeding a critical threshold does it result in instability in our system (Mishel, 1990). By assessing that future interactions are unlikely and that neither harm nor benefit is likely to occur, or by segmenting uncertainty into types, we create a tolerance of uncertainty. In addition, those of us who are low self-monitors appear to have a higher tolerance for uncertainty. As long as the uncertainty remains below our tolerance of uncertainty level, it fails to create motivation to seek additional information to reduce uncertainty.

Assimilate the Uncertainty.

Another cognitive process for managing uncertainty once it is experienced without seeking additional information involves assimilating the area of uncertainty with other cognitions that are more certain. Assimilation involves the process of incorporating two previously separate entities, ideas, or experiences into one. Three strategies have been identified in previous research that are particularly adept at accomplishing this.

One common strategy for assimilating uncertainty is the use of categorizing or stereotyping. In the best of all possible worlds, people do a thorough information gathering process before making any judgments about other people or about situations. This is frequently not the case in day-to-day interactions. People have a tendency to simplify issues, ignore evidence that conflicts with their already held beliefs, and use the most easily available information to make assessments (Nathan et al., 1992). For example, in job searches individuals appear to stop seeking information once they determine a job is incompatible, rather than continuing to seek information to determine if any disconfirming information exists (Rubin, 1977). Categorizing or stereotyping provides a cognitive shortcut for transforming an uncertain situation into one that is predictable and certain without information seeking. As a result, people frequently seek information that triggers or confirms stereotypes and expectations rather than doing a thorough information search (Baldwin & Hunt, 2002).

Tversky and Kahneman (1974) suggest that people use three general heuristic principles in making judgments about people or experiences. Each of these potentially contributes to categorizing and helps produce certainty: (a) representativeness—does it fit into an existing category or group; (b) availability—what is the most easily retrievable category; and (c) adjustment and anchoring—bias toward confirming an initial evaluation of appropriate category. Thus in a situation of uncertainty, if the interaction partner appears to represent a known category, if that category is easily recalled, and if assignment to that category confirms a bias about that category, then relying on categories or stereotypes will reduce uncertainty in the situation.

Relying on categories or stereotypes to classify partners or situations makes them seem more predictable and less uncertain. By assigning someone to a category we reduce uncertainty by being able to analyze them based on our knowledge of the category instead of individual characteristics (Kellerman, 1993). We expect them to behave in a manner that is typical for that category. The categorizing may be based on clothing and nonverbal communication or on the basis of a brief inquiry. Even though categorizing individuals by group membership is generally thought of as negative, it is not always. Sometimes positive social identity is assigned although this is probably much more rare than negative labels. Categorizing someone as part of my own group or as a member of a group to which I aspire probably categorizes them with a positive identity. Whether the category is positive, negative, or neutral, an individual who can assign an experience or another person to a category reduces uncertainty and believes that he or she knows how to react appropriately to the situation.

Of course, categorizing or stereotyping is not always accurate; misrepresentation is common. In a simple contextual relationship (customer) versus a complex one (spouse) prediction can be obtained rather easily without exploring many areas of potential uncertainty. As a result, individuals may only seek information to the point where they are satisfied with impressions that are formed (Rubin, 1977). Even though this is probably a common experience and even a regrettable experience when inaccurate categorization occurs, this is not critical for understanding the process. Imperfect knowledge still guides and directs behavior (Berger & Calabrese, 1975). The attributions made to explain observed behaviors still influence communication and behaviors even when they are inaccurate (Berger, 1975). Regardless of its accuracy, categorization provides the individual with certainty about the pattern of behavior to enact and expect. For example, based on a friendly greeting and neat appearance, I may decide that my new barber is a talkative person and so without seeking additional information, I enter friendly conversation of the day's events. I may ignore that he appears reluctant to talk and fail to recognize that my categorization is inaccurate.

Research on interethnic and intercultural communication suggests that people use categories or stereotypes to reduce uncertainty. When an interaction partner is viewed as a prototypical member of an ethnic group, individuals were more confident in their ability to make attributions about the partner relationships (Gudykunst & Hammer, 1988). Of course, only to the degree that the individual behaves in a way that is congruent with typical members of that category is the categorizing accurate (Kellerman, 1993). People are generally overconfident about the certainty of their ability to make predictions and lack awareness that their "knowledge" is based on tenuous assumptions (Slovic, Fischoff, & Lichtenstein, 1982). Similarly, members of high-context cultures make more assumptions about an individual's attitudes than members of low-context cultures (Gudykunst, 1983). This suggests that members of high-context cultures use categorizing by social class to reduce uncertainty more than members of low-context cultures. These stereotypes can occur concerning a group and not just on an individual basis.

Categorizing often continues to promote certainty because individuals tend to attend to information that confirms their expectations while discounting information that contradicts them. Categorizing individuals reduces uncertainty if we can assign them to the category with reasonable confidence and have knowledge of the typical behaviors of members of that category (Kellerman, 1993). Once the category has been determined, individuals frequently use communication strategies that confirm their expectations about the other person, making it difficult to notice the unique qualities of that person (Swann & Ely, 1984).

An example of categorizing is perhaps unnecessary because we are aware of the negative repercussions that stereotyping based on racial, ethnic, gender, or religious categories has had on individuals. It is useful to recognize that other less politically sensitive labels often categorize people into positive or negative categories, as well. We may identifying someone as "on the fast track" rather than "on the mommy track," as "union" rather than "management," as "full-time," not "part-time." In each of these instances, the category reduces uncertainty because we think we can now respond to them on the basis of our knowledge of the group, but each can also have a negative or positive impact on the person regardless of the accuracy of the categorizing.

A second cognitive strategy for assimilating uncertainty is to look for cultural similarities. If we are uncertain about someone we meet, we can create certainty about them by determining that there are cultural similarities between us. In essence, we reduce our uncertainty by identifying the person as an ingroup rather than an outgroup member (i.e., he or she is a member of my social class or cultural group). Again, nonverbal communication and appearances are frequently used to assess cultural similarity. Once we have determined that they are like us, we experience less uncertainty about them. We expect them to behave similarly to us.

Again, research from intercultural communication indicates that people use assessments of cultural similarity to reduce uncertainty. Cultural similarities appear to reduce uncertainty (Gudykunst & Nishida, 1984). In interactions within cultures individuals were less likely to intend to self-disclose, to interrogate, and to use nonverbal expressiveness than they were in interaction between cultures (Japan and United States). This suggests that they felt less uncertainty in the within-culture context than the between-culture context and therefore less need to exchange information.

An example of two coworkers meeting on casual dress day might illustrate this process of assimilating uncertainty through identifying cultural similarities. The two have limited interaction based on their jobs and as a result have a very limited personal relationship with each other. They rarely communicate. Because it is causal dress day, both decide to wear the sweatshirt of their alma mater. When they meet each other, they recognize that they both attended the same university;

they find a commonality. The nonverbal cue of the university sweatshirt provides them with a specific cultural similarity. Based on this cultural identity, both reduce uncertainty about each other in numerous areas and develop expectations and interactions based on the common cultural background. As a result of cultural similarity, they engage in intense conversation unlike they had previously experienced. The perception of cultural similarity reduced uncertainty for them.

A third cognitive strategy for assimilating uncertainty is based on perceived attitude similarities. Perceptions of attitude similarity are associated with reductions in uncertainty (Prisbell & Andersen, 1980). When meeting a stranger, we reduce our uncertainty about them if we perceive that they have similar attitudes to us. Perhaps they express a similar attitude of enthusiasm or cynicism in their nonverbal communication. If this is similar to our own attitude we feel that we can better predict how they will behave and perhaps develop explanations for those behaviors. By identifying attitude similarities, we have reduced our uncertainty about them.

My brother-in-law provided me with an example of relying on attitude similarity to reduce uncertainty. He and his family recently visited the Baseball Hall of Fame in Cooperstown, New York. In describing the visit to the museum, he commented that it was very interesting that he had had a number of conversations with complete strangers as they stood admiring the exhibits. In most settings the uncertainty created by strangers in a public setting prevents communication from occurring. In this case, the mere presence of these individuals at the museum indicated an attitude similarity (baseball fan) between them and my brother-in-law. The reduction of uncertainty between these strangers allowed for conversations that normally would not occur between strangers. Of course, the reduction of uncertainty was domain specific; uncertainty was reduced about interests in baseball. As a result, the conversations were focused on baseball rather than some of the other common introductory conversation topics such as demographics and background.

In sum, cognitive processes can be used to reduce uncertainty after it is experienced in situations by assimilating that uncertainty into previous information or knowledge. By categorizing or by identifying cultural and attitudinal similarities, we develop certainty about other people. Even though these perceptions are not always accurate, they become the basis for feeling certain about the appropriate communication and attitudes to assume in situations.

Acceptance of Uncertainty.   A strategy that is quite similar to tolerating uncertainty is simply accepting uncertainty. The differences between tolerating and accepting uncertainty relate to attitude and time. In tolerating uncertainty, there is often the recognition that the uncertainty is short term because, for example, future interactions are unlikely. Tolerating uncertainty involves an attitude of temporarily allowing uncertainty to remain with the expectation that it will dissipate over time. Acceptance of uncertainty recognizes the uncertainty and chooses to endure it with the recognition that it may continue for extended periods of time or indefinitely. In support of this, Emmers and Canary (1996) found that even in intimate relationships people sometimes simply accepted uncertainty about their partners. They seemed to figure the situation may work itself out sooner or later, but if it does not, it does not really seem to matter. Similarly, Brashers et al. (2000) reported that patients who experience chronic uncertainty about their illnesses often felt relief when they resigned themselves to the fact that some things are never certain, thus accepting the uncertainty. Accepting uncertainty even has positive outcomes such as leading to growth, new roles, and an appreciation of the complexity of life for chronically ill patients (Mishel, 1999). We practice acceptance of uncertainty when we conclude that we will never understand our boss (or coworker, subordinate, spouse, and so forth); we accept the uncertainty and discontinue information seeking to reduce it. My experience with some people who complain about the "politics" at work is that the phrase is often a catch phrase that indicates they have resigned themselves to the uncertainty they experience about certain aspects of their work place such as how decisions are made or how rewards are determined. By blaming it on "politics," they resign themselves to not being able to understand the situation and thus accept it.

Imagined Information Seeking. One final cognitive strategy that an individual can use to reduce uncertainty in a situation is to imagine the results of information seeking rather than actually seeking information. Honeycutt (1993) recognized that expected or anticipated responses to inquiries without any actual interaction, that is imagined interactions, can reduce an individual's uncertainty. By mentally determining the information likely to be gained through interaction, an individual reduces uncertainty. The once popular WWJD (What Would Jesus Do?) bracelets among some Christians appear to be an example of this strategy. When faced with situations in which they are uncertain how to act, individuals are encouraged to ask themselves "What would Jesus do?" After they ascertain his likely response through cognitive processes, they then are to act based on imagined directions from him. In work settings, individuals may ask, "What would the boss do if he or she were here?" and reduce uncertainty by imagining the response.

Summary. Individuals can use a variety of strategies to reduce uncertainty through cognitive processes. These strategies fall under five main headings: deny the uncertainty, create a tolerance of uncertainty, assimilate the uncertainty, accept the uncertainty, and use imagined information seeking to reduce uncertainty. Several of these strategies manage the uncertainty by reevaluating the uncertainty rather than actually reducing the uncertainty. For example, determining that future interactions are unlikely does not actually reduce uncertainty about another person, but it manages the uncertainty by creating tolerance of the uncertainty. The characteristic that all of these strategies share is that the individual uses his or her internal resources to manage uncertainty without seeking information from external sources.

Group and Organizational Level of Analysis

In the same way that an individual can use the strategies already mentioned to reduce uncertainty without seeking information beyond his or her own internal resources, members of groups and decision makers in organizations use similar strategies to minimize their efforts at seeking information. They rely on their own internal resources or collective cognitive processes, to reduce uncertainty rather than seeking information from others in their external environment. In the group or organizational setting, interactions within the group or organization represent collective cognitive processes whereas interactions with external sources represent information seeking. Previous research and a number of examples illustrate these strategies at work in group and organizational settings.

Deny the Uncertainty. After experiencing uncertainty, members of groups or organization may collectively deny the existence of the uncertainty in their environment. Researchers have identified the strategy of dissociation as a way that members of groups and organizations deal with uncertainty in their environments (Downey & Slocum, 1975; Emery, 1967). Dissociation is a tendency to treat some aspect of the environment as if it is irrelevant. Similarly, decision makers may not be motivated to seek information in response to environmental uncertainty because they fail to notice the changes or uncertainty, or consider such changes unimportant (Beam, 1996). Through communication members of a group or organization may determine that some aspect of the environment that is creating uncertainty for them does not actually effect the group or organization. Through this process the members collectively deny the uncertainty. As an example of this, during the waning weeks of the Clinton administration a federal advisory committee recommended a number of changes for the way human subject research should be conducted (Brainard, 2001). These recommendations created a great deal of uncertainty for the future of Institutional Review Boards, such as the one on which I served. When we met and discussed the article briefly, we collectively decided that because these were just recommendations, they were unlikely to be adopted soon, if ever. As a result, we simply denied that the uncertainty existed for us, at least at that time.

Tolerance of Uncertainty. Individuals can create a tolerance for uncertainty by assessing that future interactions are unlikely, or that neither harm nor benefit is likely, or by segmenting the uncertainty. Evidence suggests that members of groups and organizations use these same strategies when dealing with uncertainty in their environments. For members of groups and organizations the perceived uncertainty in the environment varies by characteristics such as how dynamic or complex it is and by individual cognitive differences, but also by processes involving the tolerance for ambiguity of their members (Downey & Slocum, 1975). Through communication, members can collectively determine to tolerate the uncertainty.

Members of groups and organizations can collectively decide that some uncertainty will not influence them in the future or produce any noticeable harm or benefit. Believing that an aspect of the environment is likely to impact the organization is necessary to motivate decision makers to seek information (Milliken, 1987). Trivialization involves treating issues as small or insignificant or restricting the range of conditions to which one responds by treating them as being simple instead of complex (Downey & Slocum, 1975; Emery, 1967). If an impact is unlikely or trivial, then members can tolerate the uncertainty. For example, our city council has been considering changing the requirements for the width of sidewalks. This creates uncertainty about costs to businesses, as well as homeowners. Managers of most businesses appear to have collectively decided to tolerate the uncertainty created by this issue because it seems unlikely that it will actually affect their future or cause them any harm or benefit. Most have not appeared at city council meetings protesting the new requirements because they know that if they are adopted, the new requirements will most likely apply to new construction only. Managers of companies involved in new construction, however, cannot create enough tolerance of uncertainty in this situation because future impact and harm are likely. It is not surprising that managers of these companies have appeared at city council meetings seeking information, as well as trying to influence decisions.

The strategy of fragmentation, similar to the individual process of segmenting the uncertainty mentioned above, assists members of groups and organizations in creating a tolerance for uncertainty in their environment. Fragmentation involves breaking an issue into small parts (Downey & Slocum, 1975; Emery, 1967). Uncertainty is reduced for each of the small, tolerable parts so that any overall uncertainty is no longer a concern. Faced with uncertainty about meeting a deadline on time, many groups divide the process into small parts, delegating parts to various members. Through this process of fragmentation, uncertainty about the overall goal is significantly reduced. Members can tolerate the remaining uncertainty because it seems plausible that each individual part can be accomplished.

Assimilate the Uncertainty.   Individuals assimilate uncertainty by categorizing or by identifying cultural and attitudinal similarities. In a similar manner, members of groups and organizations can use cognitive processes to reduce uncertainty without seeking information. The research on groupthink (Janis, 1972) provides ample evidence of this process. One of the characteristics of groupthink is a tendency for members of the group to view opposition as enemies while perceiving themselves as morally right. This process involves categorizing opposition, in a sense demonizing them, to produce a singular attitude toward them. At the same time, group members view themselves as having a similar attitude and cultural identity. This process of categorizing both the opposition and group members creates certainty about appropriate attitudes and behaviors. At the societal level, Ronald Reagan's references to the former Soviet Union as the "evil empire" and strategic defense systems as "star wars" provide examples of these cognitive processes. As a society we were certain about our enemy.

Accept the Uncertainty. Individuals sometimes resign themselves to uncertainty in situations. In a similar fashion, members of groups and organizations can collectively accept uncertainty through communication interaction. Perhaps this is most clearly demonstrated in the way group members manage uncertainty created by contradictory regulations and procedures. Whether these contradictions occur in government regulations and procedures or directions in manuals, work frequently must continue without resolving the uncertainty. People simply accept the uncertainty, do the best they can to make sense, and then move on.

Imagined Information Seeking. Certainly no specific research has explored the way that members of groups or organizations use imagined information seeking to reduce uncertainty. However, apparently group members do use imagined communication to make decisions from time to time. According to an article I once read, for a period of time after the death of their founder, decision makers at the Disney Corporation supposedly asked themselves, "What would Walt (Disney) do?" when faced with an uncertain situation. Only after the new CEO announced that they would no longer ask, "What would Walt do?" was the company able to begin to produce movies like "Pretty Woman," a romantic comedy about a prostitute, under the name of a subsidiary, Touchstone Pictures. Prior to that, they apparently imagined what Walt would do to reduce their uncertainty in making decisions and they apparently felt that Walt would not make such movies. Once they quit relying on imaginary information seeking from Walt, they managed uncertainty in other ways and made different decisions.

Summary

Overall, various cognitive processes work to decrease the experience of uncertainty and the motivation to seek information by creating tolerable levels of uncertainty and thereby reducing cognitive involvement (Heath & Gay, 1997). By denying uncertainty, tolerating it, assimilating it, accepting it, or seeking information through imaginary interactions, individuals or collections of group and organizational members can manage uncertainty so that information seeking is unnecessary. However, if these cognitive processes are unable to reduce uncertainty sufficiently, if the uncertainty passes some threshold of tolerance despite these cognitive efforts, then motivation to seek information remains.

MOTIVATION TO REDUCE UNCERTAINTY

The result of the previously mentioned cognitive processes is some level of uncertainty with a resulting level of motivation to reduce uncertainty. In situations where the cognitive processes have successfully managed the reduction of uncertainty for individuals or collections of individuals, little or no motivation to reduce uncertainty exists. As a result, limited information seeking would be expected. An example at the individual level of analysis illustrates this.

I experienced a moderate amount of uncertainty when I met a sales clerk with unusual hair color and body piercing at a specialty shop. I was able to assimilate most of the uncertainty by deciding that she was probably just another typical college student experimenting with rebellious appearance. I concluded that she would follow most of the behavior norms for sales clerks. In addition, I expected that I would probably not interact with her in the future because I rarely shop at the particular store. Through these cognitive processes I managed my uncertainty in several ways. I reduced both my cognitive (what kind of person is this?) and behavioral (how will she act?) uncertainty. I experienced little or no motivation to ask her about the reasons for her appearance (explanatory uncertainty) because I believed I knew her motivations. Although I might have been incorrect in my explanation of her behaviors, those assumptions were never challenged because I have not seen her again. I reduced my behavioral uncertainty about her, and because she behaved within a very wide range of acceptable store clerk behavior, I did not need to seek information to understand her behaviors better. Finally, I also created a tolerance for any uncertainty I might still have experienced about her because I believed I was unlikely to interact with her in the future. Little or no motivation to seek information existed in what was initially an uncertain situation despite the fact that no intentional interaction to reduce uncertainty occurred. The reduced uncertainty resulted in low motivation and no information seeking.

Not only do individuals behave in this manner, but also at the group or organizational level of analysis, a group involved in groupthink might behave quite similarly. For example, members of a cult may initially experience uncertainty about the local police force. With little or no interaction outside their group, they may use internal interactions to determine that the local police force is the same as most—intolerant of those who behave differently. Having reduced their uncertainty internally, whether correctly or incorrectly, the cult members have little motivation to seek information to confirm or deny their characterization of the police. Their behavior toward the police force is based on their reduced uncertainty toward the them.

By contrast, in situations where the cognitive processes discussed in the previous section do not successfully reduce uncertainty, motivation to seek information remains high according to TMU. In such situations, TMU is in agreement with the basic tenet of URT that the experience of uncertainty motivates individuals to seek information (Axiom 3, Berger & Calabrese, 1975). However, as the previous section suggests, the proposed TMU model accepts that this general premise occurs only under certain circumstances. Only if the cognitive processes fail to reduce uncertainty will motivation to reduce uncertainty result in information seeking. Again, an example illustrates this type of motivation.

In response to a general inquiry about a past weekend, a fairly new coworker mentioned that she had a relaxing weekend by staying home the whole time except for attending church Sunday morning. She had never mentioned attending church to me previously. The information she gave created uncertainty for me because I did not know what church she attends, how regularly she attends, what her beliefs are, and so forth. There are elements of cognitive and behavioral uncertainty for this topic area. Because she had not mentioned this previously and does not have any obvious religious symbols in her office or on her person to suggest anything about her beliefs, I could not rely on any cognitive processes to reduce my uncertainty. Further, I knew that I was going to continue to interact with her and so knowing more about her would help me in future interactions. Because I could not easily reduce uncertainty through cognitive processes, I remained motivated to seek information and as a result asked her what church she attended. Her response was followed by additional questions that further reduced my uncertainty about her. She told me what churches she and her husband attended prior to marrying, and provided some explanation of her reason for choosing the particular church. Because this was an initial conversation about religion, I did not push the issue too far, but at least reduced some of the behavioral and cognitive uncertainty that I experienced. Subsequent interactions were able to further reduce uncertainty about other areas concerning her religion and faith.

Collections of individuals respond similarly when they are unable to reduce uncertainty about some individual or event using internal resources. When a merger is announced for a company, the individual employees experience a great deal of uncertainty. In groups they may discuss what they know about the merger. However, if this amounts to little more than shared ignorance, their motivation to seek information remains high and they frequently interact and seek information from the media, supervisors, and union officials. As they acquire information from external sources and then share the information with each other, they are able to reduce their collective uncertainty.

The discussion of the level of motivation to seek information has so far focused on two of the three variables that seem to influence information acquisition according to Heath and Gay (1997). Cognitive involvement, the degree to which the issue relates to the self-interest of the individual or group, and uncertainty, the degree to which potential risks or rewards are unpredictable, are both evident in the previous examples. In the previous examples, lacking a need for more cognitive involvement and reduced uncertainty resulted in reduced motivation to seek information from the sales clerk or the local law enforcement agency. Continued cognitive involvement and uncertainty result in information seeking in response to the coworker's comment about religion and the announcement of a company merger.

Heath and Gay (1997) identify a third factor that can influence motivation to seek information, a desire for control of the situation and the degree to which control of the uncertainty is perceived as possible and desirable. In situations in which there is low motivation to reduce uncertainty, a strong desire to have control over situations could lead someone to seek information, but control would most likely not be perceived as desirable given that uncertainty has already been managed. As a result, motivation to seek information would remain low. In situations with high motivation to reduce uncertainty a perception that control of the information is not possible might lead to low motivation to seek information. For example, if employees perceive that management will never provide valuable information about a potential merger, they may become unmotivated to seek information from management because they perceive it as a futile effort. Thus, the perceptions of the ability to control would increase or decrease motivation to seek information.

Overall, then, the cognitive process and perceptions of the ability and desirability of controlling the uncertainty impact motivation to seek information to reduce uncertainty. When cognitive processes reduce uncertainty and control of the uncertainty seems unnecessary or impossible, motivation to seek information remains low. When cognitive processes fail to reduce uncertainty and control of the uncertainty seems possible or desirable, motivation to seek information to reduce uncertainty remains high.

COMPETING MOTIVES

If the level of motivation to reduce uncertainty were the only predictor of behavior, then once the levels of motivation were determined there would be a simple relationship between motivation levels and communication behaviors. As the cognitive processing is completed, if low levels of motivation exist, then it would be expected that information-seeking behaviors would not follow. If high levels of motivation exist, then information-seeking behaviors would be expected to follow. Previous research indicates that these simple relationships do not always occur. For example, Planalp and Honeycutt (1985) found that events that increased uncertainty in a relationship often resulted in little or no information seeking. Sheer and Cline (1995) found that the desire for information was unrelated to any measure of uncertainty. Heath and Gay (1997) found that there was no correlation between uncertainty and general information seeking by industrial hygienists; these individuals monitored the media to gain a sense of issues, but not to gain technical information to actually reduce uncertainty.

TMU suggests that the reason there are not simple relationships between levels of motivation to reduce uncertainty and actual behaviors is because these relationships are influenced by competing motives or goals. Certainly, social interaction is goal oriented; people generally interact to accomplish something, not just for the sake of interaction (Berger, 2000). Anderson (1996) points out that a problem with URT is that it typically assumes that uncertainty reduction is the solitary determinant or goal of communication behaviors. Clarity or uncertainty reduction is not always the ideal, and there are multiple goals in communication interactions (Eisenberg, 2001). Other competing motives may occur simultaneously. In his criticism of URT theory, Sunnafrank (1986a, 1990) attempts to place the goal of affiliation or outcome value as the primary determinant of communication behaviors instead of uncertainty reduction. However, Honeycutt (1993) notes that attraction or positive outcome value is also not always the immediate, primary goal of communication. For example, he suggests that individuals may focus primarily on enhancing self-concept, maintaining appropriate image, securing resources, or managing arousal rather than reducing uncertainty.

Support for the notion of multiple goals in interactions is found at both the interpersonal and organizational levels of analysis in previous research in organizational settings. The presence of multiple goals in interactions makes it difficult to design messages to accomplish all of the goals (O'Keefe, 1991; O'Keefe & Sheperd, 1987). For example, Bingham and Burleson (1989) examined the importance of multiple goals or motives in responding to situations involving sexual harassment. Their factor analysis results indicated four primary clusters of goals for communicators: maintaining relational rapport, maintaining the victim's social image, addressing the harasser's behaviors, and addressing the victim's self-feelings. Messages designed to meet these multiple goals were generally perceived as more effective than messages designed to meet single goals. These results suggest that in a similar manner competing motives would intervene in the relationship between uncertainty and behavior. In addition, it suggests that messages designed to balance the competing motives are more effective than ones designed only to accomplish one goal, such as reducing uncertainty.

The literature examining environmental uncertainty at the organizational level similarly provided evidence of the importance of considering multiple goals. Child (1972) notes that the reason there is not a direct relationship between decision makers' perceptions of the environment and their organizational strategy is that the decision makers may have other important referents to consider besides purely economic issues related to environmental uncertainty. Thus, even though the goal of reducing environmental uncertainty may be important to decision makers, they may prioritize other goals, such as maintaining a positive public image or balancing the competing goals, instead of maximizing uncertainty reduction.

The following section identifies some of the competing motives that have previously been identified in organizational settings. These competing motives complicate the relationship between uncertainty and communication behavior. Examples are provided of both the individual and collective levels of analysis.

Impression Management. An important competing motive in communication situations involving uncertainty is the simultaneous issue of impression management. Public image concerns influence the decision to seek information (Morrison, 2002). An individual may be motivated to seek information to reduce uncertainty, but the person may be equally or more concerned about creating the appropriate impression and therefore not seek the desired information. Interaction frequently focuses on the verbal and nonverbal presentation of a specific impression of the self to others (Honeycutt, 1993). Seeking information may not present the desired impression. The simple act of seeking information may suggest that the person is incompetent or insecure (Morrision & Bies, 1991). As a result, when people believe that seeking information will make them appear insecure, uncertain, or incompetent, they are less likely to request information (Ashford & Northcraft, 1992).

For example, an individual recently promoted to manager may be expected to know many aspects of the new position based on tenure in the organization, but may experience uncertainty about many of the particular details having never actually done the various tasks involved. Asking questions, especially too many questions, may reduce uncertainty for the manager, but may also create a negative impression of incompetence among coworkers and supervisors. Similarly, it may be acceptable for a newcomer to ask for directions about how to complete a new job, but if it has already been explained once (or more than once), the information seeking may create the impression that the newcomer is a slow learner or incompetent.

Not only does the act of seeking information create impressions, but the particular type of information requested may also create impression management issues. If the either the manager or the newcomer seeks feedback concerning the quality of their work and the quality is poor, then by requesting the feedback, they draw attention to the poor work, creating an even more negative impression of their competence (Morrison & Bies, 1991). Individuals with low self-esteem are particularly reluctant to draw attention to their efforts by seeking feedback for fear it will damage their self-esteem even more (Morrison, 2002). The unfortunate aspect of this scenario is that the person who most needs the feedback, the one who is performing poorly and has low self-esteem, is the one who may be most inhibited from seeking the feedback.

Awareness of these impression management concerns may prevent the manager or the newcomer from seeking needed information. They may choose not to seek information they need in order to avoid appearing incompetent or to avoid drawing attention to their poor performance. Even if they decide to use indirect information seeking, such as monitoring, in order to save face, such indirect approaches may not result in gaining the desired information, or they may misinterpret the information they do gain (Afifi & Reichert, 1996). The end result is that their concern over impression management inhibits them from seeking and gaining the information they need to reduce uncertainty.

Whereas the previous examples suggest that impression management concerns inhibit information seeking to reduce uncertainty, impression management concerns may also encourage information seeking even when uncertainty has been managed. Requesting performance feedback after doing an effective job can increase a positive image (Morrison & Bies, 1991). Seeking performance feedback after successful completion of a task draws attention to a positive performance and helps create a positive impression. Research suggests that individuals who perform well continue to seek feedback to assist others in recognizing their positive performance (Ashford & Northcraft, 1992). Thus, the previously mentioned manager and newcomer may seek feedback after they do a good job to help enhance their image in the eyes of their supervisors even though they are not experiencing uncertainty.

Research by Callister, Kramer, and Turban (1999) found evidence that both uncertainty reduction and impression management motives influenced the communication behaviors of transferees. Consistent with uncertainty reduction, transferees gradually decreased their requests for information from their peers over time as they became more certain of their jobs and reduced their role ambiguity. However, transferees continued to seek feedback from their supervisors after they reduced such requests from their peers. Apparently, transferees continued to seek feedback from their supervisors who controlled rewards in an attempt to help create positive impressions. This suggests that their communication with their supervisors was being influenced by impression management concerns, while their communication with their peers was influenced more by uncertainty reduction motives.

At the group level of analysis, similar impression management concerns may compete with uncertainty reduction motives to influence communication behaviors. Again, the impression management concerns may result in a failure to seek needed information or promote information seeking after uncertainty has been reduced. For example, a team of employees who are struggling and need additional information for their project may well present an image of confidence and control to their supervisor rather than asking for the information and assistance that they need. Likewise, a team that has recently been successful may ask whether their supervisor has had a chance to examine their report, not to reduce uncertainty but to draw attention to their success to increase their image in the supervisor's mind.

At the organizational level of analysis, research clearly indicates that organizations use annual reports as a means to communicate a positive image rather than as an information-seeking tool. The attributional bias of taking credit for successes while blaming failures on external sources indicates that organizational decision makers use annual reports to suggest that they are competent and in charge to the degree possible (Clapham & Schwenk, 1991). Any uncertainty that they may be experiencing is attributed to external sources beyond their control. There is no attempt to seek information from the audience of the annual reports to reduce this uncertainty.

Overall, previous research suggests that one motive that competes with uncertainty reduction to influence communication behaviors is impression management. Whether it is an individual trying to maintain a competent self-image, group members trying to appear on top of their project, or the public relations official's efforts at providing an image of stability, the desire to communicate the appropriate image or impression may have a stronger impact on the communication behaviors than the desire to reduce uncertainty.

Social Appropriateness.   Behaving in a socially appropriate manner can be another competing motive with uncertainty reduction. Certainly, it could be argued that behaving in a socially appropriate manner is a subset of impression management because both involve presenting an image of oneself. However, whereas impression management involves presenting a particular image, for example as knowledgeable or confident, social appropriateness involves a more general presentation of oneself as an individual who knows and understands social norms and rules for communication interaction. Communication interactions are guided by rules of appropriate behavior (Shimanoff, 1980). The communication context constrains what are perceived as appropriate or inappropriate behaviors (Rubin, 1979). In some cases the rules are implicit, although in other cases they are explicit. Social appropriateness is demonstrated by following these communication rules. This motive can work either to discourage or to encourage information seeking despite levels of uncertainty.

Even though an individual may feel motivated to seek information, the desire to appear socially appropriate may inhibit requesting information from the source of uncertainty. In some instances, any effort to seek information might be socially inappropriate. In meeting a businessperson from another culture, an astute or culturally sensitive individual might recognize that to request information would be an insult to the member of the other culture. Thus, only if the behavior is deemed socially appropriate and the partner allows it would information seeking occur (Kellerman, 1986). Individuals must also balance their need for efficiently seeking information with their need to display socially appropriate behaviors (Douglas, 1988). Information exchange is constrained by expectations that interactions begin with more superficial questions and move to more intimate ones later (Kellerman, 1986). Although this gradual increase in topic depth may be inefficient, following it demonstrates socially appropriate behavior. In addition, even when seeking some information is appropriate, there is a limit to the amount of information seeking that is considered appropriate in a particular setting. A continuous, relentless asking of too many questions may be perceived as intrusive and inappropriate, thus constraining the use of direct inquiry during face-to-face interaction (Kellerman & Berger, 1984). After asking for certain amounts of information, discontinuing such inquiries may be the socially appropriate behavior even though uncertainty has not been reduced sufficiently.

Alternatively, asking too few questions, not seeking information, may also be perceived as socially inappropriate. Certain role restraints or expectations of the interaction partners may compel information seeking when levels of uncertainty do not motivate it (Kellerman, 1986). As part of the role of an experienced employee, an individual may feel the need to ask a newcomer basic initial interaction questions, like demographics, even if not motivated by uncertainty because future interaction is unlikely. Most of us have had conversations with people at a social gathering whom we have politely asked the typical questions that occur in initial interactions. We may have little interest in the responses because we never expect to meet these people again. We simply ask questions to behave politely, in a socially appropriate manner, not out of any particular motivation to reduce uncertainty about the other people. At one time or another, individuals who fail to reciprocate by asking us about our background have probably bothered most of us. We may have left such conversations judging them as egotistical or self-absorbed. Research suggests this type of negative evaluation of those who fail to politely reciprocate information-seeking norms. Individuals instructed to seek limited amounts of information asked fewer questions of their partners and as a result were perceived as demonstrating significantly less appropriate behaviors (Berger & Kellerman, 1983).

In a variety of situations, social appropriateness may be emphasized at the expense of efficiency in reducing uncertainty (Berger, 2000). Recently I observed a member of my church who was visibly distraught. She was at the time surrounded by a number of other people. Had uncertainty reduction been my only motive, I might have walked up to her and asked her what the problem was. I suspect that I would have been judged rather rude had I done so, particularly because the person was only a casual acquaintance of mine. So to demonstrate socially appropriate behavior, I waited until later when I could ask another person who I knew better if she knew why the woman was so upset. This more subtle or indirect approach was not as efficient, but it was more socially appropriate.

Similar concerns for socially appropriate behaviors may influence the collective behaviors of members of groups or organizations. Our college's promotion and tenure committee relied on social appropriateness as determined by the rules. Until recently, the only choices for the committee were to recommend or reject a candidate for promotion and tenure. Frequently the submitted materials were less than complete, creating uncertainty about a candidate's promotion. Rather than seek information, the committee would follow the rules and behave accordingly. This too often resulted in them rejecting a candidate, the candidate appealing and providing the additional information needed, and then being recommended for promotion. Of course, being initially rejected often left a bitter taste in the mouth of the candidate. Some candidates left even after they successfully appealed the decision due to the negative impact of being initially rejected. Recently, the committee was given a third option, to table the candidate and seek information. Now they can follow the rules to behave in a socially appropriate manner and seek information to reduce uncertainty at the same time, instead of rejecting the candidate.

At the organizational level, there are sometimes even rules that determine socially appropriate behaviors that inhibit information seeking to reduce uncertainty. A university needing to hire a new coach may be quite uncertain about the availability and interest of a particular candidate for the job. Direct inquiry of the target coach would be the most efficient way to address this. However, many colleges in the National Collegiate Athletic Association (NCAA) work under the agreement that they will not contact a coach under contract with another school about a job opening without first receiving permission from the coach's current employer. Although it would probably be impossible to know if this rule is carefully followed, university officials maintain the appearance that the rule is followed. They behave in a socially appropriate manner at first by not seeking information until permission is granted. This pattern of behavior is frequently mentioned in news releases such as, "The University of LSRS has been granted permission to contact Coach Champion at the University of WNRS."

Together, this suggests that behaving in a socially appropriate manner can have a stronger influence on communication behaviors than the desire to reduce uncertainty. An individual may follow norms for questioning behavior, group members may follow the communication rules, and organizations may follow legal requirements rather than pursue uncertainty reduction. The importance of appearing to behave in a socially appropriate manner competes with uncertainty reduction motives to influence the communication behaviors.

Social Costs.   The social cost of seeking information is also a competing motive with uncertainty reduction that influences communication behaviors. Because social interaction is a symbolic process in which resources are exchanged (Roloff, 1981), there is always a cost involved in seeking information. Organizational members must weigh the perceived cost of seeking accurate and reliable information with the value of the information to be gained (Morrison, 2002). In some situations the cost of seeking information is higher than in others, and higher than the value of the information sought. For example, if individuals think that seeking information will appear as bugging the individual or are afraid that reprimands are likely to follow for not already knowing certain information, then the cost is perceived to be quite high (Miller & Jablin, 1991). If individuals perceive that they are expected to ask questions and seek information, then there is little cost associated with information seeking. Along these lines, Sias, Kramer, and Jenkins (1997) theorized that newcomers would perceive higher social costs for seeking information than temporary employees would. On one hand, newcomers need to maintain relationships with their peers because presumably they will be working with them for an extended time period. Asking for too much help and seeking too much information from their peers would put them in debt to those peers, potentially hampering future relationships with them. On the other hand, temporary employees do not need to maintain relationships with the people in their temporary assignment, unless perhaps, they are trying to gain permanent employment. Any indebtedness resulting from asking for help or seeking information will most likely never be repaid, making the social cost of such requests much smaller. Confirming this, Sias et al. found that new hires perceived the costs of seeking appraisal information as significantly greater than temporary employees.

In many instances, the social costs of seeking information include more tangible costs than simply avoiding a sense of indebtedness to the sources of information. Social costs can include expending resources such as time or money to seek information to reduce uncertainty. Some information is simply more difficult to obtain and incurs higher costs (Morrison, 2002). Faced with a complex decision, an employee must gauge how many resources to expend in order to gather information to reduce uncertainty to the point that a good decision can be made. Given the availability of potentially unlimited information sometimes, the decision maker must decide when enough resources have been expended so that a good quality decision can be made. A former sales representative told about how she had spent a considerable amount of time gathering information before making a presentation to the client. When her boss asked her if she had made the presentation yet, she said she was still gathering information. Her boss sat her down and told her to make the presentation and then to adjust accordingly rather than expending more energy collecting more information. Her boss's comments indicated that she had spent too many resources gathering information to reduce her uncertainty and needed to move on.

At the group or organizational level, the idea that decision makers often seek only enough information to reduce uncertainty to the point that a good decision can be made has been termed *satisficing* (e.g., Connolly, 1980). In satisficing, the decision makers do not necessarily reduce uncertainty until the best or maximum decision can be made. Instead, rather than expending more time and resources, the decision makers arrive at a satisfactory decision and then monitor and adjust the impact of the decision after it is enacted. Such an approach is less costly for the decision makers because it consumes fewer resources.

Because information seeking involves costs, consideration of those costs may inhibit information seeking that would be motivated by uncertainty. Individuals may choose not to seek information if they perceive the cost to be too great. Group and organizational decision makers may similarly make satisfactory decisions rather than expending the resources necessary to reduce uncertainty so that a best or maximum decision can be made.

Utility of Information Seeking. Even though individuals may experience uncertainty, they may feel that seeking information may not have any real advantage or utility for them. The competing motive, utility, may prevent information seeking. One reason that may result in a negative assessment of the utility of information seeking is the belief that the information needed to reduce uncertainty is simply not available. Uncertainty may result in seeking information only so long as the search is perceived as likely to provide additional relevant information; once it becomes apparent that additional searching is unlikely to reduce uncertainty, predictions or guesses are made based on the available information instead of continued information seeking (Acredolo & O'Connor, 1991). An assessment that the goal of reducing uncertainty for a particular situation is not important could also result in an assessment that it is not useful to seek information. Only if seeking information is likely to assist individuals in completing a task or goal that has salience to them would they be motivated to seek information. Sunnafrank's (1986a) "predicted outcome value" is really a similar concept. Information seeking is based on whether a positive outcome is expected. In support of this, Pavitt (1982) found that in some situations individuals experienced more uncertainty (about some third party) but did not seek information (from a partner) apparently because they did not believe that seeking information would be useful.

Similar concerns can influence information seeking by group and organizational decision makers. Only if the decision makers perceive that seeking information is possible or will result in valuable information will they seek information to reduce uncertainty. Duncan (1973) found that when decision makers perceive that they have little potential influence on their environment, they simply rely on standard procedures instead of seeking information and using flexible approaches. This suggests that they see little value in seeking information to reduce uncertainty because it will provide them little advantage over following a standard operating procedure. Similarly, a team of workers might decide not to consult their coordinator because he or she does not know any more about the issue than they do and make decisions without seeking additional information to reduce uncertainty.

To summarize, when individuals or groups of decision makers are faced with uncertainty, they may not seek information if they do not perceive that there is utility in doing so. If they do not believe that the issue is important enough or do not believe that seeking information is likely to result in uncertainty reduction, they may simply act on the basis of the information they already have or choose not to act at all.

Competence.   Being motivated to reduce uncertainty and having no other competing motives may still not result in information-seeking behaviors. Competence in communication is also a necessity. If individuals do not feel competent at seeking information, they may not seek the information despite their levels of uncertainty. Along these lines, Douglas (1991) demonstrated that those individuals who experience a general, global uncertainty in interpersonal relationships seemed incapable of seeking information in what might be the most appropriate way. For example, those high in global uncertainty asked fewer questions but did more self-disclosure in the first minutes of interactions. So even if direct inquiry might be appropriate, they seemed to lack the skill to manage their uncertainty by directly seeking information. Lack of knowledge or experience may result in some plans for uncertainty reduction being carried out ineptly because of ineffective strategies (Honeycutt, 1993). As evidence of the opposite effect, communication competence is associated with lower levels of uncertainty. Research on clergy in nonprofit organizations found that those high on communication competence and low on communication apprehension experienced less uncertainty (Forward, 1997). Apparently, their competence enables them to successfully seek information to reduce uncertainty.

Similarly, group or organizational decision makers might not feel competent to seek the information they need to reduce their uncertainty. For example, owners of a small business may be uncertain whether a particular tax break or government program applies to them. Even though they would like to seek the necessary information to answer this question, based on previous experiences, they believe that they are not capable of seeking the information from the government (of course, the real fault may be the incompetence of the government agency rather than their own incompetence). As a result, they make a determination on their own and respond accordingly. Similarly, a group of decision makers may believe that the information they need to reduce uncertainty exists somewhere on the World Wide Web. However, because they do not feel competent to begin searching for the information on the web, they may never begin their search, or they may give up after a brief, unsuccessful attempt at gaining the information on the web. In the end, they make a decision without gaining the available information.

The point is that when faced with uncertainty, an individual or group of decision makers must feel that they are competent information seekers before they will exert the effort to seek the information they need. When they do not feel competent, the motivation to reduce uncertainty no longer is the primary motive. As a result, information seeking does not occur.

Emotions. URT assumes a very thoughtful, rational process in which an individual is aware of his or her uncertainty and takes appropriate action to reduce it by seeking information. Such an approach fails to consider the role of emotions in interactions. Emotions may become a primary motivator of communication behaviors rather than uncertainty reduction. Strong negative emotions may be particularly significant as primary motives for communication behaviors. Planalp and Honeycutt (1985) conclude that strong negative emotions lead to avoiding unpleasant interactions. This suggests that avoiding negative emotions may override uncertainty reduction concerns. For example, if an individual has had very negative interactions with someone previously, even though he or she is experiencing a great deal of uncertainty about some current situation, he or she may not seek the needed information from that person in an effort to end the interaction as quickly as possible. Avoiding negative experiences becomes a more important motive than uncertainty reduction.

Similarly, a team of employees may have been reamed out by their supervisor on more than one occasion. Now they are in a situation where they would benefit from some additional direction from their supervisor. However, based on their previous experiences, they would rather not interact with the supervisor and so do not seek the information they need. Asking the supervisor will guarantee another (negative) interaction with the supervisor. Although not seeking information could lead to another reaming out, it may not if things turn out right. So the potential avoidance of a negative interaction takes precedence over uncertainty reduction. At the organizational level, a restaurant management group may have sought information from the county health department on a previous occasion to clarify an issue. Not only did the county health department provide them with the needed information, but in the process also found several previously missed code violations, resulting in the restaurant being written up. Remembering this negative experience, the managers decide to go it alone when a new uncertainty arises and ask for forgiveness rather than permission if the issue ever is actually uncovered by the health department.

Avoiding negative emotional experiences is a powerful motivator of human behavior. When individuals or decision makers associate seeking information to reduce uncertainty with negative emotions, they are likely to act in such a way as to avoid those experiences. As a result, negative emotions become a more powerful motivator of communication behavior than uncertainty reduction.

Maintaining Uncertainty. Although reducing uncertainty is often a primary goal, maintaining or increasing uncertainty may be a competing goal at times. Maintaining or increasing uncertainty can be accomplished with either of two strategies. In a situation with uncertainty, failing to seek information can maintain uncertainty because no additional information can clarify the situation. In a situation in which there is certainty, seeking additional contradictory information can help to create uncertainty. In both instances, information can be used to manipulate uncertainty in the desired manner (Brashers, 2001).

The motive of maintaining (or increasing) uncertainty has been particularly noted in health situations. When negative outcomes are expected, seeking information may be avoided to maintain uncertainty, whereas when negative outcomes are certain, information may be sought to increase uncertainty (Brashers et al., 2002). Maintaining uncertainty may allow for denial of certain negative consequences or increasing uncertainty may allow for increased hope in situations where certainty would create fatalistic attitudes (Brashers et al., 2000). As a result, individuals who suspect that they may have AIDS or cancer sometimes fail to seek information because the information would make it impossible for them to maintain hope in the face of negative information. Alternatively, when they receive an apparently definitive diagnosis, they may seek additional information to create uncertainty so that they can continue to maintain hope.

Maintaining uncertainty can be a powerful motive in a number of other situations unrelated to health. For example, employees who hear rumors that they are about to be laid off or fired may not make any effort to seek additional information. Seeking such information could confirm their worst fears. By avoiding information seeking, they can dismiss the information as rumor and deny the certainty of the negative future. Alternatively, if the rumor is from a reliable source, they may seek information from another reliable source that will deny the rumor. The conflicting information from alternative sources creates uncertainty so that the employees can hope that they will have jobs in the future.

Group or organizational decision-makers may similarly be motivated by a desire to maintain uncertainty. Although I have never been a basketball coach, I can imagine how the coach of the fifteenth seed maintains uncertainty for his players as they prepare to play the second seed of the Men's NCAA Tournament. Of course, there is little uncertainty about the game. Only something like three times in the history of the tournament has the fifteenth seed defeated the second seed (for example in 2001, when Hampton beat Iowa State). To create uncertainty for his team and perhaps for himself, too, the coach focuses on the fact the opposing team has been beaten a number of times this past year and will be tired after their league tournament. From the game films he points out their weaknesses and develops a strategy for defeating them. He might mention reports of injuries or illnesses of key players that could affect the outcome. He mentions how top teams sometimes look past their first opponents and underprepare so that upsets are possible. He reminds his team of the Cinderella teams of the past who have made it deep into the tournament. He of course reminds them that fifteenth seeds have won in the past, even if only rarely. He reminds them that "it ain't over until the fat lady sings." All of this information seeking and sharing seems designed to create and maintain uncertainty about the game so that the players (and he) have hope as they begin. They need enough uncertainty about the outcome of the game so that they can imagine themselves winning. Of course, this challenge to maintain uncertainty is even more challenging for the coach of the sixteenth seeded team because a sixteenth seeded team has never defeated a number-one-seeded team.

These examples illustrate how creating or maintaining uncertainty can be a motive for individuals and group and organizational decision makers. Even though at times reducing uncertainty can be a positive thing, sometimes by creating or maintaining uncertainty, individuals and groups can maintain an optimistic outlook and avoid feeling hopeless. Managing uncertainty does not always mean reducing uncertainty.

Information Variety.   Many of the previously mentioned motives would inhibit information seeking motivated by uncertainty reduction for reasons such as avoiding costs or feeling incompetent to seek information. Other motives could inhibit or promote information seeking in different circumstances, involving issues such as impression management or social appropriateness. This final motive is different from the previous ones in that it seems to promote information seeking in situations in which uncertainty is low, contrary to URT. Some individuals seek information, not so much to reduce uncertainty but out of a need for variety. It is not unusual to do casual information seeking due to the need for variety (Nigg, 1982). These individuals might be called the curiosity seekers. These are people who love information about people, about places, about organizations, about just about anything, just because it is interesting to know. Although it could be argued that at some level these people are reducing their uncertainty about the world at large or people in general, it seems more appropriate to consider them people who just enjoy new information even if it has no particular value or addresses any area of uncertainty. Some organizations have a sort of priest or storyteller who seems to know everything about the history of the organization, its myths and legends (Pacanowsky & O'Donnell-Trujillo, 1983). Such a person serves as a source of information for others in the organization, but seems to gather information for the fun of knowing it, not in response to particular uncertainties. At the group or organizational level, decision makers may justify keeping in touch with their environment because it will help them strategically. However, it seems likely that much of the information seeking fulfills the need to seek novel and interesting information more than it provides information that reduces any real or imagined uncertainty. So whereas information seeking may be the result of an uncertainty reduction motive, in some instances, information seeking occurs primarily out of a desire to seek novel information.

Summary

It is important to end this discussion of motives by recognizing that motives are fluid. The idea that a preset motive governs action is an oversimplification, as is the argument that intention is purely retrospective (Poole et al., 1985). Although uncertainty reduction is an important motive for determining communication behaviors, it rarely works independently of other motives. People are generally motivated to promote positive outcomes and prevent negative ones (Morrison, 2002). A variety of competing motives may hinder information seeking because it may result in negative outcomes, such as impression management, behaving in a socially appropriate way, avoiding social costs, and avoiding negative emotions. Feeling incompetent to seek information or believing that there is little utility in seeking information can also hinder information seeking. Alternatively, a number of motives can result in information seeking behaviors that are not the result of uncertainty reduction. A desire to appear socially competent or to find new information can motivate information seeking even when there is little or no uncertainty. These behaviors may result in positive outcomes apart from reducing uncertainty. As a result of these competing motives, there is not a simple relationship between uncertainty and information seeking. At times, information seeking does not occur even though the levels of uncertainty would predict that it should.

At other times, information seeking occurs despite the fact that there is little or no uncertainty. Competing motives in TMU can be used to explain these behaviors.

COMMUNICATION BEHAVIORS

Whereas the early conceptualizations of URT focused on seeking information by direct inquiry only, later elaborations recognized that people can seek information through a variety of interactive, active, and passive strategies (Berger, 1979). Some of the critics of URT fail to include the possibility of various indirect and passive information seeking strategies in their experiments and critiques of URT. The importance of examining different communication strategies of gaining information is emphasized by results suggesting that 65% of social information is gained through direct interaction *or* observation, 30% through indirect or third-party interactions, and 5% through other sources such as media (Hewes et al., 1985). Along these lines, Planalp et al. (1988) found that indirect discussions with third parties were common ways of gaining information in uncertain situations in personal relationships.

A variety of scholars have developed slightly different typologies to describe the interactive, active, and passive communication behaviors that individuals use to seek information in organizational settings. In one of the most comprehensive and more frequently cited lists, Miller and Jablin (1991) developed a typology that includes seven strategies:

1. *Overt question or direct inquiry* involves asking a source for information to reduce uncertainty in a direct or straightforward manner.
2. *Indirect questions* involve asking for information from the source of uncertainty in a more subtle or roundabout manner with the hope of receiving the needed information.
3. *Third-party inquiry* involves requesting the information from someone other than the target of uncertainty.
4. *Testing limits* involves using trial-and-error strategies, including possibly breaking apparent norms in an attempt to gain information from the reactions.
5. *Disguising conversations* involves seeking to gain information by disclosing and expecting reciprocal self-disclosure or joking about the topic to gain a reply.
6. *Observing* involves actively monitoring the environment in order to gain specific information.
7. *Surveillance* involves passively attending to information in the environment and making sense of it retrospectively rather than to address a particular uncertainty.

The following section integrates several different typologies in an attempt to provide a comprehensive but succinct list of strategies. These are divided into interactive, active, and passive strategies.

Before examining these strategies, it is important to note that not all information useful for managing uncertainty is gained strategically. Berger (2002) notes that it is "extremely shortsighted to conclude that individuals acquire information about others exclusively through strategic means" (p. 280). Individuals gain information when they are not seeking information, gain more information than they sought at times, and sometimes gain information when they are actively avoiding it. For example, one employee may accidentally discover that there will be no raises this year, another may find the information about no pay raises that he was looking for and also find out that two people will be laid off as well, and a third may be avoiding reading any information about the economic situation of the company and be told about it by a coworker anyway. So, although what follows are the strategic ways that people gain information, it is important to note that people receive information useful for managing uncertainty through a variety of other means, as well.

Interactive Strategies

Interactive strategies involve clear, observable communication behaviors between individuals and some potential source of information. Sometimes this is a direct interaction with the primary source of uncertainty. At other times, the communication may involve interaction with a secondary source of information.

Interactive Communication Behaviors With Primary Sources.   The most obvious interactive, communication behavior is simple inquiry or request for information from the source of uncertainty to reduce uncertainty. Miller and Jablin (1991) called this *overt question* or *direct inquiry*. Similarly, Morrison (1993a, 1993b) used *inquiry to peers and supervisors*, Kramer (1993) named it *solicited information*, and Kramer et al. (1995) labeled it *initiating information requests*. This is a basic strategy of asking a specific question to reduce a specific uncertainty. For example, a newcomer who is uncertain which forms to use can simply ask the staff accountant whether to use Form A or Form B to receive cash reimbursements for meal expenses. Alternatively, a veteran who is uncertain whether the newcomer has experience with a particular procedure for finding inventory reports on the computer system can simply ask the newcomer, "Have you done this before?" In either case, the response will reduce the uncertainty.

The second interactive strategy is more subtle, involving indirect strategies for information seeking. This broader category includes indirect inquiry and disguising conversations (Miller & Jablin, 1991). Instead of directly requesting needed information to reduce uncertainty, an individual creates an opportunity for someone to provide information. Even though this strategy can help save face or manage impressions, it also has the potential to be less successful because the desired information may not be provided or the information provided may be interpreted incorrectly because it is not discussed explicitly

(Miller & Jablin, 1991). Applying this strategy to the previous examples, the newcomer might say to the staff accountant, "At my old job, we used a form like this one to get our meals reimbursed." The staff accountant might give the needed information by saying, "Well, here we use Form A for meals for day trips, but Form B if the trip includes an overnight stay in a motel." Alternatively, the accountant might just say, "We do it differently around here. You'll get it figured out after a while." In the first case, the indirect approach produces the needed information, but in the second it does not. Similarly, the veteran employee might joke, "I remember how I used to really waste time and screw things up using the computer system to find inventory information. It was almost embarrassing until someone finally helped me." The newcomer might reply, "Yes, I had the same problem until someone showed me last week," or "Yeah, at my old job, there were guys who were the brunt of jokes because they were so computer illiterate. I have decided not to be one of those." Again, the first reply reduces uncertainty for the veteran employee by making it clear help is not needed, whereas the second reply really does not make it clear whether help is needed or not. The value of these indirect approaches is important to note. Afifi and Reichert (1996) concluded that there is a preference for indirect information seeking over more direct approaches. These indirect approaches do involve interaction with the source of uncertainty, unlike the following strategies.

Interactive Communication Behaviors With Secondary Sources. Although asking the source of uncertainty for information either directly or indirectly can be effective, it is not unusual for individuals to seek information from a third party instead of the source of uncertainty. For example, the newcomer might ask a peer, rather than the staff accountant, about the appropriate forms to use. The veteran employee might ask a supervisor if the newcomer has received any training on the use of the computer system rather than asking the newcomer. Asking a third party can be a particularly good way of managing the competing motives of impression management and uncertainty reduction. By seeking information from a third party, there is limited chance of making a negative impression on the source of uncertainty. The newcomer does not come off as uninformed to the staff accountant and the veteran does not come off as condescending to the newcomer if it turns out that the training has already been given.

For individuals in organizations, third-party inquiry of secondary sources can include sources such as customers, newspapers, spouses, friends, and other family members (Napier et al., 1989). Newcomers rely on these extra-organizational sources in other organizations for information to reduce uncertainty (Morrison, 1993b; Teboul, 1997). The importance of these third-party sources has been found in a number of areas. In religious organizations, spouses are important sources of information for married clergy, whereas friends are more important for unmarried clergy (Forward, 1997). Conrath (1967) found that in more uncertain situations decision makers relied on informal communication, which would seem to include some third-party sources.

Active Strategies

Unlike interactive strategies, active strategies do not involve direct communication interaction with another person. They do involve actively seeking information nonetheless. In active strategies, individuals assume the role of active receiver of information without assuming the sender role needed for interactive approaches. Ashford (1986) was one of the first scholars to emphasize that individuals could actively seek information or feedback without direct interaction. By actively paying attention to the surroundings, individuals can gain information without interaction. A variety of scholars refer to this strategy as *monitoring* or *observing* (Kramer et al., 1995; Morrison, 1993a, 1993b; Teboul, 1994). Organizational newcomers might use this strategy to reduce uncertainty about many aspects of their organization. Through monitoring their peers they can determine appropriate apparel norms for communicating the company image. They learn whether business causal is acceptable and whether jeans can be considered business casual. They can watch the reactions to other newcomers making suggestions in a meeting to determine whether newcomers must pay their dues before they will be listened to in a meeting or whether they are accepted as part of the team right away. A student told me about an organization that had very clear norms about newcomers contributing during meetings. The norm was simply that they did not participate, but talked to their supervisors outside the meeting. Although newcomers may be told this information, it is more likely that they gain this by monitoring. Through their observations, the individuals learned that they should not contribute during meetings.

One particular type of monitoring may be to pay attention to the social context for cues that will reduce uncertainty and prescribe appropriate behaviors. Examining the context often reduces uncertainty and the resulting need for information seeking. As Berger and Calabrese (1975) argued, meeting a stranger at a political rally provides more information for making attributions than meeting a stranger on a public street. Rubin (1977) found support that context influences uncertainty and information-seeking. Participants used different information seeking strategies when in an ambiguous situation of getting to know someone compared to a task of determining whether a person fits a particular job. In the ambiguous situation, demographic questions dominated the initial minutes of interaction whereas questions of opinions and values became prominent later in the conversation, typical of initial interactions. In the job-fit situation, questions of opinions, values, and work ethics occurred throughout the interaction. This suggests that in the context of the job situation uncertainty was reduced by providing a focus for information seeking.

Testing limits is another active strategy for seeking information (Miller & Jablin, 1991; Teboul, 1997). In this approach individuals make an effort to push the limit of some norm or deliberately break a suspected norm in an effort to gain information to reduce their uncertainty about the norm. For example, if newcomers are uncertain whether the half-hour lunch break is a general guideline or a strict rule, they may come back after 35 minutes one day, then try 40 minutes after a few more days, and so forth until they receive some sort of negative feedback. That feedback could take many forms from dirty looks from their peers, to biting remarks from coworkers about work habits, to an official reprimand from a supervisor. By actively testing the limits in this way, they eventually receive the information they need to reduce their uncertainty about the lunch policy without ever directly asking for the information. Again, the individual receives information often without direct communication with others.

Passive Strategies

Passive strategies rely on the information coming to the individual rather than on the individual seeking the information or trying to create opportunities to gain information. In the passive strategy, the individual does not make any effort to gain information to reduce some experience of uncertainty. Rather, the individual simply is open to receiving information, and some source provides information without any request or prompting for it. This passive strategy would include surveillance in which information is not sought, but some attention is paid to the environment so that information can be received (Miller & Jablin, 1991). Such causal scanning may occur simply for information variety (Nigg, 1982).

This passive information acquisition can occur quite rapidly and subconsciously. Berger (2002) reports that a variety of research demonstrates that people are influenced by stimuli outside of the consciousness and sometimes in less than a second. This includes the observation of nonverbal characteristics. For example, brief exposure to pictures of pleasant or unpleasant faces influenced subsequent ratings of others even though research participants could not recall the initial faces. Passive information acquisition can include other types of verbal and visual information, as well.

Research on newcomers and transferees has demonstrated that this kind of unsolicited information or passive information received is an important source of information for them as they are socialized (Kramer, 1993; Kramer et al., 1995; Morrison, 1993a). In each study, this passive information explained a significant reduction in uncertainty for the organizational members. Although we know little about why some employees receive more of this unsolicited information than others, it has a significant impact on uncertainty reduction and adaptation to the organization. This approach involves organizational members providing information perhaps out of friendly concern for the new employees or from remembering what information was helpful to them when they were new employees.

Alternative Activities

Sometimes individuals cope with uncertainty by doing seemingly unrelated activities that do not involve information seeking. Although not all of these alternatives may be communication behaviors, they are substitutes for communication behaviors in the face of uncertainty. Perhaps due to a sense that nothing productive can be done to reduce uncertainty or that there is no adequate source of information, individuals may simply choose to ignore uncertainty and talk about something else or do something else. For example, faced with possible layoffs due to a bank merger and having no satisfactory source of information to reduce uncertainty, some employees simply updated their own resumes and considered various internal and external employment opportunities (Napier et al., 1989). Although such strategies perhaps prepared them for actions to take after an eventual reduction in uncertainty, they did nothing to reduce current levels of uncertainty. Their communication about their resumes and job opportunities prepared them for potential realities, but did nothing to reduce uncertainty about those possibilities.

Group and Organizational Level of Analysis

Most of the examples provided so far concern the communication behaviors of individuals seeking and receiving information. Members of groups and organizations can collectively use all of these same communication strategies to seek and receive information. Members can use direct strategies to seek information. For example, team members may ask their coordinator for information to clarify some aspect of their project that is unclear to them. Organizational leaders may directly contact a government agency for an explanation of a new safety policy. Members may use indirect strategies, as well. Rather than ask their coordinator for clarification about their project, team members may ask other teams how they are approaching a problem in order to better understand what the coordinator might mean. A business owner may ask fellow Chamber of Commerce members how they are handling the safety policy. Passive strategies can also be used. The team may decide to just wait and see, knowing that eventually the coordinator will let them know. Organizational decision makers may casually monitor their environment for safety policy issues until the needed information comes their way. Finally, group and organizational members may simply do nothing to reduce uncertainty. If they believe that the environment is too turbulent or that there is no reliable source of information, they may simply go about their business and ignore their sense of uncertainty. By staying busy with unrelated communication and activities, they avoid confronting the uncertainty they are experiencing.

Summary and Implications

Faced with various levels of uncertainty, individuals and members of groups and organizations can respond with a variety of communication behaviors.

These communication behaviors range from very active strategies, such as direct inquiry, to very passive strategies, such as waiting to receive unsolicited information. They may interact with a wide range of primary information sources as part of these communication behaviors, including internal organizational sources such as peers, coworkers, and supervisors, or a variety of secondary sources, such as people in other organizations, friends, and relatives. According to TMU there is no direct link between the level of uncertainty and the particular strategy used due to the competing motives discussed in the previous section. Individuals with high levels of uncertainty may use direct inquiry if there are no competing motives, but may use a more passive strategy in order to create or maintain a certain impression for themselves. Alternatively, members of a group experiencing low levels of uncertainty about their task may rely on passive strategies to gain information, or they may use direct inquiry in order to behave in a socially appropriate manner, such as following protocol that says it is important to consult with your supervisor.

In addition, the type of uncertainty itself and the source of information may influence the choice of communication behavior. Morrison (1995) reported that certain strategies are associated with certain types of information needs. Employees were more likely to use direct inquiry for technical or job-related information, but more likely to use monitoring for social, appraisal, normative, or political information. They relied equally on inquiry and monitoring for referent and organizational information. Teboul (1994) reported that the source for the information seeking seemed to influence the frequency and strategy used as much as the particular type of uncertainty. Together these findings suggest that different types of uncertainty and different sources of information produce different levels of motivation and that different competing motives influence the choice of communication behavior. It is this recognition that competing motives and different levels of motivation to reduce uncertainty can influence communication behaviors that makes TMU a more comprehensive model of information seeking than URT.

IMPACT ON UNCERTAINTY

The strategic communication behaviors enacted in response to various levels of uncertainty have some impact on those levels of uncertainty. Additional information may be gained when it is not sought or even when it is being avoided; the unintentionally acquired information maybe as important as that gained through strategic information seeking (Berger, 2002). In the original URT, it was postulated that information gained resulted in reduced uncertainty and increased liking. Even though those are potential outcomes of the communication behaviors, based on more recent research, TMU suggests that a number of possible outcomes occur.

Whereas communication may result in decreases in uncertainty, there are times when communication results in increases in uncertainty instead. This can occur at either the individual level (Planalp et al., 1988) or at the collective level (Driskill &

Goldstein, 1986). An individual may leave a meeting with a supervisor feeling more uncertain despite the effort to reduce uncertainty by seeking information. When the information gained is unexpected, such as discovering that the supervisor deliberately hid information about the matter on a previous occasion, an increase in uncertainty is possible. The new information brings into question whether the new information is any more accurate than previous information and brings into question the relationship with the supervisor. Driskill and Goldstein provided an example of this problem at the collective level. The management team put out a memo to all organizational members in response to uncertainty concerning a planned plant closure. Despite this effort, there appeared to be more uncertainty afterwards. Although the memo adequately addressed uncertainty about the company's long-term viability and stability (collective level), because it did not address uncertainty concerning individual job security (individual level), it actually increased rather than decreased uncertainty for the employees.

An alternative way to think about the impact of information gained through communication is suggested by Honeycutt (1993). Honeycutt suggests that the outcomes from interaction about uncertainty can result primarily in either assimilation or accommodation of the prior expectations. Assimilation occurs when the behaviors are accepted as fitting the expectations. Accommodation occurs when experiences result in changes in expectations. So, for example, at the individual level, my initial interaction with a new employee may begin with uncertainty. After exchanging information for a while, I may discover that the person fits into my schema of a typical, just out of college, enthusiastic employee. I assimilate the new employee into my expectations for a group of new college graduates. In essence, I develop a stereotypical set of expectations for the person and reduce uncertainty in the process. Alternatively, my interaction with the new employee may go quite differently than I expected. Even though the person is also a new graduate, I find the person to be very secretive, private, and unenthusiastic. Having never met such a new graduate in my company before, I must accommodate this unusual individual and so broaden my categories for employees who are recent graduates. The group or collective level of analysis may have similar reactions. As a group they collectively make sense of the new employee to reduce their uncertainty either by assimilating or accommodating the newcomer with their previous notions of new college graduates.

The same information gained through communication may not have the same impact on uncertainty, depending on the source and situation. Ellis (1992) found that in high-uncertainty situations, information from a highly credible source (perceived as competent and similar) reduced uncertainty, compared to information from less credible sources. Not surprising, in low-uncertainty situations, information had limited impact. These findings suggest that in an organization facing potential layoffs, the source of the information is likely to have a greater impact on uncertainty than the information itself. If a recent hire reports that there really will not be layoffs due to the number of back orders according to the person who interviewed him, this may not reduce uncertainty for the veteran employees. If, while managing by walking about, the vice-president of operations says that they have way too many orders to be able to afford to shut down even one assembly line for a week, veteran employees may feel that their uncertainty has been reduced. Again, the collective group reaction to such reports could be quite similar. If the source is reliable and credible, then the members of the group or organization may accept the explanations and reduce their uncertainty. If the source seems unreliable, the information may not impact their uncertainty at all.

URT seems to suggest that there is an immediate impact on uncertainty when information is gained. Individuals seek information, receive the information, and then the uncertainty is reduced. However, the impact of information seeking on uncertainty may not be immediate. Inferences made in recalling interactions may be more important in reducing uncertainty than inferences made during the interactions, making those instances which are easily retrieved very important (Berger, 1993). An employee may leave a meeting with the supervisor feeling no more certain about which project he should focus on for the next month. But after reflecting on it later in the week, he concludes that she was subtly telling him that one project has less upper management support and that he should focus on the other instead. This inference may be incorrect, but it still reduces his uncertainty. The members of a team or organization may similarly have a delayed reaction to the information gained. The initial response to a clarification from the safety commission may be no change in uncertainty as they muse, "What is that supposed to mean?" However, a few weeks later, after trying to make sense of it, they look back at the memo and draw conclusions about what it really means.

CONCLUSION

Regardless of whether the behaviors increase or decrease uncertainty, whether the information is assimilated or accommodated, whether the source is credible or not, and whether the response is immediate or delayed, the process frequently begins again. For example, if the communication increased uncertainty, then the process of TMU can begin again. The previous episode or event triggers new levels of uncertainty or certainty, which must be managed. If the communication reduces uncertainty, then there is little motivation to seek additional information. However, managing uncertainty does not end when one uncertainty is resolved, as new uncertainties emerge (Babrow, 2001b). In addition, a competing motive, such as a desire to appear polite, may cause an individual to continue to request additional information even though uncertainty is no longer a concern.

At this point, the model described may seem like a very linear process in which the components follow each other in a very methodical pattern. As stated at the beginning of the chapter, this really is not an accurate portrayal of how TMU always works. An analogy to the garbage-can model of decision making (Cohen, March, & Olsen, 1972) might provide an appropriate explanation of the process of TMU.

In the garbage-can model of decision making there are solutions, problems, participants, and attention milling around in the organization. Sometimes the process of decision making appears very organized and linear. Someone attends to a problem and gets others to focus attention on it as well, a solution is suggested, and the problem is solved. At other times the process is not so simple or linear. Sometimes a solution is created first but addresses no known problem. It may be some time before someone pays attention to the solution and then notices that it could solve a recently developed problem. Gradually people pay attention to the situation and the solution is used in a successful way. Here the decision making process is much more fluid, with solutions occurring first and problems occurring later. Only when someone pays attention to both does the solution get applied to the problem.

TMU actually works quite similarly. Sometimes it works in a very methodical, almost linear, cyclical process. First, uncertainty is experienced. Then cognitive processes are unable to reduce uncertainty. Motivated by the uncertainty with no competing motives to interfere, interactive communication occurs to seek information. When the information is gained, uncertainty is reduced. Then, the process begins again when another event triggers uncertainty. At other times the process is much less organized or the process is much more fluid. An individual may be having polite conversation with a friend, passing time. The friend makes an off-color remark about a mutual acquaintance, causing some uncertainty for the individual. Although not understanding the remark, the individual tries to maintain a polite conversation. In recalling the conversation the next day, the individual remembers something from a previous conversation that makes the off-color remark perfectly understandable; it fits into the individual's schema for the friend. Ultimately, uncertainty returns to its previous state, more or less. In this second example, the parts of TMU are mostly present, but they occur in a rather random or haphazard order.

Along these lines, Berger and Calabrese (1975) discuss the possibility of retroactively explaining the other's behavior. The retroactive uncertainty reduction that can occur is similar to the cognitive uncertainty reduction processes discussed previously. It differs from the cognitive reduction processes in that it occurs *after* the communication instead of *prior* to the communication. Then, instead of continuing to seek information, the process of cognitive uncertainty reduction adequately addresses uncertainty concerns. However, this makes retroactive uncertainty reduction almost identical to sensemaking (Weick, 1995).

This chapter, then, has delineated the parts of the process that TMU proposes. It suggests that uncertainty may be experienced for a variety of reasons. An individual or group of people can often reduce their uncertainty through cognitive processes without interaction or communication. At other times, unable to reduce uncertainty, information may be sought, but only if competing motives do not interfere with the need for information. Communication behaviors from interactive to active to passive may be used to gather information. Depending on the nature of the information, uncertainty may be reduced or increased. To verify this model of TMU, the following three chapters include three examples of research that explore some of the components of TMU.

Cognitive and Behavioral Processes for Managing Uncertainty: A Qualitative Study of Car Salespeople

Most adults in the United States have had some interactions with car salespeople. Sharing stories, often negative ones, about these experiences is a common conversational topic among adults. As consumers we typically focus on our experiences of attempting to decide what type of vehicle to purchase and of determining if we got a "good deal." We consider how we manage uncertainty as we make a major purchase. We rarely consider how car salespeople manage their uncertainty in interacting with us.

This chapter reports the results of a study designed to investigate and verify aspects of the TMU in an organizational setting. Because much of the research on URT has focused on initial interactions, it seemed appropriate to examine TMU in an organizational context in which there were a large number of initial interactions.

Car salespeople were selected for the study because they routinely interact with strangers as part of their work. Indicative of this, one salesperson in this study indicated that he sold a car to about one in ten customers on whom he waited and sold more than 300 cars a year. By this estimate, he has significant interactions with over 3,000 customers per year. Even though some of the interactions are with previous customers, assuming this is fairly typical of car salespeople, it demonstrates how frequently they must manage uncertainty as they interact with strangers. As a result, car salespeople likely develop some system to cope with the constant uncertainty of meeting people. This coping system would likely have well-developed cognitive processes and information seeking strategies for managing uncertainty in their initial interactions with customers, like those suggested by TMU. The constant use of such a coping system could result in it being either more sophisticated or more efficient than people use in other initial interactions. However, the coping system would represent an extension of the cognitive and behavioral processes used in initial interactions in a particular organizational context.

In addition, the principles of TMU seemed to be likely to be especially pronounced for salespeople of "high dollar" or "big ticket" items such as automobiles. Automobiles are typically second only to home purchases as the most expensive items individuals buy. This makes car buying an important event for a customer. Because most car salespeople are paid on a commission basis, car salespeople are also highly motivated by these interactions. This should provide incentive for car salespeople to reduce uncertainty about their customers. For car salespeople, knowing when to take the time for an extended sales effort and when to avoid interacting with customers has far greater potential for affecting their income than it does for many salaried salespeople. Overall, car salespeople provided an excellent context for examining the cognitive and behavioral aspects of managing uncertainty in organizational settings suggested by TMU.

RESEARCH FOCI

The study examined three specific issues related to TMU. First, the study examined the cognitive processes that car salespeople have that work to preclude or prevent the experience of uncertainty in their interactions with customers. TMU suggests that individuals may experience little or no uncertainty if they have cognitive scripts or schemas to provide a framework for understanding a particular situation. The situation seems certain to them, rather than uncertain, because they have a script or schema for the situation. The same situation may cause a great deal of uncertainty to others facing the same situation because they do not have an available script or schema.

Because salespeople continually meet new people, they likely have some scripts and schemas that enable them to reduce or avoid the experience of uncertainty in their initial interactions with customers. These schemas and scripts would allow them to predict their own or customers' behaviors without direct communication interaction. As a result, the first focus of this study was to explore the scripts and schemas that salespeople have that reduce or prevent the experience of uncertainty when meeting customers.

Second, the study examined the cognitive processes that car salespeople use to reduce the uncertainty they experience when they do meet customers, especially new customers. TMU suggests that individuals may use a variety of cognitive processes to reduce uncertainty when they experience it without interacting with the source of uncertainty. These cognitive processes include denial of uncertainty, tolerance of uncertainty, assimilation of uncertainty, acceptance of uncertainty, and imagined information seeking. These cognitive processes allow individuals to reduce uncertainty with little or no information seeking. Even if a car salesperson's script or schema does not prevent the experience of uncertainty, salespeople may rely on these cognitive processes to quickly manage uncertainty without interacting with a customer.

All five cognitive strategies suggested in TMU (denial of uncertainty, tolerance of uncertainty, assimilation of uncertainty, acceptance of uncertainty, and imagined information seeking) could be used be car salespeople, although two of them seemed to be more likely to occur than the others. In particular, tolerance of uncertainty seemed like it would be particularly useful. Because car salespeople recognize that they often do not see a customer more than once, it seemed that they would be quite tolerant of knowing very little about the customer. In addition, they probably assimilate the uncertainty by assuming that a current customer is like another customer with whom they previously interacted and, as a result, may make very little effort to actually seek unique information or may not be very thorough in their information seeking. With limited verbal interaction, they may rely on appearances and observations of nonverbal communication to categorize individuals, thereby reducing the uncertainty they initially experience with limited interaction. Even though these two strategies seemed most plausible, a case could be made for all five strategies being used for reducing uncertainty. In addition, car salespeople might have developed cognitive processes that allow them to reduce uncertainty that have not been suggested in previous research. In light of this, the second focus of this study was to explore the cognitive processes salespeople report using to reduce their uncertainty in initial interactions with customers.

Third, the study explored communication behaviors that car salespeople use to reduce uncertainty in their interactions with the customers. TMU suggests that when cognitive processes fail to prevent or reduce uncertainty, individuals may rely on various information seeking behaviors to gain the information they need to reduce uncertainty to acceptable levels. These include a variety of behaviors, from direct or indirect communication strategies to observation.

Even though salespeople may be able to reduce uncertainty about many customers, either because they apply scripts to the situation or because they reduce uncertainty through cognitive processes, it was obvious that they also rely on information-seeking behaviors to reduce some of their uncertainty. Car salespeople approach customers and directly seek information, such as asking customers about the type of car they desire. Alternatively, it seemed likely that they often combine questions with observations simply to gain information about customers' likes and dislikes, such as watching a customer shake his or her head after glancing at a price tag. It seemed possible that they may also rely on information from coworkers who may recognize customers from previous visits. The third focus of the study was to explore the various strategies car salespeople use to gain information to reduce uncertainty about their customers.

RESEARCH PROCESS

The Car Salespeople

Given the foci of the study on gaining an understanding of the scripts and schemas of car salespeople, of the cognitive processes they use to reduce uncertainty, and of the behaviors they use to gain information, it was important to interview a number of experienced car salespeople. Because I personally knew two car salespeople at local dealers, I began by asking them to participate in the study. After interviewing them, I asked them for names of additional salespeople who might be willing to participate in the study. Through this snowball technique, I was able to contact addition salespeople. If they agreed to be interviewed, I asked them for names of additional salespeople at the ends of their interviews. This eventually led to a total of 20 interviews out of 24 car salespeople I contacted. Although I had additional names to contact, I did not conduct any additional interviews because at this point it appeared I had reached theory saturation (Glaser & Strauss, 1967). As is typical with this type of study, the last few interviews provided information that was consistent with the pervious interviews without providing additional or unique insights. This indicated that the completed interviews could give a fairly thorough description of how car salespeople manage their uncertainty.

The snowball sample provided a range of participants, although all were from the same city in the Midwest. The salespeople represented eight different car dealerships. They included domestic, import, and combination dealerships. All the dealerships and salespeople sold both new and previously owned (used) cars. From one to four salespeople from each of the different dealerships participated in the study. The salespeople were predominantly male (95%) and Caucasian (95%). Their average age was 45 (S.D. = 7.5) and they were experienced salespeople with an average of 12.3 (S.D. = 6.3) years in the car business. Some had only finished high school (15%). Some had completed a college degree (40%), with the rest having attended college without earning a degree (45%). This seemed fairly representative of my experience at car dealerships in this particular community.

Interviews With the Car Salespeople

Based on the model of TMU, I created an interview schedule to explore the cognitive and behavioral strategies car salespeople used to reduce their uncertainty in interactions with customers. The questions (see Appendix) explored how salespeople approached customers, classified customers, and adapted to customers as part of their initial interactions.

At the beginning of the interviews conducted at their dealerships, I asked the car salespeople for permission to record their interviews so that I could do more detailed analysis of their answers. Even though most (18) agreed to allow this, a few (2) did not. In addition, the tape recorder failed to function correctly in two cases. During all interviews, I took extensive field notes. Verbatim transcripts were made of the available audiotapes. In the instances in which there were no tapes, the field notes were transcribed and elaborated on as soon as possible after the interviews so that additional details would not be forgotten.

Analyzing the Interviews

Although TMU suggested that the car salespeople would use some specific strategies, a grounded theory approach was still used in which categories were allowed to emerge from the data (Glaser & Strauss, 1967). This allowed additional categories to emerge beyond those suggested by TMU. This represents an interpretive-symbolic or interpretive paradigm with a focus on meanings and how individuals understand or make sense of their situations (Fisher, 1978; Krone et al, 1987; Putnam, 1983). As such, I looked for meaningful topics or themes rather than sociolinguistic or technical patterns of speech (Lindlof, 1995). Topics or themes were developed inductively. Specifically, I read the field notes and interview transcripts repeatedly to identify possible themes or topics. Once these themes were tentatively identified, I reread them again to confirm their importance and searched for further examples of the same themes. This allowed for a comparison on the same theme across instances. The analysis continued through a three-step process of reducing the data texts to themes, then developing explanations for those categories, and finally using theory to relate the themes to the research concerns (Lindlof, 1995). In developing explanations for categories, the themes were compared to those identified in the TMU model. Whenever there seemed to be a match, the category label identified in TMU was adopted. Labels for the remaining themes were developed inductively. In the following section, exemplars from these themes are used to illustrate and address the research foci.

FINDINGS

Scripts and Schemas That Reduce or Prevent the Experience of Uncertainty

Schemas That Preclude Uncertainty About Customers. TMU suggests that salespeople might not experience uncertainty about some customers if they had schemas for customers that would prevent uncertainty about the customer by classifying them based on little or no information. Along these lines, many of the salespeople interviewed warned against judging potential customers based on preconceived notions of who can or cannot buy a car based on first impressions with no direct interaction. In addition to warning against making quick judgments without interacting with customers, most denied that they personally ever made such determinations and most said they always spoke with customers before determining if they had eligible buyers or not. They often provided specific examples to support their point. A few specifically mentioned an old cliché, such as a 51-year-old salesman with 13 years of experience who supported the cliché with this example:

> You can't judge a book by its cover. During my first year of selling ... I saw a gentleman in bib overalls and an old rusty jeep drive up and no one seemed to want to

wait on him. Well, I went out and he wouldn't talk to me much, wouldn't give me much information, wouldn't give me his name, or anything. Finally at the end, he gave me a card with his name on it, and left. Two days later he bought a car from me for $45,000. It turned out he owns a couple of cement factories and quarries and has a lot of money.

This example illustrates that apparently other salespeople did not wait on this customer because he did not look like an eligible buyer. They did not experience uncertainty about him because they were certain he was not an eligible buyer. Even for this salesperson, the interaction did not suggest that he would gain a sale because the customer did not seem very cooperative. However, the example demonstrates that any judgment about this customer's eligibility to make a purchase based on first impressions was incorrect.

While denying that they personally made such judgments of customers without interactions, most were more than willing to admit that other car salespeople practice this, particularly inexperienced or ineffective ones. A number of them used terms like "prequalifying" or "curb-qualifying" or "showroom qualifying" to refer to the process by which a salesperson makes a determination that a customer is not qualified to buy a car without interacting with them and therefore decide not to approach a customer. This apparently was the case for the other salespeople who did not wait on the customer in bib overalls in the previous example. In addition to admitting that others did this, they also readily provided suggestions about how such prequalifying is accomplished by other salespeople. Some mentioned prequalifying based on the car the people were driving. A 45-year-old salesman with 9 years of experience put it this way:

> When you first start, and you've been there maybe a year and you've been successful, and you think you know everything, you see a car come in, it's an old clunker, you're thinking, um, those people couldn't buy anything and so you sit around or some people smoke cigarettes and just ignore them. But if you're in the business long enough, you'll realize that those people, too, uh, er, can buy and will buy.

Interestingly, driving a very new car was also mentioned as leading to prequalifying judgments. Salespeople recognize that many people driving a 1- or 2-year-old car cannot afford to purchase a new vehicle. Often these individuals have signed a lease that they cannot afford to break or owe more than the vehicle is worth because of a low down payment and the high depreciation on the value of vehicles during the first years of ownership. A 42-year-old sales manager with 15 years of experience in the sales described how salespeople sometimes work:

> A lot of times if they have a real old car, you're more apt to wait on them than if they had a real new one because the salesmen make the assumption that they owe more on this new car than they could ever trade out of it. So it's not necessarily someone drives in, in a nice new car, everybody wants to jump on them.

As these two excerpts illustrate, car salespeople recognize that the appearance of the car a customer drives causes some salespeople to prequalify and thereby not experience uncertainty about specific customers. A very old car may lead a salesperson to conclude that the individuals cannot afford a better car and a very new car may lead the salesperson to conclude that the individual is "upside down," owes more on the car than it is worth, making the owner ineligible to purchase a different vehicle. In either case, the salespeople do not experience uncertainty about the customers and may not speak to them as a result. Of course, salespeople were more likely to attribute these cognitive processes to other salespeople than to themselves and frequently said that they know such conclusions are not always accurate.

In addition to not experiencing uncertainty about customers based on the cars that they were driving, others mentioned prequalifying based on their general appearance including race, age, or weight. A 40-year-old salesman with 15 years of experience commented on how other salespeople act:

> Some of it is prejudice. Prejudice exists. There are certain ethnic backgrounds and groups of people that aren't waited on readily. There are some salespeople that absolutely refuse to wait on certain ethnic groups.... There is some qualification based, you know, on looks, demeanor, personal appearance. You see a '62 Plymouth with holes in the side of it pull up, some people won't [wait on them]; some people will. Sometimes it's more of an economic evaluation made just by looking. You can't tell by that. I can't.

In cases like this one, the salespeople were suggesting that there are some salespeople who do not experience uncertainty about some strangers (potential customers) based on first impressions without interacting with the individuals. As the end of this excerpt illustrates, the salespeople generally maintained that they do not personally respond this way because they know it is invalid to make those kinds of conclusions. They indicated that such prequalifying judgments are sometimes or often incorrect.

A few salespeople actually admitted that there were certain people that they would not approach based on first impressions without additional information seeking. In essence, they did not experience uncertainty about the individual so that they did not feel the need to interact with them. A 36-year-old salesman with 3 years of experience admitted the following:

> We're trained and told not to, so called cherry pick, like, you know, prejudge anyone. Except for you do get to the point you can tell sometimes without talking to somebody if they're, if they're just simply not eligible buyers at this lot because we don't carry, um, too much low-cost used vehicles.

He later added:

> As far as what I won't approach, like I said, uh, the suspicious appearance as far as drugs or alcohol. Um, I'm uncomfortable with, I'm uncomfortable with, uh, vehi-

cles, people drive in regardless of, of race, creed or color, it doesn't matter to me, but loud music, that kind of thing.

Similarly, a 42-year-old saleswoman with 4 years of experience indicated that she sometimes did not approach customers, in effect, prequalifying them. She said:

Sometimes I don't have a comfortable feeling about them. I'll say that's just maybe two percent of the time that I have that vibe. But, I would say, other than that, I'll approach them.

When I asked her if she could identify what gave her the uncomfortable vibes, she said:

Um, I don't know. It's like just, their looks, you know. Um, and it's usually, like if it's a group of three men or more, um, it'll make me uncomfortable. Um, and not always. It just, it just depends on the person.

A couple of other salespeople mentioned concern over their own personal safety as a factor in their choice to either not interaction with customers or cut those interactions short. They were aware of incidents in which car salespeople were hijacked and even killed by supposed customers.

In each of these examples, the salespeople admitted that they drew conclusions about customers based on very limited information generally obtained without ever interacting with the customers. Based on their schemas, they felt certain about these customers because of experience, feelings, or intuition. In some cases, they had trouble verbalizing exactly what it was that caused them to draw their conclusions. They did not experience uncertainty based on first impressions without direct information exchange.

In addition to these admissions of making prejudgments about customers based on appearances, the responses of others who warned against prequalifying suggested that they did in fact at times use schemas to avoid experiencing uncertainty about customers. For example, salespeople have schemas based on their previous experience with customers. When they see these customers come to the dealership again, they can rely on previous experience to manage their uncertainty about the customer. In most instances, the relationship between a customer and a salesperson is positive and the salesperson can rely on that to understand the customer as they approach them when they return to the dealership. Some salespeople have so many of these repeat customers and receive so many referrals from satisfied customers that they rarely have to meet an "up," a stranger who walks up into the dealership lot or showroom. When salespeople know the customer already they experience limited uncertainty in the situation. This decreases the amount of time needed to create a relationship and complete a sale, because their previous knowledge prevents the experience of uncertainty about how to conduct the transaction.

But because not all previous interactions with customers are positive, salespeople also have schemas for previous customers with whom they do not wish to interact again. Many of the salespeople mentioned that there were a small number of previous customers that they would avoid interacting with if they saw them again. Usually this was because they had a negative experience and did not care to repeat the experience. A 39-year-old car salesman with 14 years in the business said this:

> Then sometimes you go up and talk to somebody and you just don't hit it off, and so maybe when that person comes back, and you're, and you're doing them a favor, just like, and what I mean by that, uh, they need to be talking to somebody that gets along with them, that's on their same playing ground instead of it being a, a constant fuss back and forth.

Although such instances were reported as rare, they did indicate that car salespeople included in their schemas a category of customer that they were certain they did not want to interact with in the future. When these customers appeared again, the salespeople did not experience uncertainty due to their schemas. Rather, they recognized the customer as one to avoid and allowed another salesperson to serve the customer.

Two specific types of previous customers also created certainty for salespeople so that they did not want to interact with them. Sometimes they knew that a customer was not eligible to purchase a car due to being "upside down," owing more than the value of the car, making it impossible for the individual to purchase a different car. They knew this from having worked with them previously or from talking with other salespeople. A 52-year-old salesman with 17 years of experience put it this way:

> There's people that you, that you've worked with before, that you know, that they, that they have to trade their, their present car in order to buy another car and you know for a fact that they owe $6,000 more on their car than what it's worth on the trade and they don't have any cash to put down because they were upside down when they traded their other car in on that one.

A 35-year-old salesman with 4 years of experience put it this way:

> If I'm going to avoid someone, I know who they are. I might know they can't buy the lettuce on a Big Mac. Or I might know they can't buy anything. Or I might know they're so far upside down in their car. There's a deaf gentleman who comes in here. I talk to him all the time cause I'm one of the only guys [he knows], but, I'm very, hey, Teddy, you know and I know, you're not trading. You come in here everyday. And if someone, there, there's nothing worse in our business than spending two or three hours with someone that wasn't honest about credit.

In these situations, because they are already certain that this previous customer cannot purchase a different vehicle, the salespeople will generally avoid talking to them or at least avoid spending much time talking to them about purchasing a different vehicle because they know it is not a productive use of their time. However, if it is a slow day and they are not busy, they may have brief friendly conversations with these customers without discussing purchasing a car.

Some salespeople also avoided interacting with another type of previous customer that they sometimes called "lot lizards." A 48-year-old salesman with 8 years of experience described these people:

> These people are professional shoppers. And they spend a lot of time going from dealer to dealer to dealer and normally if you did sell one it would be like winning the lottery.... And it's more, your time is better spent someplace else.

When I asked him how he could know which people were lot lizards, he said:

> 'Cause I've seen them. You know, I mean, I've been in the business long enough to know and I've worked some of them in the past and it's kind of an ongoing joke, you know. If one of them comes in and somebody sees them and then one of the new guys goes down there excited because he thinks he's going to sell something, but he's not.

In this case of "lot lizards" salespeople developed the schema for these individuals based on prior observation or experience or interaction with peers. They reported they did not experience uncertainty about these individuals when they saw them again, even if they had never personally interacted with them. They did not experience uncertainty about them because they had already made a determination about the type of customer they were. They felt certain that there was no point in interacting with these customers because as another one put it, "It's just luck if you ever sell to one of them."

Scripts That Preclude the Experience of Uncertainty in the Situation.

Whereas the previous section discussed how car salespeople avoid the experience of uncertainty about customers prior to interacting, car salespeople also experience limited uncertainty about the car sales situation by having tentative or flexible scripts for interacting with customers. Most talked about a standard process of meeting the customer and then asking what many referred to as "qualifying questions." Although these qualifying questions varied some from person to person, they included general questions such as these:

Can I help you zero in on anything today?

Is there anything in particular you are looking for today?

What kind of car are you currently driving?

Will you be trading in a vehicle?

What kind of payment are you looking for?

These were clearly flexible scripts that were adapted to the specific customers. A couple of the salespeople even made fun of inexperienced salespeople or the way certain dealerships train their salespeople so that the individuals have their list of 10 questions on their clipboard and try to go through those questions with the customer no matter what the situation might be.

Most felt confident about the value of their script for reducing the experience of uncertainty in the interaction. A number mentioned being able to determine in a very short period of time whether they had a potential buyer or not. A 48-year-old salesman with 9 years of experience put it this way:

> You learn early, hopefully, now some of them don't, uh, that everybody that comes on, it should take you 5 minutes, if you've been properly trained or have any smarts at all, to determine if you have a potential prospect.

Others made similar comments such as this from a 35-year-old salesman with 4 years of experience:

> If you do your job right, you can tell within 4 or 5 minutes, 10 minutes, well, this person's blowing smoke or if this person really truly, truly wants to buy a car.

These experienced salespeople felt that they had flexible scripts for their interactions with customers that enabled them to quickly make assessments of their customers, thereby reducing their experience of uncertainty about the situation. A number of them also made fun of inexperienced salespeople who spent long periods of time with customers and were not able to tell if they had a potential buyer because they failed to use appropriate qualifying questions to gain the information needed to reduce their uncertainty about the customers. These car salespeople seemed to think that the key for success in interacting with customers was having a script that managed the uncertainty about how to interact with the customer while they gathered the information to reducing uncertainty about the customer's needs and wants.

Summary.   The interviews revealed that car salespeople do have scripts and schemas that reduce or prevent the experience of uncertainty in their initial interactions with customers. Even though most warned against prequalifying individuals based on the cars they drive or their appearance, they indicated that other salespeople do this and a few admitted to doing this in a small percentage of cases. Those that did admit to prequalifying at times used schemas to avoid the experience of uncertainty about certain individuals such as customers whom they perceived as threatening or unsafe, previous customers who they did not get along with or who were ineligible to buy a new vehicle, or customers labeled "lot lizards" because they constantly shop for cars. This prequalifying was generally based on visual information gained by observing the customers briefly. These prequalifying schemas help create certainty in the situation.

In addition, car salespeople developed scripts that reduced or prevented the experience of uncertainty in the situation by giving them a structure for interacting with new customers. These scripts typically included a greeting followed by a set of "qualifying questions." These scripts provided a flexible structure to work with for seeking information about the customers so that in a relatively short period of time, they could reduce uncertainty about the individuals to determine if they were potential buyers. The scripts greatly reduced uncertainty about managing the situation, although not necessarily about the particular customer.

Focus Two: Cognitive Processes for Reducing Uncertainty

The preceding section examined ways that car salespeople may not even experience uncertainty concerning some customers who enter their lots or stores. At other times, the scripts or schemas do not preclude the experience of significant amounts of uncertainty in the situation. When that occurs, the car salespeople sometimes rely on their own cognitive processes to reduce uncertainty rather than seeking information. They reported using a number of different cognitive strategies along these lines.

Denial of Uncertainty.   TMU suggests that sometimes individuals deny that they experience uncertainty as a way to manage uncertainty. Salespeople provided some evidence of using this strategy. As discussed previously, salespeople admitted that there were certain customers that they would either not approach or rarely approach. These were customers that were either prequalified based on some visual information or previous customers who owed too much on a vehicle (were "upside down") or had been identified as professional shoppers (lot lizards) who never buy. When asked if they were concerned about missing a possible sale to these individuals, some salespeople replied no. Others responded a little less definitely such as, "Rarely, it rarely bothers me that I might have [missed a sale]." Although a couple admitted that they were a little concerned about missing such sales, they did not worry about it much because the odds against making a sale to these customers were very low. A 52-year-old salesman with 17 years of experience described the very low probability of making a sale by not approaching a customer based on prequalifying them this way:

> [Not talking to them is] like, that's like not going to buy a lottery ticket with somebody in your, somebody you work with offered you to go in [on lottery tickets] with them and [you] didn't.... But I don't worry about it.

As these examples suggests, the salespeople basically denied that there was any real chance of selling vehicles to these customers who they did not approach and so they denied the uncertainty that they experienced. In this way, even though they may be uncertain about whether a customer's situation has changed, making them an eligible buyer, the salespeople deny that they experience uncertainty in the situation. For the most part, they were confident that they did not miss a sale.

Tolerance of Uncertainty.   TMU suggests that people will tolerate uncertainty about someone for a variety of reasons, such as expecting no future interaction or expecting little harm or benefit from the interaction. Salespeople suggested some use of this strategy in their dealings with customers who appeared to be at the dealership for service on their current vehicle rather than purchasing a new vehicle. For example, a few salespeople mentioned that if they see someone walking in from the service department, they are less likely to approach them because they expect that they are not there to purchase a car. A 40-year-old salesman with 15 years in the car business mentioned this:

> Now, I can ascertain being in the business long enough that a guy's going to service. I can watch him and his wife pull in in two cars, and I know with them that the one is [domestic brand] and the one is a [import brand], and you can pretty much ascertain by watching them.

His dealership sells and services both brands of cars and so the salesperson experienced uncertainty when such customers drive up, but he then concluded that the customers were dropping off one car for service. This made it unnecessary to approach the individuals because the salesperson reduced his initial uncertainty and felt certain that they were not there to purchase a vehicle.

But even in situations where they believe the person is a service customer, a few mentioned that they might ask the customer if they have been helped "because sometimes people come out of the service department and may have decided they don't want to fix the car and [want to] buy a new one."

As these two examples suggest, salespeople tolerate their uncertainty about a customer based on very little information gained through observation or a single question. They then can tolerate their uncertainty about the customer because it seems unlikely that they will need to interact with the customer, at least in the near future, and they consider it likely that there is neither any benefit from approaching them nor any loss for not approaching them.

Assimilating Uncertainty.   Each of the salespeople had at least a minimal category system that they used to help classify customers into types. The existence of these category systems suggests that salespeople manage their uncertainty about new customers by associating them with a category or prototype of customer so that they could direct their sales presentation at the customer's needs or wants. By assimilating new customers into their category system, salespeople can manage their uncertainty about how to approach the customers.

The difference between these category systems and the schemas mentioned previously for not experiencing uncertainty about a potential customer has to do with interaction. In the previous discussion of schemas and pre-qualifying customers, salespeople made judgments about customers without communicating with the customers and experienced little or no uncertainty about the customers as a result. In using the following category systems to assimilate their uncertainty, the salespeople experience uncertainty about customers, but then quickly classify individuals based on minimal communication interaction with the customers to reduce the uncertainty they initially experience. A 50-year-old salesperson with 22 years of experience emphasized this point:

> You can't tell that [what type of customer] till once you get to, to spend a little time with them. Because you can always get fooled, you know. Um, if, if you talk to the guys who have been in the business a while here, that, that are successful, that sell most of the cars in the dealership, they're all going to tell you the same thing.

So gaining information from the customer through interaction allows the salesperson to classify the customer more accurately into a category system than prequalifying them based on some external factor, such as the car they drive or their appearance. However, the category system is a cognitive process for quickly assimilating the experience with the new customer with very limited interaction.

Some had more complicated or refined category systems, often involving more than five distinct types. Others had rather uncomplicated or simple category systems, reporting as few as two or three main categories. No two salespeople had exactly the same category systems. However, even though the category systems were quite varied, there were some commonalities across many of the salespeople. Among those with more complicated categories systems, there were a few types that appeared with some regularity. However, no one had all of the following types in their category system.

The most frequently mentioned type of customer was one who has done a lot of research before coming to the dealership. Salespeople used a variety of names for these buyers. They were variously referred to as analytical, educated, or Internet buyers. They were also known as clipboard commandoes or authors because they frequently came with a notepad or clipboard and wrote down details of what was said during the transaction for further consideration. They could sometimes be classified quickly because they were literally carrying a clipboard or computer printouts as they got out of their vehicle. These buyers were often, but not always, described as being more formally educated and associated with professional people, including professors. They had done a lot of research either through consumer reports or on the Internet. They were often comparing a number of vehicles by different manufacturers and comparing price and availability in the local car market. They frequently bought imports and wanted a lot of technical information about the car. Sometimes they knew more about the technical aspects of the car than the salespeople. They liked to control the sales process rather than have the salesperson in charge. The salesperson simply provided information to answer their questions. The analytical buyer usually took more than one trip to a dealer before making a purchase.

A somewhat similar category that was mentioned regularly was a conservative or cautious buyer. These were described as customers who ask a lot of questions and also take more than a single visit to purchase a vehicle. They usually asked questions, listened to the responses, and then thought it over. They were also often professional people. They were not as informed as the analytical buyer, perhaps arriving on the lot the first time without having done any significant research about vehicles they might buy. They had a general idea of what they needed or wanted, but were probably not committed to purchasing a particular make of vehicle. They were not as concerned about technical aspects of the car as the analytical buyer. They were described as impossible to sell to on the first visit.

The next category mentioned regularly was the older customer, sometimes called blue-haired ladies or gray-haired couples. These were customers in their 50s or older who have resources to buy any car that they might like. They typically were driving an older car that was obviously paid for already. Given a choice of customers to approach, these were often mentioned as a first choice. Because financing was usually not an issue, it was much less trouble to complete a sale with them, saving the salesperson time.

At the other end of the age spectrum was a category for young male customers. Often these customers showed up as a group with a "leader" who wanted to take a test drive. They may have had loud music coming from their car when they drove up. They most often arrived during lunch hour at the local high school or just after school got out. One salesman described them as "a kid with his baseball cap on backward. We call those catchers. I've had salesmen tell me, I'm not waiting on any more catchers today." Frequently these are not really eligible buyers. Fortunately for most salespeople, it is illegal to provide pricing information or to allow for a test-drive unless the person is 18 or accompanied by an adult. However, in a few instances these young men were actually ideal customers because their parents were purchasing a car for them and they were just shopping around to pick it out and then bring in the parents to close the deal.

A few customers arrived at the dealership ready to complete a deal that day. These were called various names such as the direct buyer, a lay down, cash buyers, or buying today customer. Sometimes, the salesperson could even see that they were carrying the title to their old car in their pocket, indicating that they would not even have to go home to retrieve the title before completing the deal. These were obviously considered hot prospects. In these cases, the salesperson's job was relatively easy. They just needed to help these customers find the right vehicle on their lot so that they did not go somewhere else to buy.

Another type of customer that was frequently mentioned was the rude or un-responsive customer. These customers often seemed mad at the salesperson. They were unresponsive and provided very little information to the salesperson. They frequently said, "I'm just looking," and sometimes walked away from a sales- person who was trying to speak to them. They sometimes treated the sales-person as if he or she did menial work. One salesperson thought that these cus-tomers are actually afraid of salespeople, afraid that they will sell them a car they do not really want or at a price much higher than they could have. They do not be-lieve much of what the salesperson says because they do not trust them. It is not surprising that salespeople were reluctant to work with these customers and often avoided them if they returned to the dealership.

Another negative category of customer was the arrogant and overbearing cus-tomers. These customers seemed to want to impress salespeople with how im-portant and impressive they were. One salesperson described them as Type-A personalities. They often bragged about how much money they had and informed the salesperson that money was no object in the purchase of the vehicle. They were usually looking to purchase a more expensive vehicle than what they already had. They wanted to control the sales presentation because they felt superior. As a result, they often told the salesperson how things were going to go. They fre-quently acted as if they knew a great deal, although it was not unusual for them to have inaccurate information and they often had unrealistic expectations about the value of their current vehicle. This was also a category of customers that some salespeople would prefer not to work with.

Sort of the opposite of the arrogant buyer was the friendly buyer. This in-cluded those referred to as "good old boys." The friendly customers liked to sit back and chat, sometimes for a long time. They wanted to become friends with the salesperson before they would even consider buying a car. The only problem with this type of customer is that some of them just wanted to talk to someone and were not very serious buyers. Salespeople were annoyed when they end up wasting time on these customers if they were not serious buyers and if there were other potential customers with whom they could have been interacting instead.

A few salespeople mentioned a category of first-time buyers. These were de-scribed as young people, perhaps in their early 20s, perhaps working their first job after high school or college. Some had recently established a credit history and could now manage a loan, whereas others needed to establish credit for the first time. These customers sometimes needed a cosigner or borrowed some of the money for the down payment from a relative. At some of the more upscale dealer-ships, these were not considered very good prospects because they did not have the resources to purchase the more expensive vehicles.

A few salespeople mentioned the hurried or rushed buyer. These customers were often eager to find out what their current car was worth and what the differ-ential was between their trade-in and the cost of a new vehicle. They were often trade or payment buyers who are more concerned about cost differential than the features of the car. Because of their focus on cost and price, some did not even want to take the time to actually drive a new car to see if they liked it. Some of the salespeople felt that these customers simply used them to get an estimate on the value of their trade-in so that they could go down the road to another dealer with that information. A couple of salespeople refused to give out pricing information to these customers unless they took the time to test-drive a vehicle.

A single woman on the lot created an interesting situation that many of the salespeople discussed. They warned against asking questions like "Will your husband be coming to look at the car, too?" or saying, "Why don't you bring your husband in?" They said such questions were professional suicide. These women were often professional people who can afford a vehicle and had done enough research to know what they wanted. The one saleswoman in the study was particularly anxious to help these customers. The consensus seemed to be that although a man might go look at cars without his wife knowing about it, women who go to a car lot are probably serious buyers. These were considered potential sales and were quickly approached.

A few salespeople mentioned impulse buyers. Impulse buyers make a purchase based on it "feeling right." These were customers who saw a vehicle and just fell in love with it and had to have it. These were often the easiest deals to close, assuming the customer can afford the vehicle. One salesperson mentioned that there were very few true impulse buyers anymore, perhaps due to the cost of the vehicle.

A few salespeople described a type of customer as brand-loyal buyers. These people drove a certain make of car, which may be domestic or import, but did not consider buying other brands or makes of cars. In some cases they were loyal to a domestic car company because a relative worked for the company or was a member of the United Auto Workers Union, but some were equally loyal to an import company based on positive experiences with a previous or current car. Because they were loyal to a brand name, the salesperson presented a focused sales presentation.

A few salespeople also mentioned the old-fashioned customer who wants to do business the way it used to be done. One labeled these horse traders. Another spoke about how these customers kept grinding the salesperson down. In these situations, the salesperson thought they had reached an agreement on everything and then the customer comes back and wants to negotiate one more concession on pricing or features. Even when the salesperson has given the rock bottom price, the customer wanted it to be even lower. Even though repeat business is very important in car sales, some salespeople said they avoided doing repeat business with these horse traders because it was just not worth the trouble working with them.

Two categories of customers are actually nonbuyers, one by choice and the other due to circumstances. A number of salespeople referred to the first group as "tire kickers." These were typically males who were not serious buyers by their own choice. They were often out looking at cars on their own without their spouses even knowing. In other instances they were looking at cars while their spouses were doing something like shopping at the mall or going to the doctor's office. They might be in town early for a sporting event. They were usually just killing time waiting for something else to happen. They simply were looking at the latest models and had no real intention of buying in the near future. Salespeople did not like to spend much time with these customers.

The other type of nonbuyer was ineligible due to circumstances. These were customers who owed too much on their current cars, had bad credit so that no bank would finance them, or who were in other similar situations, such as filing for divorce or recently divorced. These were referred to as "buyers who can't be bought" or customers who are "upside down" or "get me done." These customers were often desperate to purchase a different car, having been turned down at one or more other dealerships already. Sometimes these customers volunteered that they had recently filed for bankruptcy or had been turned down for financing at other dealerships. Frequently, they did not negotiate the price of the vehicle because they were willing to buy at any price or they expected to be turned down (again), when they submitted their paperwork for financing. Salespeople were particularly unhappy if such customers were not up front about their financial situation.

The salesman with perhaps the most complex classification system included a number of the categories already mentioned, but then further delineated visual, touching (kinesthetic), and feeling buyers. A 48-year-old salesman with 8 years in car sales described these three this way:

> Visual, everything has to look right, look all right. And they would be color people as well, uh. You know, if everything looks right, it doesn't matter how it feels when it drives, as long as it looks good.... Most of your women are feeling people. They, everything has to feel right, you know.... The kinesthetic would be your touching people. It does have to feel right when you touch it, you know. When you, when you do your presentation you work your presentation if you can get a clue up front what kind of person they are. If it's, if it's a kinesthetic people, you wouldn't say, "Well, how's it look to you?" You'd say, "Well, how does that feel to you?"

This salesman not only has a very complicated category system for his customers, but he clearly uses the categories to adapt his sales presentation. In his example, he uses the sense of touch to appeal to the kinesthetic customers.

Some of those with less complicated category systems seemed to suggest a slightly different focus for the salesperson than the previous examples. For example, a 34-year-old salesman with 8 years in the car business primarily classified customers as either need buyers or want buyers. He described need buyers this way:

> Those are customers that have needs. They need you to, they just need a car to get back and forth to work. They don't care about all the frills or all the extras. It's nice

that they get them sometimes, but, um, but they just really just need dependable, dependable transportation.

He described a want buyer this way:

A want buyer is ... first of all, they want the nicest minivan out there for the least price. And you know, they feel their car is worth retail but they want to buy the new car at wholesale. And it's hard to make a match when a customer has preconceived notions as to what they think their car is worth and you know how much they want to spend on, on the new one. So that's a want buyer. Uh, he wants this. He wants the, he wants the side air, impact airbags on his van and all the, you know, things that make it worth what it is, but he only wants to pay, you know, for what maybe an LX is, you know.

Given these descriptions, it is not surprising that this salesman preferred to work with need buyers. He felt a sense of satisfaction from helping a need buyer and felt bothered by dealing with want buyers who seemed much harder to please.

A 48-year-old salesman with 9 years of experience really suggested that he only had two main categories for customers, those looking for a free ride and those who were actual potential buyers. Those looking for a free ride might simply want to go joy riding with no intention of buying or might want to use the car to run an errand because they do not own a car. They seem suspicious because they often walk up rather than drive up, speak hesitantly when asked questions, perhaps volunteer more information than would seem appropriate, or provide contradictory information. In dealing with these customers, he might ask for a driver's license and limit a test drive to 15 minutes in order to discourage them. This often worked for him. The other category, potential buyers, actually were considering purchasing cars and were put through a serious of qualifying questions to determine their needs and wants. Although these were the only two categories he mentioned, his other responses suggested that as he got to know potential buyers he did further classify them as buying in the short term or more in the distant future, those who could afford to buy a vehicle and those who could not and so forth, some of the categories mentioned earlier.

Although these last two examples suggest that some car salespeople used rather uncomplicated classification systems, their category systems provided each of the salespersons with a set of categories for classifying customers so that a particular sales strategy can be used. They relied on these category systems to manage the uncertainty they initially experienced from customers based on limited information gathering.

One additional finding related to different types of customers was that a couple of the salespeople mentioned that they were actually taught category systems at one point in their career. A 52-year-old car salesman with 20 years in sales mentioned this:

> I used to teach other sales people how to peg customers into certain groups. You have your four main groups, the dominant, the follower, and so forth. But it's been ten years since I've done that.

When I asked him if he still used this system, he said that he really did not because he usually worked with repeat buyers and so this was not an issue for him.

A 48-year-old salesman with 9 years of experience reported having been taught a similar system when he first became a salesperson, but also denied using it anymore:

> They, a long time ago, they used to have these profiles … which to me is a stereotype, which you usually got into a lot more trouble if you did, trying to justify if somebody is a doer or thinker, a plotter. Uh, by that a plotter takes their time calculating, very slow. A doer just needs to be stroked a little bit and probably will do it at that point. Uh, I don't think [it's accurate], and that's probably why I don't use those.

Each of these salespeople denied using the category system that they were taught. However, because the last excerpt includes descriptions of the categories, it suggests that the salesperson was still conscious of the category system and may still occasionally use some revised version of the system, for example when he notices that a customer is the epitome of one of the categories that he previously learned. In addition, the brief description of the plotter seems to have much in common with the analytical buyer that many of the salespeople mentioned. So while they denied using the category systems that they were taught, these systems may have influenced the category system that they currently admit to using.

The value of these classification systems was that they reduced the initial uncertainty about customers with limited information. By classifying customers into the categories, the salesperson could gear the sales pitch toward that particular buyer. One salesperson made this quite clear when he said this about an analytical buyer, "So if they're a *Consumer Report* kind of person, then I've got to back my stuff over facts like that, too." Classifying the customer into a category enabled salespeople to take a particular approach that was suited for the customer.

A few of the salespeople made a final point about these more complex category systems. They suggested that their category systems were less than perfect and that customers sometimes did not fit neatly into the categories. Instead, some were combinations of categories. As one said quite pointedly, "And again, I mean, it's just, there's so many different mixtures because some of these people can be a combination of these. And most people are." So even though these category systems were used, they were also flexible for many of the salespeople.

Overall, the results suggest that car salespeople frequently assimilate their uncertainty about new customers by categorizing them into types. Based on limited verbal and nonverbal cues, the salespeople classified the customers into categories, although the categories were somewhat fluid. The category systems varied from salesperson to salesperson. However, whether sophisticated or simple, these category systems helped the salespeople reduce their initial uncertainty about the customers by providing a prototype from which to work in continuing their sales presentation with them. They could assimilate the person into their category system to manage their uncertainty about the customer and choose an appropriate sales strategy without going through an extensive information-seeking process.

Imagined Information Seeking.   Although none of the salespeople volunteered that they had imaginary conversations with potential customers as a way to reduce uncertainty, their responses suggested that they possibly make some use of this strategy anyway. When salespeople indicated that there were customers that they would not approach, I would sometimes ask them what they thought these people would say if they did approach them. They had no trouble imagining what the interaction would be like. For example, in avoiding interacting with a previous customer with whom he had negative interactions in the past, a salesman imagined this is what would happen:

> What happens most generally with those, those people, is they, if you were to walk past them and say something, a lot of times the people will ignore you, you know, like you weren't even here.

In considering an interaction with a "capper," the 16- to 20-year-old male with the hat on backward, one salesman imagined the conversation would go like this:

> "Can I drive this Prelude?" That's basically the way they... cause they're usually sixteen to twenty, and they're looking at a twenty-five thousand dollar sports car.

Because there was generally no way that the "capper" can afford to purchase the vehicle, there was no point in having the conversation and no point in letting them take a test drive. Imagining that the interaction would go this way reduced initial uncertainty about the situation, making interaction unnecessary.

Summary.   The responses of the car salespeople indicated that they did use a variety of cognitive processes to reduce the initial uncertainty they experienced about their customers. They denied that they experienced much uncertainty in cases where they had concluded that a customer was not an eligible buyer. They tolerated uncertainty about service customers after only observing them or based on minimal information seeking. Based on category systems they had for customers, they quickly classified customers and used strategies based on those categories. They were even able to imagine how conversations would have gone like with customers who they did not approach. These are all cognitive processes that can reduce uncertainty based on little or no actual information seeking.

At the close of a few of the interviews, the salespeople asked me about the nature of my study. Not wanting to bore them with a long, theoretical explanation of TMU, I would tell them that there is a theory that people seek information when they are unsure about someone they meet, but that I believe that people take shortcuts based on little or no information instead of always being thorough in seeking information and so I am trying to find out if car salespeople use shortcuts as they interact with their customers. I would then suggest that we all do this in our regular interactions, but that I thought salespeople were a particularly interesting group in which to explore this idea. Each person with whom I discussed this replied that salespeople do take shortcuts. They said that they have to because they meet so many people. In this way, the salespeople confirmed that they frequently use cognitive processes rather than information seeking in managing their uncertainty about customers.

Focus Three: Behavioral Strategies for Managing Uncertainty

Interaction Goals. Before discussing the specific information-seeking strategies car salespeople used, it is important to discuss their interaction goals. A common theme that emerged in their responses concerned two compatible goals that car salespeople mentioned. A first or primary goal that each car salesperson mentioned was to sell a car to the customer. Finding out the customer's wants and needs and fulfilling those needs accomplished this goal. However, many of the salespeople also spoke in terms of creating a relationship with the customers so that the customers became long-term customers. Previous customers are valued because of the certainty that is established in the relationship. A 50-year-old car salesman with 18 years of experience emphasized that there was more to customer interactions than just the goal of selling a car. He said:

> You're not just selling a car. If you sell them one car and then that's it, you didn't do your job. But if you're going to start a relationship from this point forward … you try to stress that.

Although there appears to be an ulterior motive for creating relationships with customers (i.e., future sales), this suggests a need to manage uncertainty about more than just the needs and wants to accomplish a sale. Salespeople indicated that they learned about customers in order to create relationships with them. These relationships sometimes went beyond a sales relationship into more of a friendship relationship:

> I mean there's a select few of them, the ones I feel like I had really good rapport with. The people sometimes even almost become friends, you know.

Along these lines, a number of salespeople reported that their customers had followed them from dealership to dealership as they changed their jobs. Others salespeople who were in and out of the business over the years let customers know that they were back in car sales and the customers sometimes followed them to their new jobs.

This discussion of relationships suggests that there are times when the car sales setting has more in common with interpersonal relationships than might be expected. Certainly, in many or most cases car salespeople do not expect any future interaction with customers, especially those with whom they have very short interactions. This no doubt influences the strategies they use to manage their uncertainty. The primary focus on sales also influences the strategy choice. However, the desire to create long-term relationships that turn into loyal customers and friendships has much in common with other interpersonal relationships away from organizational settings.

Types of Information Sought.   Given these two goals, car salespeople also reported seeking two general types of information about their customers. Most of the information seeking was focused on gaining information to complete a sale. This involved attempting to determine if the customer was an actual potential buyer and then ascertaining the customers' needs and/or wants for a vehicle. Salespeople needed to reduce uncertainty about these issues in order to accomplish the goal of selling the car.

Salespeople also sought information for the purpose of building "common ground" or "rapport" with their customers. A 40-year-old salesman with 15 years of experience emphasized the importance of gaining information to create common ground between a salesperson and a customer:

> You must establish some common ground with a customer. You establish some
> type of common ground and if it's they hunt, fish, or do something that you do
> that's establishing common ground. That a good thing. People buy from people
> they like. If they don't like you, I don't care how good of a salesperson you are,
> you're done, buddy. You're done early. In that first 10 or 15 seconds you're pretty
> much either done or not.

Another put it succinctly: "The more we get on common ground with each other, the more likely it is that they might buy some product from us."

Establishing common ground is important, not only in order to possibly make a sale that day, but to establish a relationship with the customer that might lead to future sales. One put it this way: "You're looking for some common ground so you get to know them. You may not sell them a car today, but maybe you will 6 months from now." Because repeat customers are such an important part of being a successful salesman, developing common ground leads to the type of relationship that can result in future sales. So, even though seeking information to establish common ground has utility for the car salesperson, it is not the same utility as information about the specific type of vehicle the individual would like to purchase in the immediate future.

In the effort to gain these two types of information, car salespeople reported using various strategies to gain information to reduce their uncertainty about customers. The two most common strategies were direct inquiry and observation. They also made mention of using other, more subtle strategies, as well.

Direct Inquiry.   The car salespeople made frequent mention of using direct questions or direct inquiry as their most common way of seeking information. As a number of them put it, if you want to help your customer and make a deal then, "Ask questions and be a good listener. They'll tell you what you need to know." Or another one said, "One of the most important things you do is you ask a lot of questions.... You've got to find out from them what they're all about." Another emphasized, "You don't ask questions that the customer is going to answer with yes and no. You ask open-ended questions and you, you listen to them. You listen to them."

Some of the most conscientious salespeople recognize that a question they should ask early in the conversation is something like "Have you been helped?" or "Are you working with someone else?" Salespeople do not consider it appropriate to steal other salespeople's customers. Questions like these can help a salesperson determine if it is appropriate to continue working with the customer. When a salesperson finds out that a customer has been helped or wants to work with a particular salesperson, then they are certain of how to respond to the situation; they know for certain to let the customer work with the other salesperson, assuming that person is working at that time. When the customer has not been helped and was not working with anyone, the salesperson knows for certain that they have a potential buyer, but they must still seek information to complete a sale.

The questions they asked to seek information to complete a sale were the previously mentioned "qualifying questions." There were numerous potential qualifying questions that salespeople mentioned. Some were used to determine the type of vehicle the person might be interested in, such as the following:

What are you driving now? Are you happy with it?

Are you looking for a particular vehicle?

Are you looking for new or used?

Do you want a two-door or a four-door?

Do you want a five-speed or an automatic?

Are you looking for economy or comfort?

Other questions were used to determine what financial resources a person has that might determine their ability to purchase a particular vehicle, such as these:

Are you looking to buy today or in 6 months or a year?

What type of work do you do? How long have you been working there?

What kind of payment are you looking for?

Will you be trading in the old vehicle? What do you owe on it?

How is your credit?

The response to these types of questions reduced the uncertainty of the salesperson by providing the information they need in order to continue with the transaction with the customer.

Of course, salespeople do not ask all of these questions of all customers. Instead, these were representative of a bank of questions that they can draw upon depending on the situation. As one said, "You know what information you're looking for and so you would have an idea what questions you would need to ask to get that information." There was no set formula or order for asking questions, and not all the questions were asked of each customer. However, a number mentioned listening to the answers to the questions as the critical skill in this process. One emphasized the importance of listening to gain information this way:

> Because you have one mouth and two ears, so therefore you should listen twice as much as you talk in that initial qualifying.

When they were dealing with a couple, rather than an individual, car salespeople often face the uncertainty of determining who was the real buyer of the vehicle. Although they continued to include both people in the sales presentation, they focused on the features that were important to the real buyer. Somewhat surprisingly to me, most of them mentioned that usually the woman was the real buyer. She has the final word on the deal. Some thought that the woman was the decision maker 85% of the time or more. This made it very important not to ignore her even when the man was doing most of the talking. To determine who is the buyer, salespeople usually ask a direct question, such as "Who will be driving the vehicle?" This direct method reduced some of the uncertainty about the sales talk.

Even with previous customers, the use of direct inquiry was necessary. When approaching a previous customer there was still uncertainty about their specific purpose for coming to the dealership on a particular day and so the salesperson must still gain the needed information. A common strategy for approaching a previous customer was one like this, reported by a 33-year-old salesman with 7 years of experience:

> Well, at first you ask them how they're doing and what they're doing and you build on the personal relationship. Then you ask them, "What brings you in today?"

The previous relationship with the customer reduced some uncertainty about the person, but still left uncertainty about the situation on the particular day. The salespeople used what they know about a previous customer to begin the interaction, but then used direct inquiry to gain specific information about the business that may need to be transacted that day.

Even though the results of direct inquiry reduced much of the uncertainty for the salespeople, they also recognized that the information they received may not always be accurate because people do not always know what they want. As one salesman said, "You can ask them, but in a lot instances, I've had people come in here looking to buy a sports car, and end up buying a truck at another lot." So even asking and listening and then trying to provide the kind of vehicle the person says he or she wants does not guarantee that the information will be the information needed to complete a sale. Customers may not know what they want or need or can afford and so all the direct inquiry may not benefit the salesperson.

Observation.   Observation was also a very important information-seeking strategy for car salespeople. From prior to approaching them on through the entire sales process, salespeople gained information from the visual cues that customers communicate intentionally or unintentionally. For example, salespeople gained information about possible interests of a customer simply by watching which cars a customer looked at before they were approached, although sometimes people unfamiliar with the dealership may be in the wrong location. In addition, some of the same information that salespeople said should not be used to prejudge or prequalify a customer was used to help determine the needs and interests of the customer. So, for example, the vehicle the person arrived in provided information about their past wants or needs which can then be verified as current wants or needs. In this way, salespeople gained information about the customer before they actually interacted with them, based on observing them.

During the sales process, salespeople also relied on observing nonverbal messages to assist them in determining if they were taking a correct approach with the customer. A number of salespeople specifically referred to watching customers' body language to gauge the success of their approach. A 48-year-old salesman with 9 years of experience said he could tell if he was being successful:

> Just from the body language. Um, their responses. If it's somebody that's more relaxed, smiling maybe, those are big things, uh. It, it means you're making progress. In other words, it's not guaranteeing you anything. It's just, uh, that's an open sign.

Another commented, "Well you have body language too. If they're standing with their arms crossed, you know they're not open to any kind of suggestion."

Observing body language and nonverbal communication also helped salespeople determine whether they were reaching both partners in a couple. A 50-year-old salesman with 22 years of experience explained how body language helped him determine if he is reaching both parties in a couple:

I mean, the way they look at it or the way that they, if it's a couple, or whoever, they'll, they'll look at each other and they'll give that body language, that positive, hey, you know, the nodding the head or the, I don't know, they keep looking at the car. They keep getting in it.

One salesman seemed to be particularly sophisticated in his observation of nonverbal communication to gain information about a customer. A 48-year-old car salesman with 8 years of sales experience volunteered that he learns a lot about customers by observing them without relying on verbal communication:

A lot of instances, you can tell what's going on in a person's mind without a word coming out of their mouth by just looking at the expressions on their face, looking to see if their eyes are dilated or not dilated, seeing if, uh, they're sitting with their arms crossed, if they're covering their mouth, or just the things that I have come to know that is signals. And I kind of know what to do after I see them.

Not only does this salesman indicate that he pays attention to the cues that many of the others salespeople mentioned, such as crossed arms, but he also says that he notices whether their eyes are dilated or not as an indication of excitement.

Overall, a variety of responses indicated that salespeople seek a great deal of information about their customers through observation. By observing the eye contact or lack of it, crossed or open arms, the appearance of interest and enthusiasm or not, salespeople gathered information that helped them reduce their uncertainty about the approach they were taking with a customer.

Indirect Questions.   Car salespeople reported using indirect or subtle approaches to seeking information instead of asking direct questions. In particular, if the salespeople thought the interaction was going well and wanted to find out if the customer was a real buyer, they would often use what they called "trial closes" or indirect questions that encourage the customer to provide information about the status of the sale. A 48-year-old car salesman with 8 years of experience discussed using an indirect inquiry as an alternative to a direct one:

They have what they call trial closes. And, uh, that's another way to assess whether or not you're going the right way with the car. Uh, you'll ask him, "Well, is that a car you think you'd like to own?" And if they say no, then obviously you've got them on the wrong car. Uh, you go down the road and you ask them, you know, you'll say, "Well, how's that going to look in front or your house?" or "Is that going to make your neighbor jealous?" Just silly little questions like that which even lightens up things.

This excerpt demonstrates that this salesperson knew that although the responses to the direct questions were obviously informative, asking indirect questions about how a car would look in front of the house or what the neighbors might think of provided similar information. The customers' responses to these indirect inquiries provided salespeople with the information they need to determine if they are approaching the customer correctly and whether they are getting close to closing a deal or not.

Relying on Reciprocity. Salespeople recognize that some customers were put off when they were asked a lot of questions. In those situations, salespeople sometimes used self-disclosure to promote conversation. The general reciprocity of self-disclosure can lead to customers opening up and talking more than a question would do. A 51-year-old salesman with 3 years of experience mentioned using this strategy especially for gaining information for developing common ground:

> Sometimes they don't want to answer a bunch of questions. Then I tell them about myself and that relaxes them some. They don't want me giving them the second degree. So I'll throw out some names. Oh, so you're from [name of town]. Do you know [name]? I've sold him a car. You're looking for some common ground so you get to know them.

A 39-year-old salesman with 14 years of experience explained how reciprocity works to possibly lead to a sale:

> After we're doing kind of telling stories, then I'll just kind of slowly ease back into it, and it, and it's not like an abrupt change. You know, I just, you know, pick a point and then we'll slowly go back into it. And uh, they know why you're there. Uh, you know, they're, uh, they're ready to hear what we have to say.

The reciprocity of telling stories created a common ground between the salesperson and the customer. It resulted in a situation where the customer was more open to discuss the purchase of a vehicle and exchange information needed to complete a deal.

Summary. Car salespeople reported that they seek two main types of information from their customers. They seek general information about the customer so that they can find a common ground to talk about and they seek specific information that will enable them to understand the customers' wants and needs and capabilities for buying a car. To seek this information they rely heavily on direct questions or qualifying questions. However they also seek a great deal of information through observing visual cues. In addition, they sometimes use indirect questions to get information that could be asked directly, and they self-disclose to create a situation where reciprocity occurs and they learn about the customer.

Other Themes and Results

In addition to responses related to the research focus, a number of other themes emerged from the interviews. Some of these themes suggested some other issues relating to how salespeople manage uncertainty with customers.

Negative Reputation; Creating Uncertainty. Salespeople often volunteered that an issue when interacting for the first time with customers was that the customers often had negative expectations for their interactions with car salespeople. Several made statements like, "Car salesmen have a bad reputation. I think we're pretty much below just about anything else. And so a lot of people come in with a chip on their shoulder and you have to work with them." Another said that, "About 50–70% of the people don't like me at first. They don't like car salesmen because we have a bad reputation." Another gave a slightly more elaborate explanation of how he deals with the situation:

> Car dealerships are next to, uh, getting your teeth pulled. It's just not a pleasant experience for a lot of people. So a lot of people will come in real tight like that. I've always tried to loosen them up with humor.

This negative expectation created a unique uncertainty management issue for the salespeople. Salespeople were often quickly aware of the attitude of the customers because the customers would be rude or very curt with them. The customers demonstrated by their actions that they were certain about what car salespeople were like. In order to change the customers' negative opinion of them, the salespeople then had to, in effect, work at creating uncertainty for the customer so that the customer would consider changing their schema for salespeople, or at least allow for an exception to their expectations and begin trusting the particular car salesperson. In the previous example, the salesperson used humor to try to create this change. If he could get customers to laugh, then the customers would be less certain about their negative attitude about car salespeople in general. A 35-year-old salesman with 4 years of experience would take a more direct approach to begin making this kind of change:

> If they're rude to you, I have very simple responses: "Have you had a bad experience with a car salesman, you know?" And if they say yes, this last person—because everybody thinks they got screwed, as soon as they walk out the door they think they, they've been taken.

By establishing the certainty of the customer's view of car salespeople, by showing that they were humorous or could empathize with the customers' negative experiences, these salesmen were able to begin to change the customer's certainty about car salespeople (i.e., their negative attitude) and try to change the attitude from distrusting car salespeople in general to trusting them personally.

Managing Unsolicited Information. Salespeople also reported receiving information from their customers that they were not seeking. This could be anything from customers telling stories about being in the military to details about a divorce to information about their financial troubles to stories about their children. This type of communication sometimes resulted in long conversations that had little or nothing to do with actually selling a vehicle to the customer. There were a number of reactions to receiving this unnecessary information.

Some tried to quickly turn the conversation back to topics related directly to vehicle sales. For example, if someone was telling a long golf story, one salesman reported that he would turn the conversation back to the car deal by saying, "Oh, and by the way, that car that you're looking at, you can lay clubs sideways in that trunk." This would hopefully focus the conversation on the sale of the car instead of allowing a long diversion about golf.

A few others listened politely even though they were not actively seeking that information. They listened while the customer rambled on because they were usually on test-drives and because they have already told the customer about most of the features of the car, they would rather have some conversation than silence. They also perceived it as rude to cut off the conversation too quickly and so listened until the customer finished.

Others reported that they found utility for this information even though they had not requested it. These rambling stories and details unrelated to the sale of the vehicle helped them better understand the customer for future interaction or helped them create common ground. A 49-year-old salesman with 23 years of experience said that when he is not busy, he enjoys talking with customers:

> I enjoy sitting and visiting with people back and forth. A lot of people come in here and visit with me and, and they have no intension of buying a car and that's great. I mean I had people come in and, and uh, just, you know, just to shoot the bull with. And it's, it's a, it's actually kind of a break for me to get down and sit, talk to some-body about they've been here, or been there and done that. And, and uh, you know, you don't worry about selling somebody a car. I mean, it's kind of neat that, you know, the people want to come in, and, and tell you that their son's done this or their daughter's done that. And it's, it's, it's a good, it's, it's a good thing to know that, that, that, you know, you can, you can relate back to them the next time you talk to them if they've bought a car and you can say, hey, how's the car doing and how's the kids doing. Are they still playing soccer or this that and the other. It's, it's just a, a part of the job.

This suggests that this salesperson used unsolicited information for relationship development rather than making a sale on a particular day. He saw the unneeded details and information as part of the job of maintaining relationships with his customers.

Finally, a few simply enjoyed meeting and getting to know people, even when the information did not result in any current or future sales. A 39-year-old salesman with 14 years in the business said this:

> I've had people that I've sat in here with for 30 minutes just bullshitting about stuff that didn't buy a thing, and I was still tickled to death that I met them because they

were so much fun to talk to, you know. Uh, it's not all about selling. You know, and they walk out and I'm saying to myself, "God, I wish every customer was like that."

Another one said:

I can talk to some customers for 20 minutes just because you hit it off and not even talk to them about what they're there for.

Although car salespeople clearly used active information-seeking techniques such as direct inquiry through qualifying questions and observation to gain information that they needed to complete a sale, they also passively received information that they did not request. Some politely listened. Others tried to subtly turn the conversation back to the sale of a vehicle. Others tried to find some utilitarian value for the information in terms of creating a relationship or common ground that could assist them in future sales. A few simply enjoyed meeting people, and for them reducing uncertainty was not a motivating factor.

Required Information Seeking.   Another theme that emerged involved motives for information seeking. Although uncertainty reduction to determine the needs of the customer or to find common ground motivated much of the information seeking, there was at least one other motive mentioned regularly for asking for information from customers. A number of dealerships have either a 10-foot rule or a 1-minute rule. These rules stated that salespeople should greet customers who are not engaged with another salesperson if they come within 10 feet of a customer or within a minute of the customer arriving on the lot or in the showroom. A salesperson might be busy with another customer and not be able to actually attempt to sell a car to the individual, but would still go through the motion of seeking information from them. The salesperson might ask, "Have you been helped?" or "Are you looking for someone?" not because they were experiencing uncertainty about the customer or really wanted information from the customer but because it was considered part of their job. They were not experiencing much uncertainty about this new customer but would still ask for information from them. This type of required information seeking seemed designed more to address the uncertainty of the customer than of the salesperson.

Managing the "I'm Just Looking" Response.   Another situation that was discussed a number of times was how salespeople responded to customers who say, "I'm just looking." Perhaps as customers we expect that this response should reduce uncertainty for the salespeople and that they should leave us alone as a result. However, in general salespeople reported that they do not leave these customers alone immediately or if they do leave the area initially they certainly return later because, as one salesman said, "Most people that come on a car lot and tell you they're 'just looking' will buy something within 60 days." Salespeople think that leaving such a customer alone could potentially mean losing a sale. A 45-year-old salesman with 18 years of experience put it this way:

> Well, just looking has been the word in this business for years. When somebody says they're just looking, it's a defense mechanism. I mean you don't go to J.C. Penney and try on shoes because you're just looking. I mean, ... they're just looking for somebody to make them feel good.... They're just looking. And they're, what they're looking for is somebody to sell them a car.

A 34-year-old salesman with 8 years of experience reported that he treated such customers this way:

> And if they turn back around to you and say, "Look, I'm just looking," then you know that maybe you probably better leave them alone. But I rarely let them go completely. I'll come back to the office and they'll still be out there and I'll come back there in another, you know, 2 or 3 minutes, and say "Have you found anything, gotten any closer to what you're looking for" you know. And usually, usually by then they've let their guard down. They'll, they'll at least say something to you. You know, they're, maybe they feel kind of bad that they've been rude before and, and they actually may be impressed that you came back again after the way they talked to you.

A popular response to "I'm just looking," reported to me by a few salesmen was to say, "Well, your cousin was here just last week, Ben, you know, Ben Looking." Those that used this response claimed that the humor often broke the ice and allowed them to actually assist the customer.

The interesting aspect of the "I'm just looking" response from a customer is that it probably rarely has the exact impact that the customer thinks it should have. The customer expects that this is a very clear response that should leave no uncertainty in the salesperson's mind as to the appropriate response. Instead, the salespeople interpret this as a defense mechanism, perhaps based on the negative reputation that was mentioned earlier, and so respond to it in a different manner, attempting to break down the barrier and create a relationship and a possible sale with the customer.

Managing Certainty About Disliked Customers.   A final theme that emerged was that salespeople knew for certain who they disliked as customers. Unlike URT, which suggests that gaining information increases liking, these salespeople reported learning to dislike certain customers based on information gained through communication. These disliked customers were the ones who they generally tried not to approach or ones who they would actually give to another salesperson. Although the type of customer each salesperson disliked varied, each mentioned some. Most were in the negative categories mentioned previously, such as the arrogant customer, or the horse trader who wears you down. Knowing the type of customer from previous experience led to certainty about them and then to avoidance behaviors.

DISCUSSION

This study was conducted to examine some of the cognitive and behavioral processes suggested by TMU in interactions in a specific organizational setting: the car salesperson–customer interaction. The themes that emerged in the interviews suggested that car salespeople do in fact use many of the processes suggested by TMU.

Even though they indicated that it was ineffective to do so, salespeople admitted that either they or others sometimes prequalify customers as ineligible to purchase cars and so do not approach those customers. This provides evidence that car salespeople do use schemas for customers as a way to avoid experiencing uncertainty about customers. They sufficiently reduce the experience of uncertainty about the customers without interacting with them based on visual cues, such as the vehicles they are driving, their appearance, or demeanor.

Car salespeople also have scripts for managing the uncertainty of how to interact with customers. These scripts are conceptually similar to the memory organization packets found in initial interactions in interpersonal interactions (Kellerman, 1991), although the particular details, questions asked, and so forth, are somewhat different due to the purpose of the interaction. These scripts provide car salespeople with a flexible approach for interacting with customers. Due to these scripts, they experience limited uncertainty about the sales situation, although they still are uncertain about the particular customer. These scripts are flexible enough to allow them to be adapted to the individual customer. They are also effective enough at reducing uncertainty about the process of selling that most car salespeople believe that they can determine whether they have a real potential buyer in a very short period of time, usually a matter of a few minutes. Together these results suggest that car salespeople manage or avoid the experience of uncertainty of meeting customers in part through cognitive processes, schemas, and scripts, which do not require information seeking from the customers.

The results also indicated that car salespeople use a number of other cognitive processes to manage the uncertainty they do experience during the interaction with customers. The most commonly reported one was using a category system to help them quickly choose the appropriate sales strategy for a particular customer. Based on limited information seeking, the salespeople determined the type of customer with whom they were interacting and then attempted to provide the appropriate sales message for that type of customer. In addition to this, salespeople also reported denying uncertainty when they felt certain that a customer was not an eligible buyer and tolerating uncertainty about a customer when they were certain the customer was there for service rather than to purchase a new vehicle. They also could imagine how conversations would go with customers that they did not choose to interact with. Together this indicates that car salespeople do not necessarily do thorough information seeking about their customers. Instead, they often use cognitive shortcuts to manage their uncertainty about customers.

Car salespeople had two primary goals for seeking information from their customers: to sell a car and to create a long-term relationship. To accomplish these goals, they sought information for accomplishing a sale, but also information for creating common ground with customers. They relied heavily on direct inquiry through a series of qualifying questions to gain the information they needed. However, they also seemed to make an almost equal use of observation to gain information about customers' likes and dislikes and to gauge customers' responses to their sales approach.

In addition to direct strategies, the car salespeople sometimes used indirect strategies. In trial closings, they often asked an indirect question that could provide them information about the success of their sales strategy. They also sometimes relied on the self-disclosure norm of reciprocity to gather information. Particularly when customers seemed reluctant to answer questions, salespeople would sometimes talk about themselves and then rely on the reciprocity norm to motivate customers to provide information in return. These are important indirect strategies for gaining information about customers that involve interaction with the customer without asking direct questions. Taken together, these results suggest that car salespeople do make use of most of the information seeking strategies suggested by TMU.

The findings are quite consistent with TMU, although this study has a number of limitations. For example, it is possible that the snowball sample resulted in a unique set of car salespeople that may be somewhat different from a typical salesperson. These may have been better (or worse) salespeople than most. In addition, there may have been a certain amount of self-presentation that may have skewed the results in a positive direction. For example, because they attributed prequalifying to other salespeople while generally denying that they did it themselves, they may not have presented a complete description of their actual behaviors. However, by mentioning the behaviors of others and admitting at other times that they had preferences and dislikes, they probably gave a fairly representative description of the process of managing uncertainty in interactions with customers. These descriptions are consistent with TMU.

IMPLICATIONS FOR TMU

This examination of the way car salespeople manage their uncertainty with customers has provided some unique insight into how uncertainty is managed in initial interactions with new customers and ongoing interactions with repeat customers in an organizational setting. Many of the results are consistent with TMU, although a number of unique insights are also provided. The results have applications to other organizational settings, as well.

The results suggest that car salespeople must manage two types of uncertainty when a new customer enters the lot or showroom. They must manage the uncertainty about the customer as a potential buyer and uncertainty about the process of interacting with the customer. Car salespeople have schemas for certain customers who they can prequalify as ineligible to purchase a car and thus become certain about them as potential buyers. When the customer does not automatically fit the schema of an ineligible buyer, they use their scripts for interacting with customers to make a determination of the type of customer. These flexible scripts enable them to manage uncertainty about the process of interacting with those customers. Car salespeople appear to be quite confident about their ability to manage the process of reducing uncertainty, many claiming that within a few minutes they are able to determine if they have an eligible buyer. Their process certainty enables them to manage their uncertainty about the customers in an efficient manner. It is likely that process scripts exist for many other interactions in organizational settings. These process scripts assist members in managing uncertainty as they deal with strangers. Whether it is a restaurant manager interacting with a health inspector, a small business owner interacting with a government employee, or a subordinate meeting the boss's spouse at a social gathering, individuals often develop process scripts to enable them to manage the uncertainty of how to interact with others. Having process scripts enables individuals to focus on reducing uncertainty about other people instead of having to first manage the uncertainty of how to interact with them.

The results further suggest ways that individuals may segment their uncertainty to manage it. These salespeople wanted to reduce their uncertainty about their customers in two main areas, the customers needs or wants in a vehicle and common ground for building rapport. They did not experience uncertainty about other areas of the customers' lives and often received information that was superfluous from customers. Other organizational members probably segment similarly when they meet individuals from distant departments or locations within their organizations. It seems they most often focus on reducing uncertainty about how the individuals will help them accomplish some goal or task, and also often attempt to determine if they have any acquaintances in common. Most likely they are not concerned about reducing uncertainty about the other people's family, social, and spiritual lives. They focus on accomplishing their tasks and finding some common ground. The results of this study provide further evidence that people in organizations are not necessarily interested in reducing their uncertainty about other people in all areas or topics, and may only be concerned about reducing uncertainty in areas that have specific functional uses for them.

The results also suggest some additional motives for seeking information that organizational members have besides uncertainty reduction. Two motives stand out as particularly interesting. First, sometimes car salespeople seek information simply because it is their job to do so. It is not that they are experiencing uncertainty or are particularly concerned about a customer that motivates them in all instances. Rather, sometimes they go through the motions of seeking information simply because they are supposed to as part of their job. This involves asking customers if they have been helped and assisting them if possible. They are assisting the customers as a job function rather than being motivated by their own uncertainty. Many people in other organizational positions are required to seek information as part of their jobs, from receptionists and security personnel to development and public relations officers. While it certainly can be argued that people in these positions are reducing their uncertainty about others, the important difference to note is that their motivation for seeking information comes from their job requirements, not from internal motivation to reduce uncertainty.

At other times car salespeople seek information for the pure joy of finding out new things. Some of the salespeople genuinely enjoyed meeting people and finding out about them. Particularly when they were not busy, they simply were motivated to seek information out of interest in people, not uncertainty about them. They were not motivated to reduce uncertainty and were not even concerned if their interactions did not help them make a sale. Most of us know people who seem genuinely interested in most anyone and anything. While we may complain about their productivity at work because they are constantly communicating with others about things unrelated to their work, the pleasure they receive from talking to others seems to motivate them rather than a drive to reduce uncertainty.

The results also reinforce the idea that uncertainty is a receiver phenomenon and not determined by the sender of a message. Customers probably feel that saying "I'm just looking" is a clear and unambiguous message. Salespeople understand it quite differently. They consider that the customer may have had negative experiences with other salespeople or that they simply want some time by themselves before they are helped. The salespeople respond to the message from their own understanding of the situation, not necessarily the one the customer expects. We may have similar experiences when we tell a coworker that everything is fine and to please leave us alone. We believe our message should create certainty for the coworker, but the coworker cannot determine whether we really mean what we say or whether the tone of voice indicates that we are actually sending a coded message that we wish someone would take the time to listen to our problems. As a result, the coworker may ask us if everything is okay throughout the day. Clearly, the receiver determines the uncertainty in a message, not the sender.

Together these findings suggest some areas for further examination and elaboration in the TMU model while generally supporting it. These findings have application to many other organizational settings. This study focused on examining the cognitive processes involved in managing uncertainty and methods for seeking information. The study in the next chapter was designed to examine more completely the behavioral responses to uncertainty and the role of competing motives in seeking information.

The Influence of Competing Motives on Managing Uncertainty: Responses to Organizational Scenarios

The study in chapter 5 focused on the ways in which car salespeople used scripts and schemas to help them avoid the experience of uncertainty with their customers, used other cognitive processes to reduce the uncertainty they experienced concerning their customers, and used communication strategies to gain information from their customers to reduce uncertainty. Beyond that, even though that was the focus of the study, the results also revealed that multiple motives influenced their information-seeking behaviors. Primarily, they were motivated to seek information to find out about the customer's needs and ability to purchase a car in order to meet those needs. They were also highly motivated to find common ground to build a relationship with the customer that could potentially last beyond the sale of one vehicle. In addition to these two motives, they also reported seeking information as a routine part of their job requirements and out of the curiosity and enjoyment they received from meeting people. These findings emphasize that competing motives influence managing uncertainty and information-seeking behaviors. The study reported in this chapter explored the importance of such competing motives in managing uncertainty. It focused on how competing motives influence individuals' information-seeking behaviors in various organizational settings involving uncertainty.

RESEARCH FOCI

Most of us can recall times in organizational settings where we experienced a significant amount of uncertainty and yet did not seek information. For example, in some situations we do not want to embarrass ourselves by admitting we did not already know anything about some topic that others were discussing in a matter-of-fact manner. As a result, we did not seek information and we remained uncertain. TMU suggests that levels of uncertainty are not necessarily a sufficient predictor of information-seeking behaviors because uncertainty is not the sole motivator of communication behaviors. High levels of uncertainty would normally motivate information seeking to reduce uncertainty, but competing motives, such as impression management or lack of communication skills, may inhibit information seeking.

Most of us can also recall other situations where we have asked for information even though we were not experiencing uncertainty. For example, when we are introduced to an out-of-town relative of a coworker we may ask them the typical questions about where they are from and how they like our community. Although we do not know the answers to these questions, we are not motivated to ask them by uncertainty. Rather, we are practicing social etiquette. Along these lines, TMU suggests that when low levels of uncertainty do not motivate information seeking, competing motives such as appearing polite or seeking information variety might cause information-seeking behaviors to occur anyway. To explore these possibilities, the first focus of this study was to explore the competing motives that influence organizational members' information seeking in a variety of common organizational situations.

Even when we are motivated to seek information because we experience uncertainty, we may choose to seek information in a number of other ways. Instead of asking the group of coworkers a question to clear up our uncertainty about the topic they are discussing, we may use a variety of other strategies, such listening in on conversations or asking someone else about it discreetly or indirectly at another time. TMU suggests that information seeking can occur through a variety of strategies. Although direct inquiry is one approach to reducing uncertainty, many others have been identified, such as third party inquiry or observation. TMU also suggests that rather than seeking information, individuals may use cognitive processes such as figuring it out on their own to manage uncertainty instead of seeking information. Given these possibilities, the second focus of this study was on examining the information-seeking strategies organizational members use in response to common situations that produce uncertainty.

Whereas URT originally postulated a direct relationship between uncertainty and communication behaviors, TMU suggests that a variety of motives may influence the choice of particular communication strategies for managing uncertainty. For example, we might use different strategies to manage the uncertainty we experience with our supervisor than we might use when a stranger walks into our workplace, because our motives might be quite different in those two situations. We may want to impress our supervisor, but we may just be doing our job when we greet a stranger. The third focus combined the first two areas of research to see if there were any associations between certain motives and specific communication strategies.

RESEARCH PROCESS

In order to explore these research foci, it was important to provide some common uncertainty-producing situations to a variety of organizational members to explore the motives and communication behaviors that they would invoke. The research process involved creating a questionnaire that included various common scenarios, distributing those questionnaires to a variety of organizational members, and then doing a statistical analysis of the responses.

The Questionnaire

The questionnaire asked people to respond to brief scenarios that could potentially create uncertainty for them in an organizational setting. The first scenario described a situation in which they were asked by a supervisor to do a job they had previously done; however, they had forgotten how to do the job because it was not a routine task. The second scenario indicated that they had heard a rumor that a coworker was leaving; the coworker was just a casual acquaintance, but they were now working alone with that coworker. The third scenario described an unusually dressed stranger with strange colored hair and body piercing entering their workplace. The fourth scenario asked them to imagine that they were taking their same job in a new organization with different procedures to follow and they had not yet been taught those procedures. Each scenario presented a situation where there was uncertainty about something or someone, as well as allowed for a variety of ways to gain information if so desired.

The questionnaire consisted of two parts. The first part simply asked for the demographic information about the people completing the study. The second part of the questionnaire provided the scenarios followed by a series of questions with five-point Likert-type responses from "strongly agree" to "strongly disagree." The first seven questions asked whether they would seek information, and what strategy or source they would use to seek information. The remaining questions asked which motives explained their behaviors in that setting. Because of concern that fatigue might influence the results if people had to respond to all four scenarios, each person received only two of the scenarios. Approximately half of the people received the first two scenarios and half received the second two.

Questionnaire Scales

The items for the questionnaire were developed based on TMU. First, to measure *motivation to seek information*, a two-item scale was developed on which people in the study indicated the degree to which they agreed that they would or would not seek information in that particular situation. The second item was reverse scored so that the combined score indicated their level of motivation to seek information. This two-item scale was fairly reliable statistically (α

= .82; r = .69). Then, to measure which strategies they would use to reduce uncertainty, people in the study indicated the degree to which they agreed that they would use different strategies to seek information. The first three strategies involved active, visible information seeking including *directly* from the source of the uncertainty, *indirectly* from other individuals, or by consulting *written materials*. The fourth strategy was an active but less visible method of information seeking, *observation*. The final strategy of information seeking represented a cognitive process of reducing uncertainty internally through *guessing*, without seeking information.

To indicate their motives for their behaviors, individuals responded to a series of statements developed out of the nine motives identified by TMU in chapter 4: uncertainty reduction, impression management, social appropriateness, social costs, utility of information seeking, competence at information seeking, emotion avoidance, maintaining uncertainty, and seeking information variety. Three statements were developed for each motive to allow for the possibility of reliability estimates.

Reliability estimates for the nine proposed scales ranged from good (five scales were in the α = .69 to .78 range) to very poor (four scales were in the α = .30 to .54 range), with an average reliability a of .61. These results suggested that the nine strategies were not completely distinct, apparently due to some overlapping motives. As a result, a factor analysis was conducted. A factor analysis helped to determine if there were any broader, more reliable, underlying motives instead of the nine originally suggested.

Factor analysis results (using a standard varimax rotation, eigenvalues > 1) indicated that there were five overall motives rather than the nine originally expected (see Table 6.1). The first factor, *uncertainty reduction*, generally combined uncertainty reduction and maintaining uncertainty motives (reverse-scored) into a single reliable factor (α = .89). It included six items that indicated the individuals felt they did not know enough or wanted to seek additional information. The second reliable factor (α = .86), *inquisitiveness*, was primarily a combination of the utility and variety motives. It included five items indicating that individuals thought it might be interesting or useful to seek additional information. The third reliable factor (α = .76), *negative impacts*, was a mixture of various negatively worded statements from various motives. It consisted of five items that indicated that individuals thought that things might get worse if they sought information, that the effort might not be worth it, and that people might think negatively of them for asking. The fourth factor, *incompetence*, consisted primarily of items associated with competence and utility. It contained three items indicating that the individuals felt it took too much effort, they did not know how to go about seeking information, and they were not good at finding out what they wanted to know. Due its relatively low reliability (α = .57), a fourth item designed to assess competence

TABLE 6.1

Factor Analysis Results for Motives Scale Development

Items	Uncertainty Reduction	Interest	Negative Outcomes	Incompetence	Impression Management
It would bother me to not find out.	−.84	.16	−.21	.06	.17
I don't need to know about this.*	.82	−.30	.18	.18	-.15
I would really want to know this.	−.79	.28	−.09	.03	.14
There would be no point in finding out.*	.78	−.24	.09	.28	−.11
Sometimes it's better not to know.*	.58	−.08	.37	.33	−.21
I already know what I need to know.*	.50	−.39	.06	.28	−.02
It's interesting to find out new things.	−.10	.83	−.07	−.15	.06
I might find out something interesting.	−.27	.76	−.20	.09	.09
You never know what you find out.	−.21	.75	−.17	.03	.04
It's good to learn new things.	−.17	.74	−.04	−.22	.17
I might find something useful by asking.	−.39	.65	−.23	−.07	.22
People might think less of me if I asked.	.10	.20	.81	.18	−.06
I wouldn't care what people thought.*	.07	.26	−.69	.10	.21
It would bring up emotions if I asked.	.20	−.21	.60	.24	.25
It could make things worse.	.22	−.14	.57	.49	−.03
Even if I try, I might not find out.	.32	.24	.56	.33	−.04
It would take a lot of effort to find out.	−.05	−.05	.09	.76	−.01
I'm not sure I'd know what to do.	.27	−.10	.23	.64	−.05
I'm good at finding out what I want.*	−.16	.41	−.09	−.59	−.14
I would appear impolite if I didn't ask.	−.01	.07	.05	−.03	.87
Asking would make a good impression.	−.25	.16	−.18	.04	.72
Asking would make me look competent.	−.37	.12	−.04	.03	.59

*Items were reverse scored when summing the scales.
Italicized numbers indicate items used for each scale.

(not knowing who to talk about the issue) was added to the factor. This increased the factor's reliability ($\alpha = .70$). The final factor, *impression management*, consisted of the three items indicating that the individuals felt that seeking information would make a good impression by making them look competent and polite ($\alpha = .69$). For each scale, responses were scored so that a high score indicated a high level of the motive. Means are reported as averages across the items for a particular scale.

Participants in the Study

Because I did not want to use student responses for this study, people were recruited for this study through a technique used successfully elsewhere (Nicotera, 1993; Teboul, 1995). Students in an upper level communication course at a Midwestern university were given alternative credit for a class assignment if they recruited four full-time adult employees to fill out questionnaires. This procedure resulted in a total of 80 respondents. To verify that students did not complete the questionnaires themselves, people completing the questionnaire included their first name and a phone number. I called approximately 25% of these people to verify that they had completed the surveys, and then destroyed the identifying information.

This technique resulted in a wide variety of people participating in the study. The people were 56% female and 44% male. They ranged in age from 19 to 60, with an average age of 34.97 years (SD = 12.94). They reported their marital status as 44.9% single, 48.7% married, and 6.4% divorced or separated. They represented a diverse set of occupations in a variety of organizational settings. The largest occupational groups were office/clerical work (21.5%), sales or customer service (17.7%), management (12.7%), educators (12.7%), health care providers (7.6%), and banking or financial services (6.3%). The largest percentages of types of organizational settings they worked in were a university (17.5%), banking or financial institutions (11.3%), business or sales companies (11.3%), primary or secondary schools (8.8%), government agencies (7.5%), building supply or construction companies (5%), and communication or media organizations (5%). Overall, this indicates that a wide range of people participated in the study.

Analysis

In order to address the foci of the study, a series of statistical analyses were conducted. Three statistical tests were used. The first type of analysis, an ANOVA (Analysis of Variance), tests for differences in means on a measure or outcome for different groups or situations. If the ANOVA results indicate that there are significant differences between some of the groups, then post-hoc (Latin for *after that*) tests are computed to determine which particular groups are different from other groups. The second type of analysis, a MANOVA (Multivariate Analysis of Variance), is an approach that simultaneously tests for differences in means across two measures or outcomes. The multivariate results indicate if there are significant differences across groups on both measures. The univariate results then indicate specifically which differences are significant, much like the post-hoc tests in an ANOVA. The third type of analysis, stepwise regression, is used to determine which variables are the best predictors of another variable. The results also indicate those that are not good predictors.

In order to address the first research focus, an ANOVA was used to determine if there were differences in motivation to seek information across the scenarios, a

MANOVA was used to determine if the various motives for seeking information differed across the scenarios, and a series of ANOVAs were used to determine if there were differences in motives to seek information for each individual scenario. For the second research focus, a MANOVA was used to determine if the information-seeking strategies differed across scenarios, and a series of ANOVAs were used to determine if there were differences in information-seeking strategies for each individual scenario. For the third focus, a series of stepwise regressions were conducted to determine which motives were the best predictors of information-seeking strategies for each scenario and for all the scenarios combined.

RESULTS

Differences in Motivation

In order to examine whether people reported differences in motives in response to the four scenarios, four sets of analyses were conducted. The first analysis explored whether there were differences in motivation to seek information across the different scenarios. The second explored whether the levels of each motive differed across all the different scenarios. The third examined whether the motives differed from each other for each individual scenario. The fourth examined whether there were significant differences in the motives for all of the scenarios combined.

Different Levels of Motivation to Seek Information by Scenario. In order to determine if there were different levels of information seeking motivated by the four different scenarios, an AVOVA was conducted. The four cases served as the independent variable and information seeking as the dependent variable. Results indicated that there were significant differences in information seeking across the four scenarios $[F(3,155) = 40.63, \eta^2 = .44, p < .001]$. Post-hoc tests comparing the cases to each other indicated that respondents were significantly more likely to seek information in the new job ($M = 4.59$) and the supervisor request ($M = 4.41$) scenarios than they were in the peer rumor ($M = 3.05$) and the stranger at work ($M = 3.04$) scenarios. In response to a new job and a request from a supervisor to do a job, respondents were highly motivated to seek information. The means, which were between "agree" (4) and "strongly agree" (5) on the scale, indicated that they were very likely to seek information. In response to a rumor of a peer leaving and a stranger entering the workplace, respondents were only moderately motivated to seek information. The means suggest that they were neutral (3) about seeking information in these situations. This suggests that they might not seek information in these scenarios.

Differences in Specific Motives to Seek Information Between Scenarios. To examine the motivations behind the differences in general motivation to seek information, two sets of analyses were run. The first analyses explored the level of each motivation across the different scenarios to determine if specific motives were stronger in some scenarios than others. The results indicated that there were different levels of the competing motives activated by the different scenarios. The overall multivariate results of the MANOVA indicated that overall there were significant differences for the motives for the four different scenarios [$F(15,400) = 10.84$, $\eta^2 = .27$, $p < .001$]. The univariate explored these differences more specifically. The results indicated that people reported significantly different levels of each of the five motives across the four scenarios.

People reported different levels of uncertainty reduction as a motive for seeking information across scenarios [$F(3,149) = 52.12$, $\eta^2 = .51$, $p < .001$]. Specifically, a series of post-hoc tests indicated that uncertainty reduction was a stronger motive in the new job ($M = 4.22$) and the supervisor request ($M = 4.16$) scenarios than in the peer leaving rumor ($M = 2.81$) and the stranger entering the workplace ($M = 2.76$) scenarios. This indicated that uncertainty reduction was a strong motivation to seek information when faced with a new job or a request to do a job for the supervisor, but that the uncertainty created by hearing that a coworker was leaving or seeing a stranger enter the workplace did not provide much motivation to seek information.

People reported different levels of inquisitiveness as a motive for seeking information across the scenarios [$F(3,149) = 8.47$, $\eta^2 = .15$, $p < .001$]. The results were similar to uncertainty reduction as a motive. The post-hoc tests indicated that inquisitiveness provided a significantly stronger motive for seeking information in the supervisor request ($M = 4.28$) and the new job ($M = 4.27$) scenarios than in the peer leaving ($M = 3.83$) or stranger at work ($M = 3.76$) scenarios. This indicates that being inquisitive about obtaining useful or varied information was a strong motive for the people to seek information when taking a new job or being asked to do a job by a supervisor. Inquisitiveness was not quite as strong a motive for seeking information in the peer leaving or stranger at work scenarios, although the means indicate that the people slightly agreed that it was a motive even in those situations.

People reported different levels of concern over possible negative outcomes across the scenarios [$F(3,149) = 13.95$, $\eta^2 = .22$, $p < .001$]. Here the results were in the opposite direction of the two previous results. The post-hoc tests indicated that concern over negative outcomes was a moderate motivation in the peer leaving ($M = 3.02$) and the stranger at work ($M = 2.71$) scenarios, but significantly less so in the new job ($M = 2.21$) and the supervisor request ($M = 2.21$) scenarios. People seemed more concerned over it not being worth the effort or looking badly by asking for information in the two scenarios in which they were less likely to seek information. People were more concerned over possible negative outcomes of seeking information about a coworker who was rumored to be leaving or a stranger who appeared at work than when dealing with a new job or a request from a supervisor.

People also indicated differences in concern over incompetence as motivating their information seeking across scenarios [$F(3,149) = 7.51$, $\eta^2 = .13$, $p < .001$]. Whereas the means suggest that incompetence was not a particularly strong motive for any of the scenarios, the post-hoc tests revealed that feeling incompetent was a significantly stronger motivation in the stranger scenario ($M = 2.61$) than in any of the other scenarios. In addition, incompetence was a significantly stronger motivation for not seeking information in the peer leaving rumor scenario ($M = 2.29$) than in either the new job ($M = 2.07$) or the supervisor request ($M = 1.98$) scenarios. This suggests that not being sure how to go about seeking information appropriately was a stronger motivation with a stranger at work than in the other situations. In the new job and supervisor request situations there seemed to be much less doubt about how to seek information.

Finally, people indicated difference in impression management concerns as a motive for seeking information across the scenarios [$F(3,149) = 10.21$, $\eta^2 = .17$, $p < .001$]. The post-hoc tests indicated that people were more motivated to make a positive impression in the new job ($M = 3.02$) and the supervisor request ($M = 2.91$) scenarios than they were in the stranger at work ($M = 2.39$) and the peer rumor ($M = 2.31$) scenarios. This somewhat surprising result indicated that people felt that seeking information in a new job or when they could not recall how to do something their supervisor asked them to do would not make as negative an impression as seeking information about a peer who may be leaving or a stranger at work.

Overall, then, the results from this first set of analyses suggests that people felt that reducing uncertainty, being inquisitive, and making a positive impression were significantly stronger motives in the scenarios involving a new job and a request from a supervisor. These were the scenarios in which they were highly motivated to seek information. People reported being more motivated by concerns over negative outcomes and appearing incompetent in the rumor of a peer leaving and the stranger at work scenarios. These were the scenarios in which they were only modestly motivated to seek information. This suggests that concerns over negative outcomes and appearing incompetent to seek information in these scenarios.

Differences in Motives Within Scenarios.   Whereas the previous analyses provide evidence that each of the motives varied according to the scenarios, a second set of analyses indicated which motives were the strongest for each scenario. The results of a series of ANOVAs indicated that the strength of the motives was significantly different within each scenario.

People reported significantly different motivations in response to the request by a supervisor to do a task that the employee could no longer recall how to do [$F(4,35) = 52.75$, $\eta^2 = .86$, $p < .001$]. Post-hoc tests indicated that people did not differ significantly in inquisitiveness ($M = 4.28$) and uncertainty reduction ($M = 4.16$) as motives for seeking information. However, they were significantly more motivated by these two motives than the other three motives. Also, they were significantly more motivated by impression management concerns ($M = 2.91$) than by either concern over negative outcomes or incompetence. In addition, they were significantly more concerned over negative outcomes ($M = 2.21$) than incompetence ($M = 1.98$). The interesting finding here is that people were as strongly motivated by a general inquisitiveness for gaining useful or interesting information as they were by uncertainty reduction in this situation. Apparently, in addition to reducing uncertainty by being reminded how to do the particular job, people thought that they might gain some useful or interesting information as well by asking for help.

For the scenario in which the employee heard a rumor that a coworker, who was not a close friend, might be leaving and has an opportunity to talk to that individual, people indicated significantly different levels for the various motives [$F(4,35) = 59.15$, $\eta^2 = .87$, $p < .05$]. Post-hoc tests indicate that the strongest motive for people was inquisitiveness ($M = 3.84$), which was significantly higher than the other four motives. In addition, people were equally concerned over negative outcomes ($M = 3.01$) and uncertainty reduction ($M = 2.81$), but these were both significantly stronger than impression management ($M = 2.30$) and incompetence ($M = 2.28$). However, these last two motives did not differ from each other. Overall, this suggests that finding out about why the coworker was leaving was not motivated primarily out of a desire to reduce uncertainty about the particular topic, but rather that people were looking for information more out of a general curiosity or inquisitiveness. In addition, a concern over possible negative outcomes, such as making the situation worse, competed with uncertainty reduction to inhibit information seeking.

For the third scenario, where an individual with strange dress and appearance entered the workplace, people reported significantly different levels for the various motives [$F(4,34) = 27.42$, $\eta^2 = .76$, $p < .001$]. Post-hoc tests indicated that people were significantly more motivated by inquisitiveness ($M = 3.76$) than any of the other four motives. People did not differ significantly in their motivation to reduce uncertainty ($M = 2.76$), avoid negative outcomes ($M = 2.71$), and appear incompetent ($M = 2.61$), although these were significantly stronger motivations than impression management ($M = 2.39$). Overall, these results suggest that faced with a stranger with an unusual appearance, employees are motivated to seek information more out of a desire to find out something interesting than to reduce uncertainty in the situation. In addition, two motives that might inhibit information seeking, concern over negative outcomes and appearing incompetent to seek information appropriately, compete with uncertainty reduction and inquisitiveness, which would motivate information seeking.

In the final scenario, taking a similar job in a new organization with different procedures, people also differed significantly in their motives [$F(4,33) = 47.46$, $\eta^2 = .85$, $p < .001$]. In this scenario, post-hoc tests indicated that people were equally motivated by inquisitiveness ($M = 4.27$) and uncertainty reduction ($M = 4.23$), but that these two motives were significantly stronger than the remaining three motives. In addition, people were more motivated by impression management ($M =$ 3.02) than either negative outcomes ($M = 2.21$) or incompetence ($M = 2.07$). However, they did not differ significantly on these last two motives.

Taken together, these analyses provide strong support for the idea that various competing motives interact with uncertainty reduction to influence communication behaviors in specific situations. Of particular interest is the finding that inquisitiveness, seeking useful or varied information, is as strong a motive as uncertainty reduction in two of the scenarios and a stronger motive in the other two scenarios. This suggests that people often seek information not because they are experiencing uncertainty. Rather, they are often motivated to seek information out of general curiosity or interest. They seek information because it might be useful or unusual, not to answer a specific question or concern. The other particularly significant finding is that concern over negative outcomes or not being competent to seek information appropriately seemed to reduce the desire to seek information despite higher levels of uncertainty. Taken together, these results help to explain why there is not always a clear association between the level of uncertainty and the resulting information seeking. Other motives influence communication behaviors.

Differences in Motives for the Combined Scenarios.   The final ANOVA examined whether people reported different levels of motives when the scenarios were treated as a combined or singular situation. This allowed examination of the relative importance of motives in general. Results indicate that people reported significant differences in motives across the scenarios [$F(4,149) = 155.69$, $\eta^2 = .81$, $p < .001$]. In descending order of strength were inquisitive ($M = 4.04$), uncertainty reduction ($M = 3.48$), impression management ($M = 2.65$), negative outcomes ($M = 2.54$), and incompetence ($M = 2.24$). Post-hoc tests revealed that all of these motives were significantly different from each other except for impression management and negative outcomes. This indicates that inquisitiveness was generally a stronger motivation to seek information than uncertainty reduction, but that uncertainty reduction was generally a stronger motivation than other concerns.

Differences in Information-Seeking Strategies

The questionnaire included five different strategies for responding to uncertainty in the scenarios. Three were active, visible methods of seeking information including directly asking the person, indirectly seeking information from someone else, and consulting written materials. One was an active but less obvious form of information seeking through observation. The final method was a cognitive process of seeking information internally by guessing or figuring it out by oneself. In order to determine if people relied on different information-seeking strategies in the different situations, three series of analyses similar to those in the previous section were computed. The first explored whether the levels of each type of information seeking differed across the scenarios. The second examined whether the types of information seeking differed from each other within each scenario. The third examined the relative use of the different information-seeking strategies for the combined scenarios.

Differences in Information-Seeking Strategies Between Scenarios.

The first analysis explored whether the levels of each type of information-seeking strategy varied across the different scenarios. The multivariate results of a MANOVA indicated that people reported different levels of the information-seeking strategies with different scenarios [$F(15,440) = 25.64$, $\eta^2 = .47$, $p < .001$]. The univariate results also indicated that there were significant differences for each of the information-seeking strategies across the scenarios.

The univariate results indicated that people reported different levels of seeking information directly from the source of uncertainty across the scenarios [$F(3,152) = 12.04$, $\eta^2 = .19$, $p < .001$]. Post-hoc tests indicated that this was due to the fact that people reported being significantly more likely to seek information directly in the new job ($M = 4.28$) and supervisor request ($M = 4.25$) scenarios than they were in the stranger ($M = 3.26$) and peer leaving ($M = 3.21$) scenarios. This indicates that in the two scenarios where they felt the most motivation to seek information, they were also more likely to seek that information directly from the source of uncertainty.

The univariate results also indicated that people reported different levels of indirect information seeking (from other people in the situation) across scenarios, [$F(3,152) = 12.72$, $\eta^2 = .20$, $p < .001$]. Post-hoc tests indicated that this was due to the fact that people reported significantly higher levels of indirect information seeking in the new job scenario ($M = 4.18$) than in the other three scenarios. They did not differ significantly in their indirect information seeking in the supervisor request ($M = 3.33$), stranger ($M = 3.05$), or peer rumor ($M = 2.90$) scenarios. This suggests that respondents were more likely to use a wide range of indirect sources of information, such as other peers, in a new job than in situations where there was a clear source of uncertainty (supervisor, stranger, or peer) from which to seek information.

The univariate results also indicated that people varied in how likely they were to seek information from written materials across scenarios [$F(3,152) = 104.35$, $\eta^2 = .67$, $p < .001$]. Post-hoc tests indicated that they were significantly more likely to seek information from written materials in the supervisor request scenario ($M = 4.28$) than in any of the other scenarios. They were also significantly more likely to consult written materials in the new job scenario ($M = 3.95$) than in the peer rumor ($M = 2.00$) or stranger ($M = 1.79$) scenarios. These last two did not differ significantly, and the means ($2 = $ disagree) indicate that they were unlikely to seek information from written materials in either of these situations. These results are not particularly surprising. It would be difficult to find many written materials to consult in the case of a peer rumor or stranger at work situation. There could perhaps be a memo or announcement explaining why the peer was leaving or perhaps a policy statement on what to do when unusual strangers enter the workplace, but not much else. However, there could be written procedures for handling the supervisor request or other situations a newcomer faces on the job and so consulting these could be valuable.

People also reported differences in the use of observation across scenarios according to the univariate results [$F(3,152) = 3.40$, $\eta^2 = .06$, $p < .05$]. Post-hoc tests revealed that people were significantly more likely to use observation in the supervisor request scenario ($M = 3.78$) than in the peer rumor scenario ($M = 3.08$). However, this was the only significant difference. Observation as a strategy in the new job ($M = 3.49$) and the stranger scenarios ($M = 3.45$) did not differ significantly from the other scenarios. This suggests a rather consistent and moderate use of observation across situations. People reported that they would use observation about equally in all four situations with just slightly more in response to their supervisor's request and slightly less in the peer rumor situation.

The final univariate results indicated that people reported significantly different likelihood of guessing or figuring out the situation on their own [$F(3,152) = 4.42$, $\eta^2 = .08$, $p < .01$]. Post-hoc tests indicated that this is because people were significantly more likely to guess in the stranger scenario ($M = 2.92$) than in any of the other situations. They indicated no differences in likelihood of using guessing in the peer rumor ($M = 2.39$), supervisor request ($M = 2.33$), or the new job ($M = 2.18$) scenarios. This suggests that respondents were likely to rely on guessing or figuring it out on their own in dealing with a stranger who would most likely have no direct affect on their work. In situations that could affect their work, they were significantly less likely to do so.

Overall, the results of these analyses indicate that people vary their information strategies according to the situation. They were most likely to use a direct information-seeking strategy to the source of uncertainty in situations where they were highly motivated to seek information. They consulted various indirect sources of information when there was no singular source of uncertainty. Observation was used about the same across situations. Written materials were consulted only in situations where they were likely to be available, and people were more likely to try to figure it out on their own in situations that did not directly affect them, such as a stranger at work.

Differences in Information-Seeking Strategies Within Scenarios.

Whereas the previous results indicated that respondents varied their use of information-seeking strategies across scenarios, the next set of analyses explored which strategies were most likely to be used for each situation. People reported significant differences in the use of different information-seeking strategies for each scenario.

For the scenario of being asked by the supervisor to do an infrequently used procedure that the individual could no longer recall, results of the ANOVA that indicated that people would make significantly different use of the strategies, $[F(4,36) = 32.36, \eta^2 = .78, p < .001]$. Results of the post-hoc tests indicated that people were significantly more likely to consult written materials ($M = 4.38$) and make a direct request to the supervisor ($M = 4.25$) than the other strategies. In addition, they were significantly more likely to use observation ($M = 3.78$) as an information-seeking strategy than either indirect sources or guessing. Finally, they were significantly more likely to use an indirect strategy ($M = 3.33$) than just guessing or trying to figure it out on their own ($M = 2.33$). This suggests that in a situation directly related to their jobs in which they were highly motivated to seek information, respondents actively sought information directly from their supervisor or from written materials. They also relied some on observation and indirect strategies, but were very unlikely to simply guess at how to do the procedure.

People reported significant differences in use of strategies for the scenario in which they were with a peer who was rumored to be leaving $[F(4,35) = 9.56, \eta^2 = .52, p < .001]$. Post-hoc analyses indicated that they were about equally likely to use a direct strategy of asking the individual ($M = 3.21$), observing the individual ($M = 3.01$), or an indirect strategy of asking someone else ($M = 2.90$). However, they were significantly more likely to use any of these three strategies than either guessing ($M = 2.39$) or consulting written materials ($M = 2.00$), strategies they reported relying on about equally. This suggests that although in general people were less motivated to seek information by any strategy in this situation than some of the others, they were about equally likely to use any of the three strategies that could likely reduce their uncertainty. They might ask the person, observe the person to see if they might overhear the reason for leaving, or ask someone else who might know. They were less likely to use strategies that could provide wrong information (guessing) or no information (written materials).

The analysis of the third scenario, in which a stranger with unusual appearance entered their workplace, indicated that people reported using the strategies differently $[F(4,34) = 20.98, \eta^2 = .71, p < .001]$. Post-hoc tests indicated that they were significantly less likely to use written materials ($M = 1.79$) in this situation than any of the other information-seeking strategies. The mean ($2 = $ disagree) suggests that they were unlikely to consult written materials at all. In addition, results indicated that they were equally likely to use observation ($M = 3.45$), direct inquiry to the stranger ($M = 3.26$), and indirect inquiry to others ($M = 3.05$). They were significantly more likely to use guessing ($M = 2.92$) than written materials and less likely to use guessing than observation. The results here are not surprising. First, the means are all in the neutral area, suggesting that they may not seek information at all. But it makes sense that when a stranger enters the workplace, respondents were not very likely to consult written materials, given that those materials would probably not provide useful information unless there was a policy for dealing with strangers in their organization. Guessing was a more preferred strategy than written materials. However, they were most likely going to use observation, direct inquiry of the stranger, or indirect inquiry of others in their work setting.

For the final scenario, taking the same job in a new organization, results indicated that people differed significantly on their use of information-seeking strategies, $[F(4,35) = 27.18, \eta^2 = .76, p < .001]$. Post-hoc tests indicated that respondents were equally likely to use direct inquiry of their supervisors ($M = 4.28$), indirect inquiry of other peers ($M = 4.18$), and written materials ($M = 3.95$) to gain information. They were significantly more likely to use these three strategies than observation or guessing. However, they were significantly more likely to use observation ($M = 3.49$) than they were to guess or try to figure it out on their own ($M = 2.18$). These results suggest that as a newcomer in a setting, people felt motivated to actively seek information from any available source—supervisors, peers, or written materials—and that they would use a fair amount of observation, as well. However, they were significantly less likely to simply guess or try to figure it out on their own.

Overall, these analyses comparing the use of different strategies within each scenario suggest some overall observations. In many situations respondents appeared to prefer to use multiple methods of information seeking, although the particular methods varied according to the situation. In addition, although direct inquiry to the source of uncertainty was consistently one of the preferred strategies, depending on the situation, other information-seeking strategies might be just as likely to be used. Sometimes this meant consulting written materials, and other times it meant seeking information from others who might know.

Differences in Information-Seeking Strategies for the Combined Scenarios.
The final analysis for this question examined whether there were differences in the use of the strategies for the combination of all the scenarios. This allowed exploration of whether there were preferred strategies for various situations involving uncertainty. Results indicated that people reported significant differences for the overall information-seeking strategies $[F(4, 152) = 46.46, \eta^2 = .55, p < .001]$. In descending order of use were direct inquiry ($M = 3.76$), observation ($M = 3.45$), indirect inquiry ($M = 3.37$), consulting written materials ($M = 3.05$), and guessing ($M = 2.45$). Post-hoc tests revealed that there were significant differences between all the strategies except observation and indirect inquiry. This indicates that direct inquiry may be the preferred method of seeking information to reduce uncertainty in general. However, the other strategies are mentioned regularly as potential strategies, depending on the situation.

Different Motives as Predictors of Information-Seeking Strategies

In order to explore which motives were predictive of particular information-seeking strategies, a series of stepwise regressions were conducted. For each scenario, a series of five regressions were conducted in which each of the five information-seeking strategies (direct, indirect, written, observation, and guess) served as the dependent variable and each of the motives (uncertainty, interest, negative outcomes, incompetence, and impression management) served as possible predictors. Then a final series of five stepwise regressions were conducted to examine the results across all four scenarios. The results of these analyses are reported in Table 6.2.

For the first scenario, involving the supervisor request to do a task, inquisitiveness was the best predictor of people asking the supervisor directly for information, and uncertainty reduction was the best predictor of using observation to gain information. The other information-seeking strategies did not have significant predictors. This indicates that although the previous results indicated no difference in the levels of inquisitiveness and uncertainty reduction as motives in this scenario, the level of inquisitiveness was actually the best predictor of asking the supervisor for information directly. The desire to reduce uncertainty was the best predictor of use of the unobtrusive strategy of observation. The other preferred strategy in this situation, consulting written materials, was apparently motivated by some combination of motives in which no particular one was prominent.

The second scenario involved a coworker who was rumored to be leaving. Results suggest that uncertainty reduction was the best predictor of people using both the direct strategy of asking the coworker about the situation and the indirect strategy of asking others who might know. So, whereas the previous results indicated that inquisitiveness was the strongest motive in this situation, uncertainty reduction was a better predictor of whether the respondents would actually consider asking the person or other peers about the reason for leaving. Feeling incompetent also predicted consulting written materials. However, the previous results suggest that incompetence was not a strong motive in this situation, and respondents were unlikely to consult written materials.

For the stranger at work scenario, impression management was a significant predictor of using a direct inquiry of the stranger and consulting written materials, and a negative predictor of asking others about the situation. Inquisitiveness and uncertainty reduction were predictive of using indirect strategies. So, although the previous results suggest that impression management was not as strong a motive as inquisitiveness and uncertainty reduction in this situation, it was a better predictor of whether respondents would likely ask the stranger a question directly, one of the preferred strategies for gaining information in this situation. One of the other preferred strategies, indirect inquiry, was predicted by inquisitiveness and uncertainty reduction, the strongest motives in this situation. Finally, incompetence was predictive of simply guessing rather than seeking information, and this scenario was the one in which respondents reported that they were most likely to guess about the situation.

For the final scenario, taking a similar job in a new company, concern over negative outcomes was the best negative predictor of direct information seeking from the supervisor. This indicates that the less concerned respondents were

TABLE 6.2

Significant Predictors of Information Seeking Strategies

Scenarios	Information-Seeking Strategies	Predictors (Motives)	Betas	Regression Results
Supervisor Request	Direct	Inquisitiveness	.34	$F(1,37) = 4.95$, $R^2 = .12$, $p < .05$
	Indirect	—	—	—
	Written	—	—	—
	Observation	Uncertainty	.36	$F(1,37) = 5.40$, $R^2 = .13$, $p < .05$
	Guess	—	—	—
Peer Rumor	Direct	Uncertainty	.44	$F(1,36) = 8.86$, $R^2 = .20$, $p < .01$
	Indirect	Uncertainty	.65	$F(1,37) = 26.57$, $R^2 = .42$, $p < .001$
	Written	Incompetent	.38	$F(1,37) = 6.28$, $R^2 = .15$, $p < .05$
	Observation	—	—	—
	Guess	—	—	—
Stranger at Work	Direct	Impression Management	.43	$F(1.36) = 8.22$, $R^2 = .19$, $p < .01$
	Indirect	Uncertainty	.60	$F(3,34) = 10.82$, $R^2 = .49$, $p < .001$
		Inquisitiveness	.34	
		Impression Management	−.37	
	Written	Impression Management	.38	$F(1,36) = 5.99$, $R^2 = .14$, $p < .05$
	Observation	—	—	—
	Guess	Incompetent	.42	$F(1,36) = 7.63$, $R^2 = .18$, $p < .01$
New Job	Direct	Negative Outcomes	−.35	$F(1,35) = 4.87$, $R^2 = .12$, $p < .05$
	Indirect	—	—	—
	Written	—	—	—
	Observation	—	—	—
	Guess	Impression Management	.38	$F(2,34) = 6.02$, $R^2 = .26$, $p < .01$
		Uncertainty	−.36	
Combined Scenarios	Direct	Uncertainty	.39	$F(2,149) = 26.22$, $R^2 = .26$, $p < .001$
		Impression Management	.20	
	Indirect	Uncertainty	.51	$F(1,151) = 52.13$, $R^2 = .26$, $p < .001$
	Written	Uncertainty	.57	$F(1,151) = 74.19$, $R^2 = .33$, $p < .001$
	Observation	Uncertainty	.25	$F(1,151) = 9.84$, $R^2 = .06$, $p < .01$
	Guess	Incompetent	.27	$F(1,151) = 12.00$, $R^2 = .07$, $p < .001$

about looking bad by asking for information, the more likely they were to ask their supervisor for help in their new jobs. In addition, impression management concerns predicted that respondents might guess rather than seek information, whereas uncertainty reduction concerns indicated that respondents would not guess. This suggests that newcomers with experience in another work setting are most likely to ask for information if they are not concerned about negative outcomes for doing so and most likely to guess or try to figure things out on their own if they have impression management concerns.

Finally, the analysis of results across scenarios suggests that across situations, uncertainty reduction is the best predictor of the use of direct, indirect, written, and observation strategies. Impression management also leads to using a direct strategy, whereas feeling incompetent leads to guessing. Combining these results with those for the different scenarios suggests that across a variety of situations uncertainty reduction is the best predictor of information seeking; however, within particular contexts or settings, other motives may be better predictors of information seeking than uncertainty reduction.

DISCUSSION

TMU suggests that the relationship between uncertainty reduction and information seeking is not as simple as originally suggested by URT. Instead, TMU argues that competing motives, in combination with uncertainty reduction, can increase or decrease the likelihood of seeking information in particular situations. This second study was designed to explore whether some of the competing motives as developed in TMU influence information seeking. Although the study relied on expected behaviors rather than actual communication, it still provides useful insight into the complexity of the relationships between uncertainty reduction, other motives, and communication. A number of the results are particularly insightful into the complex relationships between uncertainty, other motives, and communication strategies.

A particularly interesting finding was that people reported that inquisitiveness was the strongest motive across scenarios, either matching or exceeding uncertainty reduction as a motive in each scenario. URT is based on a very rational model of human behavior in which people act to address very specific problems or issues of uncertainty. Its premise is that information seeking is a logical response to the problem of experiencing uncertainty in the environment. Although certainly there are many times when this occurs, the results of this study suggest that people are often motivated to seek information simply out of inquisitiveness or curiosity. Although one could stretch the realm of logic and argue that this general inquisitiveness is grounded in a broad interest in reducing global uncertainty, such an argument clearly goes beyond the theorems of URT. It also involves the same sort of surreptitious logic that makes it appear that all human behavior can be explained as rational (Zey, 1992). It is more valuable to consider the implications of inquisitiveness as a motive that interacts with uncertainty reduction and other motives to produce communication. This inquisitiveness is what schools and colleges have for years desired to instill in students as part of the liberal arts education rather than technical or professional training. Perhaps this inquisitiveness simply needs more nurturing. Regardless, it suggests that people have motives that are not best explained as rational responses to reduce uncertainty in their environment. Clearly, more research needs to examine the role of this motive in relationship to communication.

Although inquisitiveness was a stronger motive than uncertainty reduction in many situations, it is important to note that uncertainty reduction still was most often a better predictor of people's information seeking than inquisitiveness. Inquisitiveness was only the best predictor of one communication strategy (direct inquiry) in one scenario (the supervisor request). This suggests that inquisitiveness, although it is a strong motive, may not be sufficient by itself to motivate people to seek information in many situations. Apparently, inquisitiveness generally must interact with other motives, especially uncertainty reduction, to cause people to seek information in many situations.

Uncertainty reduction, although not always as highly rated as inquisitiveness, was the best predictor of people's communication strategies for particular situations (five) and was a significant predictor of four of the five communication strategies across the scenarios. This emphasizes the importance of examining uncertainty reduction as a significant motive for people's communication because it is a strong predictor of information seeking in a variety of organizational settings. However, these results make the case for TMU that uncertainty reduction is not the singular motive of information seeking. Uncertainty reduction frequently works in conjunction with other motives to produce information seeking; and other motives, such as fear of negative outcomes, work against information seeking.

IMPLICATIONS FOR TMU AND ORGANIZATIONS

Taken as a whole, the results support TMU by indicating that there is no simple relationship between uncertainty reduction and information seeking because other motives influence communication behaviors. Whereas URT considers uncertainty reduction as the singular predictor of behavior (Anderson, 1996), TMU considers it one of the predictors of behaviors that must be examined in combination with other motives to understand information seeking. It is the interaction of motives that increases or decreases the likelihood of people seeking information.

This complex interaction of people's motives is perhaps most apparent in the results for the employee in the same job in a new organization. Although people rated uncertainty reduction and inquisitiveness as the strongest motives in that situation, it is a lack of concern over negative outcomes that best predicted their use of direct inquiry to the supervisor. This suggests that these newcomers were highly motivated to seek information to reduce uncertainty and to appease curiosity, but that these alone did not accurately predict whether they would actually seek information. Rather, only when the newcomers felt that it would not take a lot of effort, that it would not make things worse, and that they would not need to be concerned about what others think, did they seek information to reduce uncertainty and appease their curiosity. It is the interaction of motives that predicts behaviors, not any single motive.

A second finding also supported this conclusion. Although uncertainty reduction concerns predicted that newcomers would not rely on guessing to figure out their new jobs, impression management concerns predicted that they would try to guess or figure things out on their own. Increases in uncertainty appear to motivate additional information seeking, whereas increases in impression management concerns decreased information seeking. Because new employees frequently have both of these concerns, examining one without examining the other would fail to provide sufficient understanding of the resulting communication behaviors. The complexity of these relationships emphasizes that even though uncertainty reduction cannot be examined in isolation as the motive for communication, it is equally important not to examine other motives in isolation from uncertainty reduction.

While these scenarios involved individuals' managing of uncertainty, the results suggest that similar issues may affect members of groups or organizational decision makers as they face uncertainty. A group may be inquisitive and uncertain about whether they have enough information to make an important decision, but they may fail to seek additional information if they think it will take too much time or effort and may create a negative impression of them as indecisive or incompetent. Improper management of these competing motives by group members in the face of uncertainty can result in poor decision making.

The results also emphasize the importance of looking at multiple ways of seeking information. Too often, research on URT has focused exclusively on direct inquiry as the only indication of whether uncertainty motivated information seeking. Results here suggest that other strategies can be equally important. Observation was a highly rated form of information seeking in some of the scenarios. Observation and indirect inquiry were two of the most common ways of seeking information in these settings, and consulting written materials was common in the two scenarios in which such materials were likely to exist. Too narrow a focus on direct inquiry without considering other ways of seeking information will limit our understanding of how uncertainty reduction and other motives work to produce information-seeking communication.

To summarize, this second study examined the possibility that competing motives influence information seeking. The results strongly support the conclusion that uncertainty reduction cannot be examined in isolation as the motive for information seeking. Although uncertainty reduction is an important motive that does at times relate directly to information seeking, other motives, such as inquisitiveness, impression management, and concerns over negative outcomes, interact with uncertainty reduction to influence communication behaviors. The resulting communication behaviors include direct inquiry to sources of uncertainty, but also include other, less obvious forms of information seeking such as indirect inquiry, observation, and consulting written materials. As such, the findings support TMU as developed in the previous chapters and support the need to examine how individuals and groups of people consider competing motives as they manage their individual and collective uncertainty.

A Textual Analysis of Managing Uncertainty: A Reanalysis of the Lucille Burger Story

The previous chapters reported two original studies that explore TMU in organizational settings. One examined how car salespeople manage uncertainty with their customers using qualitative interview data. The other explored how individuals respond to the uncertainty of different organizational settings using quantitative questionnaire data. To further evaluate the value of TMU for examining organizational communication, this chapter presents a textual analysis of a previously analyzed story to further explore its usefulness as a theoretical perspective.

Theoretical perspectives are important. Examining a particular set of data or a particular artifact from a particular perspective influences what is attended to and what is ignored. "A way of seeing is a way of not seeing" (Poggie, 1965, p. 284). The perspective one takes influences the conclusions that are drawn. This chapter uses the perspective of TMU to examine a story that has previously been analyzed from two different perspectives, interpretive and critical. Both previous analyses focused on a more macro-level of analysis of the story, one focusing on the impact of the telling of the story on the culture of the organization and the other focusing on the hegemonic impact of the story. The purpose of this analysis is not to dispute or refute the two previous analyses of the story. Rather, its purpose is to see how analyzing the story from the perspective of TMU provides additional insights into the story and our understanding of how people respond to uncertainty. In particular, this is a micro-level analysis of the story, focusing on the how the participants in the story may have experienced and responded to uncertainty.

The story is known as the Lucile Burger story. Martin, Feldman, Hatch, and Sitkin (1983) report that the story was widely circulated among IBM employees. The story is in the biography of IBM's CEO Tom Watson (Rodgers, 1969). While the story may be an accurate reporting of events, an IBM employee personally told me in the late 1980s that he did not believe the story ever happened. This suggests that the story may no longer be viewed as credible within IBM although it may have been important in 1983 or earlier. Nevertheless, Martin et al. examined the story from an interpretivist perspective, and Mumby (1987) examined it from a critical perspective. According to Martin et al., the story goes:

> ... a twenty-two-year-old bride weighing ninety pounds, whose husband had been sent overseas, had been given a job until his return ... The young woman, Lucille Burger, was obliged to make certain that people entering security areas wore the correct clearance identification. Surrounded by his usual entourage of white-shirted men, Watson [CEO of IBM at the time] approached the doorway to an area where she was on guard, wearing an orange badge acceptable elsewhere in the plant, but not the green badge, which alone permitted entrance at her door. "I was trembling in my uniform, which was far too big," she recalled. "It hid my shakes, but not my voice. 'I'm sorry,' I said to him. I knew who he was all right. 'You cannot enter. Your admittance is not recognized.' That's what we were supposed to say." The men accompanying Watson were stricken; the moment held unpredictable possibilities. "Don't you know who he is?" someone hissed. Watson raised his hand for silence, while one of the party strode off and returned with the appropriate badge. (pp. 439–440)

The story is a fairly simple one of a lower level employee confronted with a dilemma as she is faced with a decision of what to do in this situation. Before examining the story from the perspective of TMU, I will briefly summarize the two previous analyses.

AN INTERPRETIVIST ANALYSIS OF THE LUCILLE BURGER STORY

In examining this story, Martin et al. (1983) draw a number of conclusions based on an interpretivist perspective. They note that the Lucille Burger story is one of a number of rule-breaking stories that they found in various organizations. The stories have a number of things in common. Each of them involved a high-status and a low-status person. In each, the high-status person broke a company rule. Also in each, the low-status person challenged the high-status person. And finally, the high-status person responded to the challenge, although the responses varied. In some organizations, the high-status person in the rule-breaking stories complied with the low-status person and even complimented or commended the subordinate; but in other organizations, the high-status person fires the low-status employee for challenging them. This variance in outcome is critical in interpreting the value of the story for different organizations.

Martin et al. (1983) point out that the Lucille Burger story contains a number of details that make the story believable as a unique story of IBM. The most obvious detail is that Tom Watson is specifically named rather than some vague reference to a position or rank. For employees of IBM, the Watson detail adds credibility to the story. The other important detail concerns the "white-shirted men" in the entourage. IBM employees were known for their white-shirted, blue suit, conservative tie appearance until well into the 1990s. This detail would not be in a rule-breaking story in many other organizations. Again, the white-shirt detail makes the story credible as a uniquely IBM story.

Martin et al. conclude that the story has a clear moral that "Even Watson obeys the rules, so you certainly should" and its corollary for lower status people, "Uphold the rules, no matter who is disobeying" (1983, p. 440). Given these lessons, both Watson and Lucille Burger become heroes as a result of their choices in this situation. In addition, the story becomes a cultural artifact that can communicate the distinctive values of the IBM culture to other employees. The story helps to create a shared understanding of what makes IBM a unique place to work.

A CRITICAL INTERPRETATION OF THE LUCILLE BURGER STORY

Mumby (1987) reanalyzes the Lucille Burger story from a critical or critical interpretivist perspective in order show how the story links organizational symbolism with legitimation and ideological domination. He focuses his analysis of the story on four characteristics of the deep structure of the organization accomplished through the story. The story represents sectional interests as universal, denies or transmutes contradictions, reifies the ideology of the organization, and performs the ideological function of control.

According to Mumby (1987), the story represents sectional interests as universal. On the surface, the story demonstrates that everyone at IBM must follow the rules. This interpretation misses a deeper understanding of IBM. The corporate elite, such as Watson, created the rules for the benefit of the corporate elite. The security procedures protected the organization from competition. As such, they were in place for the benefit of the corporate elite rather than for the benefit of employees like Lucille.

The story also denies or transmutes contradictions. According to Mumby (1987), the fact that the story is told at all is an indication that Watson was not subject to the same rules as other employees. If Watson really were subject to the rules at IBM, then an example of him following them would be of no particular interest and the story would not be told. The story fails to address the contradiction that Watson had the choice to follow the rule or not although other employees (including Lucille) do not have the same choice.

The story reifies the ideology of the organization in at least three ways (Mumby, 1987). First, the narrative form of the story makes it accessible for telling and retelling. This slice of life drama becomes real as it is told often enough even if it is an apocryphal tale. Second, the difference in description of Lucille and Watson reifies the hierarchy in the organization. On the one hand, by describing Lucille as a small, young bride, with ill-fitting clothes who was given a job until her husband returns, the story emphasizes her low status and reinforces that she fits a traditional female sex-role stereotype. On the other hand, Watson is barely described at all. But because he is followed by an entourage, typically a group of people following royalty, and the mere raising of his hand with out speaking commands silence, he becomes a hero of mythical proportions at the top of the organization. Third, the story reifies rules for the sake of rules. Lucille follows the rule because "That's what we were supposed to say." Watson seems to defer to the rule for the same reason. The story does not provide rationale for these security rules and especially not for enforcing them on the CEO of the company. Rather, the rules are followed because they are rules and are apparently a necessary part of the organization.

Finally, the story performs the ideological function of control (Mumby, 1987). Hegemony works most effectively when the subordinate groups actively support the worldview of the elite. In the story Lucille takes up the cause of enforcing the rules. This makes it appear that the rules are favored from the bottom up rather than enforced top-down by Watson. The overall effect of the story is to reinforce an ideology of control in the organization by demonstrating that everyone follows the rules.

Mumby (1987) concludes that the Lucille Burger story serves an ideological function. The repetition of the story creates and reifies the dominant meanings of the organization. Those dominant meanings reinforce an organizational structure that privileges the elite, such as Watson, while appearing to benefit the entire organizational membership.

AN ANALYSIS OF THE LUCILLE BURGER STORY BASED ON TMU

Using TMU to analyze the story provides an alternative perspective on the events of the story. A number of aspects of the story make TMU seem particularly appropriate. First, there is at least one direct reference to uncertainty: "The men accompanying Watson were stricken; the moment held unpredictable possibilities." As previously mentioned, most definitions of uncertainty include a lack of predictability as a significant component of uncertainty. In addition, according to the story, Lucille Berger was trembling in her uniform, suggesting that she was feeling a great deal of uncertainty in the situation. The lack of predictability or anxiety suggested by these references can easily be attributed to the uncertainty. TMU suggests that individuals have scripts and schemas for managing uncertainty in many routine situations. In this story, conflict between two such scripts creates uncertainty for the participants.

The first script, "Watson as CEO," says that Watson is in charge and has the right to do and act as he sees fit within very broad parameters. As CEO, he has the right to access anything in IBM because he is the highest authority among employees in the organization. He has the ability to make the rules, including rules for security procedures in the organization. This makes the act of a security guard preventing him from entering an area an affront to him and his position's authority. The second script, "Security Badge Procedures," indicates that there are certain security procedures at IBM that should be followed. According to this script, no one should enter a restricted area without the appropriate badge, in this case a green badge. The script does not contain an exceptions clause that allows some individuals, such as the CEO, not to follow it. This makes the act of a security guard preventing a CEO from entering an area the most appropriate behavior given the circumstances according to this script.

These two competing scripts, one suggesting that the CEO can enter as he pleases and the other suggesting that he must have the correct security badge, created the conflict and uncertainty. The uncertainty created by these competing scripts ultimately impacts Lucille, the entourage, and Watson. An analysis based on TMU suggests that each managed the uncertainty differently, resulting in different behaviors.

Lucille and Uncertainty

Lucille experienced uncertainty because she was clearly aware of the competing scripts. According to the story she knew who Watson was (CEO of IBM) and also knew what she was supposed to say to someone wearing the wrong color badge. TMU provides insight into how her behaviors may have resulted from her approach to managing this uncertainty.

TMU indicates that people experience less uncertainty when events fit a previous script or schema or there is no trigger event producing uncertainty. For Lucille, there is no escape from the uncertainty in this regard because she is confronted with an event that presents her with the two competing scripts. The approach of the CEO with the wrong color badge served as the trigger event that created uncertainty for her. There was a lack of predictability in the situation. She had to choose between the two behaviors, letting Watson pass unchallenged or preventing him from entering the area. Because she had scripts for both actions, she experienced uncertainty about which action to take. Her uncertainty was evident by the fact that she was trembling as she decided what to do or say.

TMU indicates that when faced with uncertainty, individuals may use cognitive processes to reduce the uncertainty without seeking information. These cognitive processes include deny the uncertainty, tolerate the uncertainty, assimilate the uncertainty, accept the uncertainty, and imagine information seeking to reduce uncertainty. Only one of these could be plausibly used by Lucille in this situation. She cannot deny that the uncertainty exists; to do so would be to deny the existence of the two scripts and the story indicates that she was very aware of both scripts—who she was confronted with, the CEO, and her job requirements.

Tolerating the uncertainty was also not feasible for Lucille. She could hardly claim that the uncertainty of the situation had no consequences for her. She was dependent on IBM and its CEO for her job while her husband was overseas. Her job dependency gave Watson influence over her. She knew that because the CEO was present she could be fired for making a wrong decision and yet she could not easily determine which choice was the right decision. If she allowed him to pass without challenging him for having the incorrect badge, he could fire her for neglecting her duty. If she challenged him, he could presumably fire her for insubordination. Being fired would have grave consequences for her due to her dependency on IBM for a paycheck. This job was apparently her only means of support while her husband was overseas. Tolerating uncertainty was not an option for her.

Lucille could not assimilate this uncertainty by associating it with some similar situation because she apparently had never experienced a similar situation. Perhaps her own supervisor had approached her in the past with the incorrect badge, which would be a similar situation. However, she had personal knowledge of her supervisor and probably knew how to react in such a situation. She perhaps knew that if her supervisor appeared without his badge, it was a test to see if she would follow procedures. She might know how her supervisor would respond to her request for the appropriate badge or respond to her allowing entrance to the restricted area. With no personal knowledge of Watson, she could not know if she could treat him similarly to her supervisor. She did not know if it was a test or how he would respond to her request. Assimilating the uncertainty was not an option.

Finally, she could not accept the uncertainty in the situation and just live with it. She was forced to make a decision between letting Watson in and making him get a green badge. Accepting the uncertainty would have the same impact as making a decision because it would involve allowing Watson to pass or not. She could not just live with the uncertainty and experience no consequences. There was no option that allowed for simply accepting the uncertainty.

It is possible that Lucille could have imagined information seeking to cognitively reduce her uncertainty. She could have had a number of quick imagined interactions. She might have imagined what her immediate supervisor would say to her if she asked what to do in this situation. She also could have imagined what Watson would have told her to do in the situation, although this would have challenged her imagination more because she did not seem to know him personally; she just seemed to recognize him. If she did have an imagined interaction with her supervisor or with Watson, she apparently concluded that one or both of them told her to ask Watson for his green badge even though he was the CEO. If this was the case, the response she imagined was probably based on her understanding of the culture of the organization as one that values employees who follow the rules. This type of reasoning would be consistent with the interpretivist analysis of the story presented by Martin et al. (1983).

Although using imagined conversation provides a plausible explanation of Lucille's behaviors, there is no particular evidence supporting this explanation in the story. In fact, because she was trembling as she asked Watson for his green badge, it seems likely that she was feeling a great deal of uncertainty as she confronted him. Either she did not have imagined interactions to reduce uncertainty, or the imagined interactions did not satisfactorily reduce uncertainty. Perhaps she imagined her supervisor giving one recommendation and Watson a different one, or she simply did not have enough confidence in what she imagined either one would say to confront Watson without fear and trepidation. She would appear to have been still experiencing high levels of uncertainty as she confronts Watson given her trembling. It seems that she was unable to reduce uncertainty cognitively or avoid the situation and so she was forced to use communication behaviors in this uncertain situation.

If reducing uncertainty were her only or primary motive in this situation, then URT would suggest that Lucille would have sought information. She could have used direct inquiry. For example, she might have simply asked Watson what to do: "Mr. Watson, I'm a security guard and my job is to keep people out of this area unless they have a green badge. I know you're the CEO and can decide what should and should not be done in the company. What should I do because you don't have the right badge?" His response to her inquiry would have reduced her uncertainty. Alternatively, she could have relied on a third party or indirect inquiry. She could have asked the entourage, including Watson, to wait one moment. Then she could have called her supervisor and asked what to do. Her supervisor's response would have reduced her uncertainty. However, she chose not to seek information in this situation, as URT would suggest she should. Instead, Lucille says, "I'm sorry … You cannot enter. Your admittance is not recognized." Her actions would suggest that she was motivated by something other than a drive to reduce uncertainty. She acted as if she knew exactly what to do, except that her trembling and her voice indicate that she was very uncertain about her actions.

So, although URT cannot satisfactorily explain Lucille's behaviors, TMU provides an explanation of why she confronts Watson rather than seeking information despite her uncertainty. Although the competing scripts created uncertainty for Lucille, competing motives suggested by TMU provided her with appropriate communication behaviors for the situation. Of the competing motives discussed in the previous chapters, impression management provides the most likely explanation for Lucille's behavior. The story provides some evidence that her actions were based on her concern for impression management rather than uncertainty reduction. She claimed that she managed to hide the fact that she was shaking, suggesting she was concerned about impressions. More important than just managing her impression by not shaking, by asking Watson for his green badge, Lucille portrayed an image of herself as a competent employee doing her job correctly. Even though she was frightened while doing this, she appears conscious of the fact that she was creating an image of a competent employee when she comments that it is "What we were supposed to say." Watson and the entourage knew that she was doing her job as she had been trained to do it.

As suggested by TMU, the response of the entourage and Watson then impacted Lucille's uncertainty. The entourage asked "Don't you know who he is?" Had this been the final comment on the situation, Lucille would have known that she should have let Watson in without the appropriate badge. Her uncertainty would have been reduced, although she would be aware that she made the wrong choice between scripts and perhaps would fear that she would lose her job. However, Watson raised his hand and someone went off to retrieve the appropriate green badge. This action reduced Lucille's uncertainty. She knew that the appropriate response for this situation of apparently conflicting scripts was to follow security procedures even when the CEO was present. Presenting a positive image as a competent employee had actually led to a reduction in uncertainty for her. As a result, she had a new script for dealing with situations like this in the future. The new script indicated that security procedures take precedence over other scripts regardless of the individuals involved. If a similar situation occurred for her in the future, she would not experience uncertainty and presumably would not tremble (or at least not as much). She knew to ask any employee for their correct badge, no matter how high-ranking the employee might be. She was certain that if she followed the security procedures rules, the CEO would support her actions. She did not need to fear what other employees might say or do to her if she asked them for their appropriate badge. One could imagine other employees attempting to pass her checkpoint with the wrong badge and arguing that an exception should be made because of their rank or because Lucille knew who they were and that they were actually cleared to enter the area. Lucille could respond, "If Tom Watson retrieved his green badge before entering this area, you can and will, too." No IBM employee could disagree with her after that explanation. The CEO provided her with a new resource for defending her actions and a new script reducing her uncertainty in these situations.

The Entourage and Uncertainty

Lucille's actions of preventing Watson from entering not only created an image of herself as a competent employee and ultimately reduced her uncertainty, but her actions also shifted the uncertainty in the situation to the other parties. Her act of refusing admittance to the CEO until he had his correct badge triggered uncertainty for the entourage. Although there is limited information about the entourage, TMU provides a framework for analyzing their actions.

Nothing in the story suggests that the entourage was experiencing uncertainty as they approached the security checkpoint. All of them, except Watson, must have had the correct security clearance badge, because Lucille only refused admittance to Watson. Apparently they expected that there would be no problem entering the area due to their understanding of the Watson-as-CEO script. However, they did experience uncertainty as soon as Lucille refused to allow Watson to enter the restricted area. This triggered their uncertainty because "the moment held unpredictable possibilities." They knew they were with the CEO Watson, and expected access to the area. Unpredictably, from their perspective, Lucille halted them. They could not avoid experiencing uncertainty because they did not have a script for managing their uncertainty in this situation, a situation in which a low-level security guard challenges the CEO.

Although there were probably different responses to the uncertainty within the entourage, none verbally disagreed with the one who hissed, "Don't you know who he is?" suggesting many apparently responded similarly. It is those that agreed with the one who hissed that are referred to as the entourage in the following analysis.

TMU suggests that members of the entourage could use cognitive processes to reduce their uncertainty created by the trigger event. Again, those cognitive processes include deny the uncertainty, tolerate the uncertainty, assimilate the uncertainty, accept the uncertainty, and imagine information seeking to reduce uncertainty. Two of the choices would fail to explain the hissing remark, "Don't you know who he is?" If the entourage tolerated the uncertainty or accepted the uncertainty, they would have had little to say. They would have relied on Watson to solve the dilemma.

If the entourage denied the uncertainty of the situation to cognitively reduce their uncertainty, it could explain the comment "Don't you know who he is?" They could deny that there was uncertainty by prioritizing one script over the other. If they thought that Watson-as-CEO was the dominant script for this situation, then the Security-Badge-Procedures script became irrelevant because the CEO was present. Denying uncertainty would lead them to hiss "Don't you know who he is?" because the Watson-as-CEO script determines what the CEO can do in this situation. Their comment tells Lucille that she should know that it is appropriate for the CEO to enter this area without his badge. By denying uncertainty through cognitive processes there is no uncertainty for the entourage.

Similarly, they may have assimilated the uncertainty into their scripts for the organization. To assimilate the uncertainty the entourage would have decided that this situation of a security guard challenging the CEO was similar to other situations they had experienced. If this were the case, then they would expect that the CEO should also be allowed to ignore procedures such as the Security Badge Procedure.

In addition, an imagined interaction with the CEO may have cognitively reduced uncertainty for the entourage. They might have imagined that Watson would say something like, "As CEO, I have access to any part of the organization. Why am I being stopped by this security guard?" If they imagined this kind of response, then they knew how to respond because their uncertainty was reduced. Their hissing remark would be to draw attention to the Watson-as-CEO script to help Lucille understand that her behavior was inappropriate.

It is not possible to tell which of the three approaches the entourage used to cognitively reduce their uncertainty. However, the story suggests that they reduced their uncertainty through one of these cognitive processes because they did not seek information to reduce uncertainty about the situation. "Don't you know who he is?" indicates that they felt that they knew what to do. Having reduced uncertainty, the person who spoke (and those who agreed) thought it was clear what to do in this situation. In this situation you let the CEO through even if he does not have the correct badge.

Having reduced their uncertainty, the entourage could have simply ignored the security guard and walked into the secure area knowing that this was the proper behavior for the situation. Instead, they hissed a remark to Lucille. An examination of the competing motives identified by TMU provides two possible explanations for their choice of communicating rather than simply entering the area without permission.

Social appropriateness provides a plausible explanation for their behaviors. Minimally, social appropriateness involves not being openly rude to people. Walking past Lucille after she refused them entrance would obviously be rude. More importantly, a common aspect of social appropriateness is to allow other people to save face in situations. Walking past Lucille or simply telling her to let them through because of Watson's position would have prevented Lucille from saving face, especially if she did not actually know who he was. By asking her, "Don't you know who he is?" they allowed her an opportunity to save face by recognizing or being told who Watson was, and then letting them through. The inquiry allowed her the opportunity to respond as they had to the situation by following the Watson-as-CEO script and letting him enter without his badge. Lucille might have done this type of self-correction and let Watson and the entourage through if Watson had not intervened and sent someone for his badge.

Impression management could also have been a motive for the entourage's communication. Here the impression management was not designed to make them look like competent employees, but rather to impress Watson with their deference to his position. Stating "Don't you know who he is?" indicated that they respected his position of authority. They were implicitly suggesting that Lucille should have similar respect for Watson. If after their inquiry Lucille had self-corrected and let them enter, they might have continued to build on this by commenting on how inappropriate her behavior was given that he was the CEO. This should have continued to demonstrate their deference to authority and presumably made a positive impression on Watson.

Based on their hissed remark, the entourage apparently expected a quick end to the uncertainty in the situation. Because they felt they knew what to do in this situation, they expected Watson and Lucille to behave in a manner consistent with their script for the situation. They probably expected Lucille to apologize and let them through. Perhaps surprising to them, Watson interrupted the situation and sent one of them off to find his green badge. However, rather than creating uncertainty, Watson's action reduced their uncertainty, just not as they apparently expected. Whereas the entourage seemed to have concluded that the Watson-as-CEO script took precedence over the Security-Badge-Procedures script, Watson made it clear that the security procedures were more important than his rank as CEO. The situation ends with the entourage having a clear script for handling future security issues. The CEO has made it clear that security procedures have a higher priority than rank. In light of this, one of them will perhaps make sure that the CEO has the proper badges with him at all times so that such confrontations will not occur in the future.

Watson and Uncertainty

Even though there is no direct evidence in the text of the story that Watson experienced uncertainty, he too was confronted with the conflict between the two competing scripts, Watson as CEO and Security Badge Procedures. Unless he had previously been excluded from an area for a lack of a badge in front of a number of other IBM executives, he had no script for dealing with the conflict between these two scripts. Lucille's action and the entourage's response triggered an unprecedented and unpredictable situation for him.

Surely, Watson experienced uncertainty because he had to consider that organizational culture is constraining on both the individual employees and management because it sets up expectations that need to be followed by both (Alder, 1997). There was uncertainty in this situation for Watson because he had to consider the implications of his choice of action. He had to try to predict the outcome of his actions. He needed to consider the impact of him going in without his badge versus waiting for an appropriate badge. Those outcomes were not readily predictable.

TMU suggests that Watson probably used cognitive processes to manage his uncertainty in this situation. Those cognitive processes include deny the uncertainty, tolerate the uncertainty, assimilate the uncertainty, accept the uncertainty, and imagine information seeking to reduce uncertainty. Although three of these cognitive processes would fail to explain why Watson raised his hand for silence and someone went off to get his correct badge, the other two are consistent with his actions.

Tolerating the uncertainty or accepting the uncertainty would involve treating uncertainty of the situation as if it were unimportant and allowing others to determine what actions to take. These options were really not available to Watson. There were already two groups of employees expressing opposing views in the situation. The entourage communicated that they favored the Watson-as-CEO script; Lucille communicated that she favored the Security-Badge-Procedures script. There was no neutral position for Watson to take to demonstrate tolerance or acceptance of the uncertainty unless he was willing to acquiesce his role as leader of the organization and allow one of these two groups to determine appropriate behavior in this situation.

It would also have been difficult for Watson to use imagined information seeking to reduce his uncertainty in the situation. Because he was the CEO it would be difficult to imagine with whom he could consult to decide what to do. Perhaps he could imagine what the board of directors, or the CEO of some other company, or some confidant might have told him to do. These all seem unlikely.

Two of the cognitive process would likely explain Watson's actions. It is possible that Watson denied that there was uncertainty for him in the situation. Although he probably recognized that Lucille and the entourage had each resolved the conflict between the two competing scripts differently and experienced some uncertainty as a result, he may have cognitively denied that there was any real uncertainty in the situation. He could deny there was uncertainty by recognizing that security rules are paramount at IBM. This means that the CEO has to follow the Security-Badge-Procedures script like all the rest of the employees. This denial of uncertainty would reduce his uncertainty in the situation and explain why he raised his hand and sent someone for his badge.

It is also possible that Watson assimilated the uncertainty of this situation with other similar situations. Perhaps there had been other situations in the past where he had the opportunity to disregard or maneuver around rules at IBM. For example, he may have had an opportunity to request reimbursement for expenses without the appropriate paperwork being completed. In this new situation, he may have considered his actions in those similar pervious situations and acted accordingly. If he cognitively reduced his uncertainty by assimilating this situation with other similar ones, then he must have also followed the rules in similar situations in the past. He could have reduced his uncertainty in the current security badge dilemma by assimilating it with other similar opportunities to break rules in his previous experience in which he had followed the rules.

It seems likely that Watson reduced his uncertainty through cognitive processes either by denying there really was uncertainty in the situation or by assimilating the situation with another, similar one. Given a low level of uncertainty, URT could explain why he did not seek information. Because he was experiencing limited uncertainty, he did not seek information. However, URT would not be able to explain his communication behaviors. TMU provides an explanation of Watson's behaviors by recognizing some of the competing motives that may have influenced his behaviors given his low uncertainty. Two motives in particular seem to explain Watson's behaviors: impression management and social appropriateness.

Watson's communication behavior, raising his hand for silence while someone goes to get the appropriate badge, can be explained as motivated primarily by impression management concerns. By communicating that he was going to comply with the security procedures at IBM even though he was the CEO, Watson set an example and made a powerful impression on employees who witnessed the event and who heard about it. Although as CEO he has a great deal of influence over the policies and procedures of the organization, he is also dependent on the employees at IBM. The company and ultimately his job rely on employees complying with the policies and procedures of the company. Watson risked losing employee support for organizational policies if he failed to abide by those policies. By visibly complying with the security procedure instead of joining those who would encourage him to break the rule, he created an impression of himself as an individual who follows organizational policy. By creating this impression, he solidified the employee support on which he must rely. TMU explains why he would be concerned about impression management even though uncertainty was not an issue.

Watson could have demonstrated that he felt there was no uncertainty in this situation and in the process chastised the members of the entourage who criticized Lucille. After using cognitive processes to reduce his uncertainty, a gruff rebuke of those who questioned Lucille doing her job, followed by a request for someone to get his badge, would have been consistent with his lack of uncertainty. TMU provides an explanation for why he instead said nothing. In addition to impression management concerns, Watson's communication indicates a concern for social appropriateness. As previously mentioned, allowing others to save face is an important part of social appropriateness. Although his nonverbal communication of signaling for silence was a rebuke of those who wanted Lucille to let him go past her check point, it pales in intensity to the verbal reprimand that he could have directed at the individual who hissed, "Don't you know who he is?" or those who apparently agreed with the comment. The nonverbal communication is less confrontational than a verbal reprimand while still clearly communicating his intention that he would follow the security procedures of IBM even though he was the CEO. Even though Watson could not escape embarrassing some of the entourage by correcting their inappropriate response, he did demonstrate concern for social appropriateness in reducing the confrontation by relying on nonverbal communication instead of a verbal reprimand.

After someone goes off to retrieve his badge, Watson appears to have reduced uncertainty for all the parties involved. Lucille knows that her response was the appropriate response. The entourage knows that their response was inappropriate, and Watson appears to have made things more predictable for himself and others in the future. This Lucille Burger story now exists as a script for other members of the organization to manage their uncertainty for the foreseeable future.

The Lucille Burger Story in Context

After using TMU to analyze the Lucille Burger story, I was curious if the original source of the story might shed additional light on it. The story must be part of some longer narrative or research project. Mumby (1987) relied on the version of the story reported by Martin et al. (1983). They reported finding the story in the biography of Watson (Rodgers, 1969). An examination of the story as recorded in context provides some additional information for examining and understanding uncertainty in the situation.

According to Rodgers (1969), the events of the story occurred as World War II was mounting in Europe. IBM was involved in highly classified production work at a number of its plants. Its equipment was being shipped to our allies, England and Russia, as part of the war effort. In addition, Watson had recently completed a tour of IBM's Poughkeepsie plant. During that tour, numerous guards had allowed him to pass despite the fact that he had not worn his security badge. After the tour, "Watson tracked down the supervisor of guards and reprimanded him for tolerating loose security measures" (Rodgers, 1969, p. 153). The story then goes on to tell that "Security at the Endicott plant was better, at least in the hands of a twenty-two-year old bride … Lucille Burger" (Rodgers, 1969, p. 153). Martin et al. (1983) directly quote most of the remainder in their version of the story. However, they omit a short closing to the story in which Al Good, the director of security, commends Lucille and explains that he understood why the men in the entourage were nervous about saying anything to Watson. "I guess it was the sort of thing they couldn't mention to him if they were close to him. With me, it was just a job, and it didn't bother him" (Rodgers, 1969, p. 154). The text then goes on to discuss details unrelated to this particular event, such as Lucille Burger's husband's prematurely reported death during the war and the exhilaration experienced by Lucille and other IBM employees when he was found alive. This additional context of the story provides addition insight into an analysis of the uncertainty for Lucille, the entourage, and Watson based on TMU.

Fear of espionage was common in the United States during World War II. The war made events and people unpredictable. For example, it was not clear who could be trusted. In an attempt to make the situation safer, more controlled, and more predictable, the United States government sent American citizens of Asian descent to prison camps for fear that they were traitors. As a company, IBM was producing classified equipment in this uncertain environment. This high level of environmental uncertainty was the setting that IBM employees faced, including those in the Lucille Burger story.

For Lucille the context provides two additional possibilities for cognitively managing her uncertainty in the situation. First, the addition of environmental uncertainty provides her with even more cognitive support for reducing uncertainty by enforcing the Security-Badge script. She could deny that there really was any contradiction in the situation. If those outside of IBM were concerned about security, then she should be as well. She should simply follow security procedures. Second, there was a possibility that she had heard of the Poughkeepsie events, although the story does not suggest that this is the case. If she heard about it, it would provide her even stronger encouragement to follow security procedures even for the CEO. Despite the fact that the additional information about the context potentially provides more certainty for guiding her actions, Lucille was still shaking as she refused admittance to the area. Apparently, even the uncertainty of war and the events at Poughkeepsie, if she were aware of them, did not prevent Lucille from being uncertain as to her behaviors.

Comments by Al Good, head of security, provide some additional insight into the uncertainty experience of the members of the entourage. His comments suggest that he did not feel particularly concerned about Watson's response. He was not so dependent on Watson because "With me it was just a job" (Rodgers, 1969, p. 154). However, he recognized that the entourage felt dependent on Watson. Because they were close to him, they did not feel like they could criticize him. This suggests that they used relational information as part of their cognitive processes to guide their behaviors and reduce their uncertainty in the situation. Rather than being motivated by uncertainty, they seemed motivated by concerns over relational maintenance. They wanted to maintain a close, supportive relationship with Watson. Supporting him meant supporting the Watson-as-CEO script.

This context provides a different understanding of Watson's communication during the story. As TMU suggests, group and organizational decision makers who experience environmental uncertainty must collectively manage their uncertainty. The context places Watson as representative of the decision makers for IBM rather than an individual facing uncertainty alone. The upper management of IBM had collectively adopted security rules in an effort to prevent foreign espionage during the war. These rules may even have been recommended to the decision makers at IBM by external parties such as military or government officials. Watson's tracking down the supervisor of the Poughkeepsie plant to reprimand him for lax security and his willingness to obey security measures at the Endicott plant as enforced by Lucille Burger suggest that his motivation was to reduce environmental uncertainty during the war. As representative of the decision makers of IBM, he was compelled by the rest of them to enforce the rules. This provides additional support for expecting that he was denying that there was any uncertainty in the situation. The environment was uncertain. Management (including him) had adopted security rules to control this uncertain environment. He had no choice but to enforce the security rules at the Poughkeepsie plant, and when Lucille enforced the rules at Endicott he also needed to follow them.

DISCUSSION

This analysis of the Lucille Burger story provides some additional insight into the story not offered in the two previous analyses. In addition, the analysis helps to further develop TMU while demonstrating its applicability to the analysis of texts, as well.

The two previous analyses of the story, Martin et al. (1983) and Mumby (1987), focused on the macro issues of the story and the telling of the story. Martin et al. (1983) examined how the action in the story and the retelling of the story contributed to the organizational culture of IBM; Mumby (1987) demonstrated how the story reified the power relations and ideology of the corporate elite at IBM. Analyzing the story with TMU provides an alternative understanding of the story by focusing attention on the communication behaviors of the individuals in the story rather than on the impact of the story on the organization.

By focusing on the micro issues of the story, this analysis considers the dilemmas the participants faced due to the uncertainty created by the events of the story and how each resolved the issue. By examining the communication of each of the parties in the story, the analysis provides insight into how they managed their uncertainty. Each party experienced uncertainty from the two competing scripts, Watson as CEO and Security Badge Procedures. Paradoxes or contradictions that cannot be resolved can be a source of uncertainty (Babrow, 2001b), particularly when equally attractive—or in this case, unattractive—alternatives exist (Brashers, 2001). And yet, although each party experienced uncertainty due to the same contradictory scripts, each responded to the uncertainty differently. Apparently unable to cognitively reduce her uncertainty, Lucille, shaking while she spoke, appeared to focus on impression management by creating an impression of herself as a competent employee following the rules of IBM rather than on reducing uncertainty. The entourage, opting for the Watson-as-CEO script, appeared to have decided that there really was no uncertainty and so expected that the CEO would not need the appropriate security badge. Watson also seemed to have cognitively disallowed that there was uncertainty in the situation, but still chose to avoid embarrassing the members of the entourage by nonverbally communicating his understanding of the situation rather than scolding them for their comments. As such, the analysis demonstrates how individuals responded differently to uncertainty in the immediate situation. This supports the idea in TMU that different people will respond differently to the same potentially uncertainty-producing events due to their differential understanding of the level of uncertainty, their abilities to use cognitive processes to reduce uncertainty, and the other competing motives they experience.

IMPLICATIONS FOR TMU

This analysis stresses the importance of the context of the events in considering how individuals manage uncertainty. Important additional insights into this story were gained by examining the context of the events of the story. Knowing that the events occurred during World War II and after a visit to another plant where security was lax helps explain the events in the story. Watson and IBM faced environmental uncertainty due to the war and their production of classified equipment. Watson and the decision makers at IBM appeared to have responded to the environmental uncertainty as defenders (Miles et al., 1978). In response to the uncertainty of war, they have created a particular response to the environment; they have created a niche by developing and producing classified equipment for the war effort. But to create stability for their product in the uncertain environment, they needed to prevent the environment from gaining knowledge of their equipment. Adopting security procedures and enforcing them created the stability they desired as defenders. Watson supported this strategy by reprimanding the head of security at the Poughkeepsie plant for lax security and by complying with Lucille's request that he have the correct security badge before entering her area.

Including the context of World War II and a previous plant visit as part of the context for analyzing the Lucille Burger story also suggests an important elaboration of the proposed TMU model. The environmental context becomes part of the experience of uncertainty for individuals and decision makers in organizations. As presented earlier, current events and their match with individuals' organizational scripts influence the experience of uncertainty. This analysis suggests that the general uncertainty in the environment has the ability to influence what may or may not serve as a trigger event of uncertainty. Events that may be perceived as creating uncertainty during one time period may not serve as a trigger of uncertainty at another time. If the Lucille Burger events had occurred during a time in which there was no war or fear of espionage, perhaps the communication and outcomes would have been quite different. Perhaps during a time of peace and certainty security procedures would only have applied to strangers and so the conflict between the two scripts would not have existed.

An example of the way that the general context of events influences the interpretation of those events occurred a few weeks after the terrorist attacks on the World Trade Center and Pentagon on September 11, 2001. Shortly after those tragic events, a passenger attacked a Greyhound bus driver in Tennessee, causing the bus to crash, killing six people. Due to the environmental uncertainty, a Terrorist Attack script was accessed by the executives at Greyhound and by the media in general. In response to this terrorist attack script, decision makers at Greyhound shut down all of their bus service nationwide temporarily. It seems unlikely that this script would have been retrieved if the incident had occurred a month earlier or that they would have shut down bus service nationwide after such an attack. At another time, the story would likely have been treated as an isolated event. At another time, the bus incident would have matched our scripts for random act of violence by estranged or deranged individuals, employees or partners. A few days after the bus attack, an executive for Greyhound released a statement that they now believed "this tragic accident was the result of an isolated act by a single deranged individual" (Bus driver gets credit, 2001). This "Deranged Individual" script would have been the only script accessed to understand the uncertainty of the bus attack if it had occurred a month earlier, prior to the attacks on the World Trade Towers. Examples such as this make the point that to more accurately view the experience of uncertainty, TMU needs to consider how general context and environmental uncertainty influence the experience of specific events that trigger uncertainty for individuals or groups.

The analysis of the Lucille Burger story also provided evidence of at least one additional competing motive that may influence communication relating to uncertainty events. The comments by Al Good, the supervisor of security, suggested that the members of the entourage were too close personally to Watson to question him or challenge him. His comments imply that the entourage was more motivated to maintain their relationship with Watson than with managing any uncertainty they may have experienced in this situation. Relationship maintenance was not presented as a competing motive in the earlier chapter. Although relationship maintenance may be considered a subset of impression management, it seems to have some distinctive characteristics. Whereas impression management focuses on self and maintaining an image, relationship maintenance focuses on the interaction or relationship between two parties. As such, the motive involves more concern for the other party than impression management.

Other examples can easily be imagined where relationship maintenance might be a more important motive than uncertainty reduction. If a close coworker goes on a tirade about your supervisor, you may not really understand what the complaint is or why the situation is so upsetting. However, rather than asking questions to reduce your uncertainty about these issues, you may choose to be supportive of your coworker, agreeing and supporting what is said despite a lack of understanding. Conversely, there may be times when you are not experiencing uncertainty about something your coworker is telling you about because it does not seem to involve you, and yet you continue to ask probing questions and listen attentively because you recognize that attending to your friend's concerns is important to your relationship even though you are not experiencing uncertainty.

Similarly, a group of organizational decision makers may experience uncertainty about one of their suppliers. They may want to question some aspect of the billing system that seems to put them at a disadvantage. However, because they value to relationship to that supplier, they may choose not to ask about the matter and focus instead on maintaining a friendly relationship with that supplier.

Overall, this analysis of the Lucille Burger story helped to increase an understanding of communication by focusing on the micro interactions of the participants rather than the macro implications of the story. The analysis also helped to emphasize the importance of exploring how the environmental context influences the scripts that are accessed in a situation that in turn influences the experience of uncertainty. The analysis also identified another potential competing motive, relationship maintenance, which can interact with uncertainty reduction to influence the information-seeking communication that occurs. Overall, this textual analysis provided support for TMU along with some useful elaborations of the model as presented in the previous chapters.

Implications and Conclusions

An ice cream store in a city I used to live in sold t-shirts with the slogan, "Life is uncertain. Eat dessert first." Even though most of us probably do not live with a feeling of impending doom in the next few hours, there are many people who feel that we live in very uncertain times in the 21st century. World events like unrest in the Middle East and the attacks on the World Trade Towers, economic instability in the financial markets at home and abroad, and a host of natural or manmade disasters contribute to the uncertainty we feel. Of course, people have been claiming that we live in uncertain times for years (Emery, 1967). Given the prevalence of uncertainty in the human condition, it is appropriate to study how people manage uncertainty through their communication.

There is a long history of studying uncertainty in human interaction in the social sciences. At least since the 1940s (Shannon & Weaver, 1949), scholars have considered how uncertainty relates to information and influences communication. In the 1970s, Berger and Calabrese (1975) first formalized a set of axioms and theorems concerning the role of uncertainty in interpersonal relationships. The first three chapters of this book reported the research that has previously been done based on uncertainty reduction theory, including research in both interpersonal and organizational contexts. The fourth chapter presented a model of a theory of managing uncertainty that addressed some of the criticisms from previous research in the area. It specifically applied the principles of TMU to organizational contexts at the individual, group, and organizational levels of analysis.

Chapters 5 through 7 reported results of three studies that helped to further validate and extend TMU. The use of qualitative methods in the first study demonstrated that organizational members use cognitive processes to manage their uncertainty and rely on a variety of methods to seek information. The quantitative methods in the second study examined the manner in which competing motives influence information-seeking strategies under different situations of uncertainty. The textual analysis in the third study demonstrated how TMU could be used to provide insight into the analysis of a particular situation in which uncertainty was experienced by a variety of organizational members interacting in a work setting. This final chapter considers the implications of these studies for TMU along with suggesting future applications of TMU to the study of uncertainty in organizational settings.

AN EXPANDED MODEL OF TMU

TMU is to be considered a work in progress, not a finalized version of a model or theory. It is expected that it will be a gradually changing model as some concepts or relationships are shown to be invalid. Other ideas or relationships will be added as researchers explore the model more thoroughly. Figure 8.1 represents the current development of TMU, although again the two-dimensional model fails to accurately represent the fluid, interactive nature of its components. It includes the concepts explicated in chapter 4 along with additional concepts that emerged from the three studies in chapters 5 through 7. The following text explains the relationships of these to the model as previously presented. In addition, a number of axioms are developed through the discussion.

Context

As presented in chapter 4, TMU did not include context as a specific part of the model, although context was implicit in the presentation. The analysis of the Lucille Burger story demonstrated the importance of adding context to TMU to understand how individuals experience uncertainty. Current events, such as World War II in the Lucille Burger story, can have a significant impact on how individuals experience uncertainty. Such events make some scripts and schemas more accessible for interpreting an uncertainty-producing event. More recently for example, in the months after the World Trade Towers attacks, every airline crash or train crash produced additional uncertainty because it was potentially another terrorist attack. Environmental uncertainty, such as uncertainty created by a falling stock market or the failure of several prominent organizations to accurately report their financial situations, such as Enron or World Com, created general uncertainty about interpreting financial information about other organizations where previously such uncertainty did not exist. These examples illustrate that the context influences the experience of uncertainty.

Not only can contextual factors influence the experience of uncertainty, but they may also influence or constrain other aspects of the TMU model, such as the cognitive processes for reducing uncertainty or behavioral choices for seeking information. For example, suppose you were in an organization where a number of employees had recently been dismissed due to sexual harassment charges. You had kept track of the cases and felt that the processes were fair. You genuinely believed the people deserved to be dismissed for their inappropriate behaviors. Then someone you knew and respected was charged with sexual harassment and claimed that the whole process made it impossible to respond appropriately to the

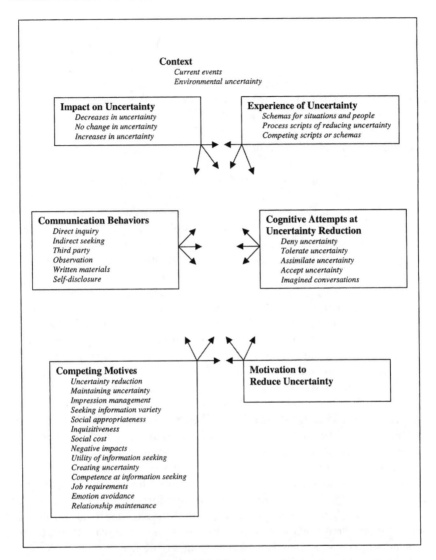

FIG. 8.1   An elaboration of the model for a theory of managing uncertainty.

charges once they were made. The context may impact your ability to use cognitive processes to reduce uncertainty and constrain your ability to seek information. If the case had occurred a number of years earlier, you may have reduced uncertainty by believing the respected friend's claim that the process was unfair. However, in the context of other cases seemly dealt with fairly, it might be difficult to accept the friend's claim. Also, the context might make it difficult to seek information. Asking your respected friend might make it appear that you have chosen sides in the case. Seeking information from a third party might accidentally give the impression of choosing the opposite side. As a result, you may feel constrained from seeking information at all except perhaps through observation. As this example illustrates, context influences the ability to cognitively reduce uncertainty and the behavioral choices for managing uncertainty. In light of this, the elaborated TMU model shows context encircling the rest of the model because it can influence all components of the model.

The Experience of Uncertainty

As presented, TMU suggests that the experience of uncertainty is related to the existence of scripts and schemas. When individuals have experiences that match scripts and schemas, they do not experience very much uncertainty. When they have no script or schema for a situation, the situation triggers the experience of uncertainty for them. They experience high levels of uncertainty because they do not understand the situation or know how to respond to it appropriately.

The studies presented led to further elaboration of factors contributing to the experience of uncertainty. Although initially the experience of uncertainty was expected to relate to the presence or lack of a script or schema for the situation, two additional concepts were delineated. The interviews with car salespeople suggested that they have content schemas and process scripts for managing the experience of uncertainty with customers. They can manage uncertainty by "pre-qualifying" customers based on the content schemas they have for customers. These schemas assist them in managing the descriptive, predictive (behavioral), or explanatory uncertainty (Berger & Bradac, 1982) they experience about their customers. Through these schemas they believe they know the customers and can accurately predict the outcomes of communication with them. In addition, car salespeople manage their uncertainty with their customers by having a process script for interacting with customers to seek information to reduce uncertainty. Having process scripts can be quite separate from content uncertainty about an event or individual. Having process scripts for managing uncertainty can assist individuals in managing uncertainty because the scripts provide the individuals with appropriate behaviors to enact in the situation even while they are experiencing uncertainty about other aspects of the situation.

Browning et al. (1999) found support for the importance of process scripts for managing uncertainty when they reported that a group of engineers were uncertain about why they were experiencing product irregularities, but certain about how to go about discovering the nature of the problem. The car valets in the same study were certain of the goal for the situation, but uncertain how to go about addressing the issue. The engineers had a process script for managing uncertainty in the situation, whereas the valets did not. Similarly, people generally have process scripts for managing uncertainty in initial interactions with others. They rely on typical patterns of questioning to meet others. These memory organization packets are routine, but adaptive (Kellerman, 1991). The scripts provide people with a process for reducing uncertainty in initial interactions. In others situations, such as an emergency, people often do not have process scripts to guide their responses to the uncertainty of the emergency. This leads to higher levels of uncertainty in such situations. Not only is there uncertainty about the nature of the emergency, but also there is uncertainty about how to respond to it. Of course, emergency personnel have scripts for such situations based on their training and experience. The distinction of a process script makes an important contribution to the understanding of how individuals manage uncertainty in organizational settings. This suggests a first axiom of TMU: Faced with uncertainty in a situation, individuals (or groups of individuals) will experience less uncertainty when they have a process script for managing the uncertainty in the situation than when they have no process script.

This axiom has some practical implications for members of organizations. Having a script or schema for a given situation reduces uncertainty in a situation by making it more predictable, a characteristic of most definitions of certainty. A novel situation creates more uncertainty because of the lack of a script or schema for the situation. This suggests that there is a great deal of value in creating crisis management policies or teams prior to actual problems. By developing contingency plans, that is to say scripts for dealing with potential problems, organizational members can better manage the uncertainty created when a problem arises. Even though it is not possible to anticipate all of the possible problems or crises that might occur, having scripts for managing uncertainty in a variety of situations will likely assist organizational members in dealing with even unanticipated problems that occur.

The Lucille Burger analysis also suggests an alternative source of uncertainty. In the Lucille Burger story, it was not the lack of a script for the situation that created the uncertainty. Rather it was the existence of two contradictory scripts (Watson as CEO and Security Badge Procedures), or two competing scripts, rather than a lack of a script that created uncertainty. Similar contradictory scripts create uncertainty for individuals in organizations on a regular basis. People receive two sets of incompatible directions. Members of groups and organizational decision makers must untangle the often apparently contradictory governmental rules and regulations. So it is not always the lack of scripts and schemas that creates uncertainty. It can be the overabundance and contradictory nature of information that creates uncertainty.

Cognitive Attempts at Uncertainty Reduction

TMU argues that, when faced with uncertainty, individuals will not always seek information. Instead they may manage their uncertainty through internal cognitive processes such as denying the uncertainty, tolerating the uncertainty, assimilating the uncertainty, or accepting the uncertainty. They may even have imaginary conversations in which they speculate about the information they would receive if they asked for it.

The research reported here found support for the concept that people use cognitive processes to manage uncertainty in situations to limit information seeking. Car salespeople used a variety of these approaches in their interactions with customers. The most common approach was to assimilate customers into categories based on limited information seeking, sometimes without interactive communication. They also may have used denial of uncertainty, tolerance of uncertainty, and possibly imagined conversations to manage their uncertainty with customers. The model also suggests that individuals can accept uncertainty or assimilate the uncertainty by viewing others as having cultural or attitudinal similarities as oneself instead of putting them into another category. Although no additional approaches for using cognitive processes to manage uncertainty were identified in this study, the results confirm the concept that individuals use cognitive processes or cognitive shortcuts to manage uncertainty in situations.

Motivation to Reduce Uncertainty

TMU indicates that individuals' motivation to reduce uncertainty is related to their ability to cognitively manage uncertainty. If they are able to manage the uncertainty on their own, they are unmotivated to seek information. If they are unable to use cognitive processes to reduce uncertainty, they remain motivated to seek information. The results from the interviews with car salespeople support this. The car salespeople suggested that when they were able to use cognitive processes to reduce their uncertainty about their customers, they did not seek information about them. If they decided the customer was a service customer or a previous customer with whom they did not want to interact again, they did not seek additional information. In addition, they typically were unconcerned about missing an opportunity for a sale in such situations. They successfully managed their uncertainty in the situation without seeking additional information. They were not motivated to seek information because they felt confident in their decision about the customers. These results suggest a second axiom of TMU: When individuals (or groups of individuals) can use internal cognitive processes to reduce uncertainty in a situation, they will be unmotivated to seek additional information.

This axiom offers some implications when observing individuals or groups in organizations. Facing a decision, an individual or a group may appear to avoid seeking information that an observer may feel would be vital for success. Such a failure to seek information is often a characteristic of the disastrous decisions made when groupthink occurs. This axiom suggests that the people in such situations do not seek information because they have been able to manage their uncertainty through internal, cognitive processes. Because they do not feel uncertain, they are not motivated to seek additional information.

Avoiding this problem will take more than reminders to be certain before act-ing or to seek enough information before making a decision, because the peo-ple involved will feel that they already have sufficient information to make a decision. Instead, it will take someone with the ability to make the individual or group feel uncertain about what they know before they will be motivated to seek information. This axiom suggests that it may take creating additional un-certainty to motivate individuals and groups to seek information beyond their own cognitive and internal processes.

Competing Motives

One of the unique contributions of TMU compared to URT is its inclusion of competing motives as explanations for communication behaviors. Where URT viewed uncertainty reduction as motivating communication behaviors in isola-tion from other motives and as the singular predictor of behaviors (Anderson, 1996), TMU suggests that other, competing motives may hinder or enhance the motivation to seek information through communication behaviors. A variety of competing motives were suggested based on previous research, such as impres-sion management, social appropriateness, social cost, and others.

The findings in the studies reported here suggest some additional elaborations and clarification of competing motives in TMU. Results from two of the studies suggest some additional competing motives that influence the relationship be-tween uncertainty reduction and communication behaviors. The study of car salespeople suggests that they sometimes are first motivated to create uncertainty for the customer about the character of car salespeople before they can begin to seek information from the customer to reduce their uncertainties. Specifically, be-cause some customers have negative expectations and stereotypes for car sales-people, car salespeople have trouble gaining information from them and must first change those perceptions by creating uncertainty about car salespeople so that the customers will consider that they do not fit the negative stereotype. By us-ing humor or expressing empathy toward the customers concerning previous en-counters with car salespeople, they are able to reach a point where the customers begin to consider that this particular salesperson may be trustworthy. When the car salesperson gets the customer to this point, they can ask the customer ques-tions they need to ask to reduce their own uncertainty.

The results of the Lucille Burger story analysis suggest an additional important competing motive, as well. According to the head guard, Tom Watson's entou-rage was motivated by a need to maintain a relationship with him and so other motives were dormant. They did not consider seeking information before re-sponding to Lucille because their primary motivation was to show loyalty to Wat-son. Certainly, the motivation to maintain relationships impacts individuals in other organizational settings as well. You may comfort a coworker after a report-edly disastrous presentation without really knowing what went wrong. You do not seek information about the presentation because you recognize that to do so would be painful for you coworker. To maintain a positive relationship, you simply provide comfort without reducing your uncertainty. Relationship maintenance is an important motive that competes with uncertainty reduction to cause or hinder information seeking.

The results from these studies and the discussion in the earlier chapter suggest the need to modify Berger and Calabrese's (1975) Axiom 3 while retaining its essence. They argued that uncertainty results in information seeking. TMU postulates this axiom: In the absence of competing motives, high levels of uncertainty cause increases in information-seeking behavior and as uncertainty levels decline, information-seeking behavior decreases.

TMU also suggests that not all information seeking is motivated primarily by uncertainty reduction. For example, to behave in a socially appropriate way people make polite conversation and ask questions of each other in social settings. The study of car salespeople also revealed another motive that may cause information seeking in organizational settings that is not motivated by uncertainty. Salespeople frequently asked customers if they were being helped or if they needed assistance as part of a job requirement. Some of the organizations had 10-foot rules or 1-minute rules that required them to speak to potential customers. Similarly, some occupations require information seeking to complete job requirements. For example, a receptionist routinely asks people for information to direct them to the appropriate places. Although it is true that the receptionist has uncertainty about the strangers, the primary motivation for seeking information is not to reduce uncertainty about the people, but to perform the job. The receptionist follows a process script for interacting with new people. The information is quickly forgotten because it was not gathered to reduce uncertainty about the person. Job requirements are another motivation for information seeking. This suggests the fourth axiom of TMU: Motives other than uncertainty reduction, such as social appropriateness and job requirements, can be the primary motivators for information seeking.

The practical implications of this axiom may be rather limited, but it does suggest some important observations for organizational settings. We have probably all been bothered at one time or another by a conversation with someone whom we politely ask about his or her background and interests, but who never reciprocates by asking us similar questions. We perhaps come away thinking that the person is a bore or has an ego problem. Although these are possible explanations, it could also be that the individual only seeks information when experiencing uncertainty and does not consider seeking information as a socially appropriate behavior in certain settings. Because future interaction is unlikely, the person may not experience uncertainty about you and may not ask you any questions. Teaching individuals like this the social skills of the politeness and reciprocity may not change how they manage their uncertainty, but it may change the kind of impression they leave on others that may influence future interactions. Teaching them to seek information out of politeness may assist them in their interactions with other organizational members.

The results from the scenario study reported in chapter 6 also suggest that the motives identified in previous research may not be as conceptually distinct as they first appeared. Although the factor analysis results from that study should be interpreted tentatively given their exploratory nature, they suggest a more complex picture of competing motives. Fear of negative outcomes reduced the likelihood of seeking information, but this scale was a combination of items designed to measure a couple of different motives. Further examination of the previously identified motives is needed. This includes the new motives identified in the studies reported here, relationship maintenance and creating uncertainty for others.

The results in the study also suggest that inquisitiveness may be an extremely important motive for understanding information seeking. Whereas uncertainty reduction motivates information seeking to address a particular uncertainty or concern, inquisitiveness is a more general motive. Inquisitiveness motivates information seeking out of curiosity and a more general desire for information without any specific concern or uncertainty. Frequently in the study, inquisitiveness was a motive that was rated as high as uncertainty reduction. The two appear to work in rather complimentary ways with each other. This deserves additional study in the future.

Other motives seem to inhibit information seeking. Relationship maintenance, impression management, and emotion avoidance are some of the suggested ones that seem to reduce the drive to seek information resulting from the experience of uncertainty. Taken together, this suggests Axiom 5 for TMU: Complementary motives, especially inquisitiveness, increase the motivation to seek information caused by high levels of uncertainty, whereas contrary motives, such as fear of negative impacts, decrease motivation to seek information.

There are a number of practical implications for organizational members from this axiom, which is really a corollary of Axiom 3. Newcomers in organizations provide an example of the implications of Axioms 3 and 5. If newcomers were only motivated by uncertainty, then seeking information would go unhindered until they become competent at their jobs and become skilled contributors to the organization. This probably only happens in rare occasions. More often, a variety of competing motives may prevent this. As the results of the scenario study suggest, the newcomers must also be convinced that there are no negative consequences for seeking information before they will freely seek the information that they need based on their uncertainty levels. Supervisors and coworkers can communicate that there are no negative consequences for asking for help. This can help to create an environment where information seeking by newcomers is not hindered by the fear of negative outcomes.

Communication Behaviors

A limitation of some research on uncertainty reduction is the focus on direct, interactive information seeking. TMU suggests that individuals use a wide range of information-seeking strategies, from direct inquiry to observation to consulting written materials. The results from the research here seem to primarily confirm the use of various strategies identified in previous research as information-seeking behaviors. The use of direct inquiry is obviously a very common approach to seeking information. Salespeople reported having a series of qualifying questions they ask as part of their process script for managing uncertainty. Respondents to the scenarios frequently indicated that they would ask the person for the information they needed. The use of indirect inquiry, third parties, and written materials were frequently reported. Car salespeople relied on reciprocity norms to seek information. They used self-disclosure to attempt to encourage self-disclosure from their customers in order to create a positive relationship with them.

The importance of observation as an information seeking strategy was emphasized in the study of car salespeople. It seemed apparent that they gained a great deal of information from their customers through what they observed, in addition to what was said. Clearly, in other organizational settings, people make similar use of observation. It is not necessary to ask some people about their mood because it is easy to tell simply by observing them. The arrangement of an office may communicate to visitors whether they are welcome or not. These results suggest Axiom 6 for TMU: Although direct inquiry is the preferred method of seeking information in many situations, individuals (and groups of individuals) rely heavily on other methods of gathering information in other situations.

Although this axiom may seem rather self-evident at this point, too often researchers of uncertainty reduction have failed to examine the wide variety of information-seeking behaviors available to people and have focused narrowly on direct inquiry. The implications for organizational members are also fairly easy to see. Whereas the savvy organizational members know to make use of a wide variety of information-seeking strategies, the newcomer or the less socially skilled member may be unaware of the many options available. Others may be aware of the choices, but not of the possible problems with relying on any particular strategy. For example, observation may be the most unobtrusive way to gain information, but it is also the strategy that can most easily result in incorrect information. Direct inquiry may be least likely to result in incorrect information, but it also has the most social cost associated with it. Increasing awareness of the choices for information seeking and the advantages and disadvantages of each strategy may assist individuals in gaining the information they need in the most advantageous manner.

As it currently is written, Axiom 6 is rather general. It does not make specific predictions as to which situations will likely produce particular information-seeking behaviors. Further research is needed to enable more specific predictions to be made as to the relative impact of various personality variables, contextual factors, and competing motives. Current research has only begun to explore these issues.

Impact on Uncertainty

As initially developed, URT suggested that information increases certainty and liking in initial interactions. A number of researchers have previously demonstrated that this is not always the case. TMU holds that information can either increase or decrease uncertainty and may increase or decrease liking. The results of the studies reported here support this more varied response to information seeking. For example, through interaction with some customers, car salespeople became certain that they did not like specific customers and did not want to interact with them any longer. The information gained resulted in a decrease of liking. Of course, if they found out that the customer was eager to buy that day, the information gained resulted in an increase in liking. Airline pilots involved in an acquisition reduced their uncertainty as they gained information, but became less positive about the transaction as they became certain that they were losing some of their seniority in the process (Kramer et al., in press). Similarly, new employees frequently receive information on the job that is not what they expect. The unmet expectations results in negative affect and lower job satisfaction. However, when they find that the new job is better than expected, they are more satisfied with the job. This suggests that the positive or negative nature of the information gained, not the amount of information, determines the affective response to the information. Thus, Axiom 7 for TMU is this: The positive or negative valence of the information gained in reducing uncertainty determines whether information gained increases or decreases liking.

The implications of this axiom are somewhat problematic. For example, an organizational representative could manipulate information given to prospective clients or employees in such a way that only positive information is given out to increase liking and increase the chances of gaining a client or employee. However, in the long run, the ethical and practical results of such a strategy may be quite negative as dissatisfied former clients and employees give out negative information after their expectations are not met. Of course, providing only negative information would also not be effective because potential clients and employees would probably go elsewhere. Apparently, some balance would be most effective. Research on realistic job previews suggests that such a balance of positive and negative information has long-term advantages (e.g., Wanous, Poland, Premack, & Davis, 1992) but does not provide a formula for balancing the information. So, although, this axiom describes the reality of information giving, it does not provide a prescription for success.

In addition to information gained from communication motivated by uncertainty reduction, the results in these studies suggest that behaviors motivated by motives other than uncertainty reduction can impact uncertainty. For example, the analysis of Lucille Burger suggests that she was motivated primarily by impression management concerns. Despite this, her behaviors resulted in uncertainty reduction. Her effort to manage her impression by demonstrating her competence in following the rules of the job by requesting that Watson have the appropriate badge resulted in Watson clarifying for her that she had done the appropriate behavior when he sent for his badge. His response reduced her uncertainty even though her motivation for the particular communication behaviors was impression management. This same type of result occurs in other organizational settings. As part of a job requirement, an employee working in the benefits department may routinely ask questions to fill in necessary paperwork. Although the motivation is completing the task, when she discovers that a new employee is from her same hometown, her motivation and uncertainty about the person changes. She now expects that they have things in common, but is also uncertain about other commonalities. The conversation shifts to one managing uncertainty as the two talk about whether they know some of the same people, attended the same high school, and so forth. Afterwards it returns to task-related communication.

Summary

Overall, the results of the research reported here suggest robust support for TMU as presented. The results did not contradict any of the ideas suggested earlier, but they did add clarification and elaboration of those ideas. TMU provides a plausible model for examining how individuals and groups of individuals manage uncertainty in organizational settings. Table 8.1 summarizes the axioms suggested by the model in the previous discussion.

UNCERTAINTY AND SENSEMAKING REVISITED

As proposed, TMU fails to maintain the distinctions between uncertainty and sensemaking research that are often made. For example, TMU suggests that scripts and schemas help prevent the experience of uncertainty, and cognitive processes can be used to manage uncertainty without seeking information. These two processes involve recalling past experiences and events to understand current situations. Based on Miller and Jablin (1991), TMU suggests that surveillance is used to gather information that may not be understood until later. TMU includes the possibility of both active and retrospective uncertainty reduction, as did Berger and Calabrese (1975) initially. As a result, TMU begins to include the characteristics of retrospective sensemaking (Weick, 1995, 2001).

In addition, TMU does not distinguish between situations in which there are multiple meanings or lack of meaning. In both situations additional information is needed to clarify appropriate behaviors. Weick (1995) discusses sensemaking as situations in which people need to know values, priorities, and preferences because of the existence of multiple meanings or equivocality. TMU would see gain-

TABLE 8.1

The Seven Axioms of a Theory of Managing Uncertainty

Number	Axiom
1.	Faced with uncertainty in a situation, individuals (or groups of individuals) will experience less uncertainty when they have a process script for managing the uncertainty in the situation than when they have no process script.
2.	When individuals (or groups of individuals) can use internal cognitive processes to reduce uncertainty in a situation, they will be unmotivated to seek additional information.
3.	In the absence of competing motives, high levels of uncertainty cause increases in information-seeking behavior, and as uncertainty levels decline, information-seeking behavior decreases.
4.	Motives other than uncertainty reduction, such as social appropriateness and job requirements, can be the primary motivation for information seeking.
5.	Complementary motives, especially inquisitiveness, increase the motivation to seek information caused by high levels of uncertainty, whereas contrary motives, such as fear of negative impacts, decrease motivation to seek information.
6.	Although direct inquiry is often the preferred method of seeking information in many situations, individuals (or groups of individuals) rely heavily on other methods of gathering information in other situations.
7.	The positive or negative valence of the information gained in reducing uncertainty determines whether information gained increases or decreases liking.

ing knowledge of values, priorities, and preferences as specific types of information needed to manage uncertainty. Situations that lack information to create meaning or have information that creates multiple possible meanings are considered uncertainty management problems.

In addition, by using quantitative, qualitative, and textual methods of analysis in this book, TMU crosses the methodological divides that have implicitly divided these two types of research. The research presented indicates that TMU can be studied through various research methods. Each method provided unique insights into TMU while addressing specific issues or concerns.

Taken together, TMU blurs the distinctions that have been made between uncertainty management and sensemaking processes. For some people (separators), this blurring of the distinctions between the two is probably a concern or even an offense. For others (combiners), further attempts at integrating the two bodies of literature may be valuable in the future.

LEVELS OF ANALYSIS

As proposed TMU can be used to examine how individuals manage uncertainty at the individual level of analysis, as well as at the group and organizational levels.

The studies reported in this volume have focused on only the individual level of analysis in organizational settings. They have provided some insight into how individuals use cognitive processes to reduce uncertainty and how competing motives influence their information seeking. They have not explored how collections of individuals manage their uncertainty. Viewing uncertainty as combination of individual, group, and organizational phenomena allows research to address multiple concerns (Driskill & Goldstein, 1986).

It would be useful to explore how groups and organizational decision makers talk to manage their collective uncertainty. Participation in groups provides us with anecdotal evidence that there is talk about these important issues. Group members and organizational decision makers may actively discuss their levels of uncertainty. During decision making, they ask questions like "What do we know?" and "What don't we know?" These seem designed to help the group assess their level of uncertainty. In addition, these questions suggest that the group members are relying on internal group processes and easily accessible information to reduce uncertainty rather than using external information seeking. These comments suggest that groups use internal processes to manage uncertainty, the equivalent of cognitive processes at the individual level.

Group members and organizational decision makers also sometimes ask questions like, "Who can we ask?" or, "Where can we get this information?" These seem designed to have the group consider what communication behaviors are appropriate given the level of uncertainty they are experiencing. This is quite similar to how individuals consider whom to talk to in order to manage uncertainty. The comments clearly indicate reliance on external information seeking rather than internal cognitive processes to gain information.

Sometimes group members and organizational decision makers ask questions like, "Do we have the time to get this information or do we need to act now?" or, "Is it worth the trouble to find out or should we just go ahead with what we've got?" Discussions like these seem to represent the ways that competing motives influence information seeking at the group level. The first question considers if they have the resources to seek information, whereas the second question asks whether it is worth expending the resources even if they are available. The questions might suggest that uncertainty reduction will not be the primary motive for the actions taken.

Group members and organizational decision makers sometimes make suggestions like, "Just ask the boss," or, "We don't want to look stupid. So hint around and see if you can get the boss to tell you without asking," or, "Do some research on this and get back to us." These all describe different information-seeking strategies that could be used. They also suggest that competing motives may or may not influence information seeking. Even though group members may rely on direct, interactive information seeking, they also may rely on a number of alternative strategies identified here, particularly if impression management (not wanting to look stupid) inhibits direct information seeking.

Finally, when someone says, "We're back to square one," it is an indication that the uncertainty in the situation has not changed significantly. Sometimes information seeking reduces uncertainty and allows the decision makers to move forward with confidence. At other times, information seeking simply makes no change in uncertainty or causes increases in uncertainty.

This volume has suggested a number of ideas about the ways that group members or organizational decision makers manage their collective uncertainty. However, only limited research has explored these issues, and the research reported here does not advance our knowledge of these processes. Future research needs to systematically examine these topics. It is not apparent how often groups actively manage their uncertainty versus allowing it to wax and wane on its own.

At the collective level it would also be possible to assess the way in which the strategies used by groups or organizational decision makers to manage their uncertainty impact their effectiveness. Prescriptive and descriptive models of decision making imply that managing uncertainty is critical to effective decision making (e.g., Dewey, 1910; Hirokawa & Rost, 1992). In addition, certain responses to uncertainty are likely to have more positive outcomes than others. It would be valuable to develop an understanding of which approaches are more effective, instead of simply predicting when groups and decision makers will respond to uncertainty (Goldsmith, 2001). It may be that those who actively discuss their level of uncertainty and seek information to reduce their uncertainty make better decisions and are more successful. Research on groupthink (Janis, 1972) and ineffective decision making (Hirokawa et al., 1988) suggests that groups that fail to address their uncertainties make ineffective decisions. However, research on newcomers (Morrison, 1993b) and transferees (Kramer, 1993) suggests that receiving unsolicited information is quite important for managing uncertainty in employee adjustment. It may be that groups that receive information without actively seeking it are most effective. It may be more important that groups monitor and observe the available information than that they actively seek information. It would also be important to examine why some groups receive more information than others without seeking it.

The amount of information seeking the group conducts may be important to consider in determining its effectiveness. Although some groups may jump to conclusions too quickly at times, other groups may become stuck in the paralysis of analysis if they continue to seek information indefinitely. For example, Ancona and Caldwell (1992) noted that members of one ineffective group never were able to stop seeking information and finalize their decisions. We can probably all think of examples of groups that took action too soon and floundered as a result or of groups that were ineffective because they were too slow in taking action. It would be useful to explore how effective groups balance the need to seek information to reduce uncertainty with the need to take action before doing a never-ending, exhaustive search for information.

Similarly, how groups or organizational decision makers go about seeking information when they experience collective uncertainty may impact their effectiveness. Some groups may be quite systematic about the process assigning responsibilities to specific individuals. Others may be quite general, asking all members to find out what they can. This could result in finding repetitive data, but not the information that is actually needed to make an informed choice. In either case the individuals may choose to present themselves as representatives of the group seeking information or not. There may be a difference in saying, "My team has asked me to find out from you" versus saying, "I was wondering if you could help me." The information the group receives may vary according to how the request for information is presented.

Although this volume has not examined the relationships between different approaches to managing uncertainty and outcomes like effectiveness, it lays the groundwork for such a line of research. Results of such research would provide additional practical advice to organizational members on the most effective or efficient ways to manage uncertainty in various situations.

AREAS OF UNCERTAINTY

In addition to concentrating on the individual level of analysis, the studies reported in the previous chapters and many of the examples provided throughout the book have focused on understanding relationships with other people. Cragan and Shields (1998) describe this as social information and suggest that URT has been limited to this examining of uncertainty of this type of relational information. TMU can be used more broadly to address many of the other types of uncertainties that exist in organizational settings. In addition to being uncertain about other individuals in an organization, people in organizations may experience uncertainty about the culture of the organization, the way communication networks work in the organization, and any number of other concerns. Many of these concerns are suggested in chapter 3 in the discussion of the types of uncertainty newcomers' experience. As indicated there in Table 3.1 newcomers experience uncertainty about their relationships with others, about their roles and how they will be evaluated in them, about the norms and culture of the organizational, about how information flows through organizational networks, and about politics or power distributions in the organization. Because the research reported in the preceding chapters focused on managing uncertainty in relationships with others, the following pages discuss a number of these other organizational topics that involve uncertainty that can be examined using TMU. Some of these topics involve more than just the individual level of analysis.

Role Negotiation and Evaluation

Organizational members experience uncertainty because they are in a constant process of negotiating their organizational roles; this process continues throughout the entire time they associate with the organization (Jablin, 2001). Role negotiation involves two or more people interacting to establish or alter the expectations about the role behaviors and how they will be evaluated (Miller, Jablin, Casey, Lamphear-Van Horn, & Ethington, 1996). It involves the interaction of role-taking, in which individuals attempt to meet the expectations of others, and role-making, in which individuals pursue their own goals and purposes (Jablin, 1987). Although newcomers may experience the highest levels of uncertainty about their roles and how they will be evaluated in them, organizational members experience varying levels of uncertainty throughout their careers in organizations including during career transitions, such as after job promotions (Kramer & Noland, 1999) or job transfers (Kramer, 1993). But even when there are no overt job transitions, roles are constantly being negotiated even if it results in maintaining the current role. This negotiation process creates uncertainty for the individual negotiating his or her role, as well as for the members of the group adjusting to the changing role expectations. Then, once roles are negotiated, feedback provides evaluative information concerning whether members are meeting their role expectations. Feedback reduces uncertainty by assisting in error detection and by providing knowledge of performance of self and groups or units (Downs, Johnson, & Barge, 1984). TMU provides a useful lens for examining how individuals manage uncertainty related to the role negotiation process.

TMU suggests that individuals with previous experience in similar roles should experience less uncertainty during the role negotiation process. Prior experience reduces uncertainty about role behaviors and provides frameworks for cognitively managing uncertainty in a given situation by assimilating it with previous experiences. But even when organizational members do experience uncertainty about their roles and are motivated to seek information, TMU suggests that they must balance their need to reduce uncertainty with other competing motives as they consider seeking information. For example, transferees balance their need for information to reduce uncertainty with their impression management concerns (Callister et al., 1999). Due to various competing motives, instead of directly seeking information organizational members may rely on indirect strategies such as indirect or third-party inquiries to gain feedback, and instead of directly negotiating their roles they may test the role limits by stretching or breaking norms to determine the real role expectations (Miller & Jablin, 1991).

The collective work group also must manage uncertainty as individual group members negotiate their roles. Changes in role expectations for one member of a group simultaneously impact the role expectations for other members of the group. For example, employees experience uncertainty about their own work situations when individuals transfer from their workgroup and as they adjust to their replacements (Kramer, 1989). TMU suggests that some workgroups may experience limited uncertainty about changing membership and roles if this is a common behavior. For example, some workgroups are regularly used as training groups for up-and-coming management personnel. Workgroup members in such groups may experience little uncertainty because they already have a process for dealing with new, temporary supervisors or because they can manage the uncertainty they experience by associating the new supervisor with some category of previous supervisor they have had. When workgroup members are motivated to seek information by their uncertainty, they must still balance uncertainty reduction with other motives, according to TMU. For example, the need to appear competent may preclude the group members from directly asking for the information they need about a new supervisor. As a result, they may rely on observation to gain the information they need instead of directly seeking information.

Role negotiation is a constant process for those associating with organizations. TMU provides a framework for examining how individuals and the collective group manage the uncertainty associated with this process. Cognitive processes assist individuals in reducing the experience of uncertainty or in managing it without seeking information. The need to balance competing motives helps explain why information seeking does not always follow at the levels that might be expected.

Organizational Culture

One of the primary areas of uncertainty facing organizational members, especially as newcomers, is understanding an organization's culture. Although there is no precise definition of culture, most scholars agree that organizational culture is the shared meanings or understandings that make up and affect the beliefs, values, and behaviors of an organization and which are manifest in members' communication behaviors including stories, reminiscences, and rituals that create a symbolic common ground for its members (Barnett, 1988; Sathe, 1983; Smircich & Calas, 1987). Because an organization's culture must be enacted or performed (Pacanowsky & O'Donnell-Trujillo, 1983), the culture is constantly changing and evolving. As a result, it continues to be a source of uncertainty for organizational members, not just newcomers, as members experience the changing norms, values, and behaviors of the culture.

Martin's (1992) work emphasizes the uncertainty of the experience of an organization's culture when she provides three cultural lenses or perspectives for examining it. From an integrated perspective, employees share meanings and behaviors, much like the general definition of culture given previously suggests. From a differentiated perspective, subgroups or subcultures exist that share meanings and behaviors within their subcultures but that may differ significantly from other groups or subcultures in an organization. From a fragmented perspective, there exist ambiguities and uncertainties with only temporary moments of clarity and agreement in the culture. Because the combination of all three perspectives provides the most complete understanding of an organization's culture (Meyerson & Martin, 1987), researchers have examined organizations using all three perspectives (Hylmo & Buzzanell, 2002; Kramer & Berman, 2001). This suggests that organizational members will experience uncertainty about the culture as they have experiences that are suggestive of the various perspectives. For example, if an event suggests lack of unity or even disputing subcultures, members will experience uncertainty about the overall culture.

TMU can provide insight into how individuals and groups within an organization manage their uncertainty about the culture. For example, Smith and Eisenberg (1987) discuss how employees at Disneyland reacted when layoffs were announced, since the organization used a family metaphor to describe itself. Because layoffs were inconsistent with the metaphor of family (you don't lay off family members), many employees experienced uncertainty and even anger. TMU could explain many of the possible responses that occurred in response to this event.

For those individuals or groups of employees who accepted the Disney-as-family metaphor, the layoffs would be inconsistent with the family schema. These individuals would experience high levels of uncertainty, not only about their own job security, but also about the true culture of the organization. Many would be unable to cognitively manage this uncertainty and so would seek information. Seeking information by discussing the situation with other similar employees probably did not reduce their uncertainty, because the others also did not know what the layoffs meant. Actively seeking information from Disney management, or perhaps passively receiving it, would help them manage uncertainty. Management explained that the correct metaphor for Disney was family entertainment, not family of employees (Smith & Eisenberg, 1987). Such information would probably not please these employees, but it would enable them to manage their uncertainty since they now know what the family metaphor means.

For those individuals or groups of employees who were more skeptical and who did not believe that Disney really was a family, the layoffs may have produced very little uncertainty about the culture, although probably more about their job security. If they did experience uncertainty, these individuals may have managed it cognitively by assimilating the situation with other situations or experiences like it. They might recall other businesses that have used a family metaphor when times are good, but laid off employees when times were bad and conclude that Disney is just like other businesses. They could reach this conclusion without seeking any addition information. If they did not manage it cognitively, they may have managed it by seeking information from other equally cynical employees who shared their differentiated subculture understanding of Disney. Through discussions with like-minded employees, they reached an understanding that Disney was a business first that protected management, but that employees like themselves were replaceable. The messages from management about Disney as family entertainment, not a family of employees, would simply confirm their understanding of a typical corporate culture that separates management and employees and focuses on the bottom line.

Employees who interacted with both the true believers of the Disney-as-family metaphor and the cynical employees might experience the most uncertainty in this situation. By being exposed to two different perspectives on the layoffs, they might experience Disney as a fragmented culture and wonder about its real culture. TMU would suggest that these individuals would perhaps be most motivated to seek information since they have no cognitive processes for managing uncertainty on their own. However, as they find conflicting ideas about what the situation means, they may continue to experience high levels of uncertainty. As these analyses suggest, TMU can be used to explain multiple responses to the same uncertainty-producing event in an organization.

Understanding the culture of an organization is a primary task for members. TMU suggests ways to examine how members gain understanding of the culture through cognitive processes and information seeking at either the individual or the collective level. In addition, TMU suggests ways people manage uncertainty about particular aspects of an organization's culture.

Emotion Management Norms.   One specific aspect of an organization's culture that involves managing uncertainty concerns the organizational norms for emotion management. The management of emotion in the workplace has increasingly been recognized as an important part of organizational life, since emotions are inseparable from life experiences (Ashforth & Humphrey, 1995). Much of the research in this area has focused on the emotion display norms for frontline employees who interact with the general public and customers (Morris & Feldman, 1996). In order to reduce uncertainty for these employees concerning emotion management, some organizations explicitly teach them to display positive emotions in occupations like flight attendants or convenience store clerks (Hochschild, 1983; Rafaeli, 1989) or negative emotions in occupations like bill collectors (Sutton, 1991). Supervisors then reinforce the display rules by observing them and rewarding them for following the norms or punishing them when they do not (Van Maanen & Kunda, 1989). In these types of frontline occupations, there would appear to be limited uncertainty after training and reinforcement for employees concerning how to display emotions appropriately, although some may resist following those emotion display rules.

While frontline employees may experience limited uncertainty about their interactions with customers and the public, organizational members have most of their interactions involving emotion with coworkers and supervisors (Waldron, 1994). For these interactions, there appears to be a general understanding that employees should act professionally. The exact nature of what is professional emotion management is rarely if ever explicitly stated, but professionalism seems to involve limiting the expression of extremely positive or negative emotions by masking them with a more neutral appearance (Kramer & Hess, 2002). To gain an understanding of the norms of professional emotion management in their interactions with coworkers, employees must reduce their uncertainty through processes like those suggested by TMU.

TMU suggests that some members will have developed schemas for appropriate emotion management through previous education and work experiences and experience little uncertainty if they have worked in a similar environment previously. Others will experience uncertainty about emotion management initially, but then rely on cognitive process to manage their uncertainty. For example, an employee might consider that there is little chance for future interaction with an employee visiting from an out-of-town facility and therefore conclude that using the same emotion management rule for working with customers of presenting a positive front would be appropriate. In other cases, employees may actively seek information about emotion management rules or professionalism by asking someone, although many seem to rely more on passively learning through observation (Kramer & Hess, 2002). If emotions are intensely displayed at an initial meeting, a new employee may ask someone about this norm or choose to observe several meetings to reduce uncertainty about this norm. Overtime, the employee gains an understanding of when emotions can be more openly displayed (e.g., department meetings), and when they should be managed (when the public is present or in companywide meetings with upper management). This allows them to manage their uncertainty about emotion display rules.

This last example suggests that at the group and organizational level uncertainty about emotion management is also an issue. For example, I have been a member of congregations in which the display of disagreement and anger at meetings was fairly routine and others where there seemed to be a conscious effort to eliminate any negative displays of emotion. Interestingly, I found both situations equally upsetting to me as a member. The display of emotions was upsetting, but the suppression of emotions was equally upsetting to me. Regardless of which is the norm, uncertainty about the norm must be managed at the group or organizational level as the collective members develop an understanding of what is the appropriate display of emotions in their particular setting. Managing emotions is a specific area of an organization's culture in which individuals and groups must manage uncertainty through the processes explained in TMU.

Work-Family Policies. A second specific area of organizational culture that could be examined using TMU is the work-family norms. Organizations and researchers have become increasingly aware that work and family influence each other. For example, there is a general spillover of work and nonwork attitudes and moods (Rousseau, 1978; Staines, 1980; Williams & Alliger, 1994). Conflicts at home impact the workplace, and conflicts at work impact home life (Frone, Russell, & Couper, 1992). As a result, organizations have developed a wide range of organizational policies in an attempt to help members manage these issues. These policies include, but are not limited to, onsite childcare, flextime scheduling, job sharing, telecommuting, and maternal and paternal leave policies.

Regardless of the intentions of the organizational policy makers, these policies potentially create uncertainty for members as they attempt to understand them as a part of an organization's culture. Uncertainty is created for members individually and collectively as they decide on the meaning of the policies for them. Employees experience uncertainty as they attempt to determine whether the company adopted the policies only to improve its image as a worker-friendly organization or if the employees are actually supposed to use the adopted policies. For example, in many organizations there is pressure within the organization against taking maternity leaves because it suggests that the individual is less committed to her career, and there is concern that she will not return (Miller et al., 1996). TMU suggests some of the ways that employees may manage their uncertainty about these policies.

Based on previous experience and the resulting scripts and schemas, individuals may not experience any uncertainty about these policies. If, in prior experience with the company, such policies proved to be window dressing that was never actually intended to be used, employees may not experience much uncertainty about the new worker-friendly policies because they are certain they mean nothing. Work will continue to be the top priority as before. For example, Microsoft has many family-friendly work policies and yet most employees work long hours and reportedly receive phone calls from Bill Gates if they do not spend enough time in the office on weekends (Andrews, 2000). Alternatively, employees may manage their uncertainty about work-family polices through cognitive processes without seeking information. For example, single employees may decide to tolerate the uncertainty they experience about these policies because they believe that the policies will not impact them, at least in the near future. Employees unable to manage their uncertainty through cognitive processes may rely on a variety of methods to gain information about the real policies. They may directly ask their supervisors if they can actually use flextime scheduling. However, if they are concerned more about creating a positive impression for their supervisors than about reducing their uncertainty, they may observe others to see if they take advantage of it rather than directly seeking information about the policies. Throughout this process they are negotiating the meaning of the work-family policies for them, as well as their own particular role in the organization.

Beyond individuals managing their own uncertainty about the policies and their roles, organizational members must collectively manage their uncertainty about the work-family policies. They may discuss the meaning of the policies to understand how the implications may differ for married and single people. Through conversation they may attempt to create informal norms about when it is appropriate to use flextime scheduling and when it is not. For example, it may become the norm that people use flextime at the beginning of projects when people can work somewhat independently, but never during the last week of a project, as deadlines approach and interdependence is critical.

The work-family policies (or lack of such policies) of an organization are part of its culture. Employees individually and collectively must manage the uncertainty they experience about such issues. This is an ongoing process, not one that is ever completed. The cultural norms for these issues formally and informally change over time. TMU provides a useful way to explore how employees manage their uncertainties about them.

Diversity.   As we embark on the 21st century, workplace demographics are changing. The workplace is becoming increasing diverse with significant increases of women, American minorities, and international employees. These changing demographics result in changes in organizational cultures through new values and beliefs and different communication patterns and rituals. A variety of evidence indicates that the changes in diversity produce increases in uncertainty for organizational members. For example, diverse workgroups initially scored lower on process and performance effectiveness as they were less certain of how to interact, but over time they scored the same or higher than homogenous groups (Watson, Kumar, & Michaelsen, 1993). In addition, the organizational context in which the diversity occurs impacts the experience of uncertainty. For example, diverse workgroups interact differently depending on whether the organization has a monolithic culture in which the vast majority of employees are of the same demographic, a plural culture in which diversity is represented in moderate numbers but mostly in lower level jobs, or a multicultural culture in which diversity is present in representative numbers at all levels of the organization (Larkey, 1996). In addition, at the group level, groups with a single minority member interact differently than those with multiple minority members (Li, Karakowsky, & Siegel, 1999). TMU provides a way of exploring and explaining the impact of diversity on workgroup members as an uncertainty management process.

Members of monolithic organizations would experience the most uncertainty in their interactions with minorities due to the infrequency of interaction with them, while members of multicultural organizations should have more developed scripts and schemas that enable them to experience less uncertainty or manage it without seeking information. In either setting, new groups with diverse members may initially experience uncertainty that causes them to be less effective than homogenous groups. However, as they interact over time, through observation and inquiries, they can reduce their uncertainty and begin interacting as effectively and productively as other, more homogenous groups.

Collectively, the organizational members must determine what the changing demographics mean for the organization's culture. The members may feel the organization is committed to creating a multicultural culture or simply a plural culture that keeps minorities out of important positions. If members feel that a glass ceiling exists this may indicate the existence of subcultures in the organization distinguished in part by the opportunities that exist depending on gender or race

(Buzzanell, 1995). Through communication with others, members gradually reduce their uncertainty about diversity and possible subcultures in the organization. They may become satisfied or dissatisfied with the organization as they
reach an understanding of this aspect of its culture. Their response may cause
them to accept the culture or act to change it.

Diversity in the workforce is changing organizations' cultures. TMU suggests
ways, individually and collectively, the members manage their uncertainty about
the changing culture. It helps explain how experience with a diverse workforce
over time results in reduced levels of uncertainty as employees develop scripts and
schemas for interacting with each other.

Communication Networks

A more functional concern than the organization's culture that creates uncertainty for organizational members would be uncertainty about the way communication networks function in an organization. Communication networks
indicate who talks to whom within an organization about what topics and with
what frequency. Because there are multiple goals and functions in organizations,
there is not a single communication network in an organization, but rather multiple networks that deal with different topics and frequently involve different people. These content-specific networks include task (how do I complete my job?),
social (who are my friends?), authority (who is really in charge?), political (how do
I get things done or changed around here?), and innovation (where do new ideas
come from?) networks (O'Reilly & Roberts, 1977; Tushman, 1977a, 1977b). Using
the lens of TMU to examine communication networks provides insight into how,
individually and collectively, organizational members manage uncertainty.

Individually, members can gain information to reduce their uncertainty through
their network contacts. Faced with uncertainty that they cannot manage alone
through cognitive processes, organizational members can rely on their network
links for information. This could include actively seeking information from their
network links, as well as passively receiving information through these contacts.
Network linkages that provide individuals with different types of information (mul-
tiplex linkages) provide the most uncertainty-reducing communication (Albrecht &
Hall, 1991). This indicates that if a specific coworker can perhaps serve as a source of
information about getting jobs done and who is influential in organization, while
being a friend, that coworker will help manage uncertainty for the individual. TMU
would suggest that the information that the coworker provides is gained both
through various direct inquiries, such as asking who to contact about a particular issue, as well as through passive receptions, such as when the coworker casually discusses how things really work in the organization. It is likely that network linkages
provide the passively received information that is so crucial to newcomers' and
transferees' positive adjustment (Morrison, 1993a; Kramer, 1993). Through com-

munication with their network linkages, members actively and passively receive information that enables them to manage uncertainty about their organization.

Collectively, as organizational members experience uncertainty about a changing environment, about simple and complex tasks, and about the interdependencies of those tasks, communication networks provide the information processing to manage those uncertainties (Tichy, 1981). The exchange of information through communication networks provides the information necessary to reduce uncertainty about the various issues and topics. For example, organizations develop innovation networks to assist them in gaining information and ideas for managing uncertainties (Albrecht & Hall, 1991). TMU suggests that it is through both internal and external processes that individuals collectively manage their uncertainty. Thus, it suggests the need to examine the information flow of both intra-organizational and inter-organizational networks. Whereas intra-organizational networks help manage uncertainties about internal processes and tasks, inter-organizational networks enable members and especially leaders to manage uncertainties about the changing environment (Monge & Eisenberg, 1987). For example, many individuals simultaneously serve on boards of directors of multiple companies. Through these interlocking boards of directors, organizations gain information to manage uncertainties about their environment, including reducing conflict between organizations (Monge & Contractor, 2001).

Communication networks are an important source of information for managing uncertainty for members individually and collectively. TMU provides insight and suggestions for exploring how members gain information actively and passively through their communication network linkages, both within the organization and between organizations.

Power and Influence Concerns

For some researchers, power is the fundamental characteristic of the process of producing, reproducing, and transforming organizations through communication (Mumby, 2001). Power exists both at a surface level that is fairly conscious and observable as members compete for limited resources and at a deep level that is less transparent and involves the way ideology serves some members, typically those at the top of the hierarchy, at the expense of others, typically at the bottom of organization (Frost, 1987). Because it is through communication that organizational members gain an understanding of power in organizations, it is not surprising that one of the content-specific networks in organizations concerns power or influence (Tushman, 1977a). This indicates that managing uncertainty about the power relationships in an organization is a major concern of organizational members. TMU can provide some insight into the way people experience and respond to power and influence in organizations.

TMU suggests that organizational members are more likely to experience uncertainty and manage uncertainty about surface-level power issues than deep structure power. Deep structure power is often enacted subconsciously and accepted unquestioningly as part of the organization's culture (Frost, 1987). These deep-level power relations are naturalized as unquestionable (Mumby, 1987). Because the experiences are consistent with the scripts and schemas they have for the organization, TMU suggests that members experience little uncertainty about deep structure power.

In contrast, organizational members are likely to experience uncertainties about the surface-level power and influence activities in the organization, frequently referred to as the politics of organizational life. Individuals or groups in organizations are likely to experience uncertainty as they observe the exchange of resources in the organization, especially if they perceive inequities. They may cognitively manage those uncertainties if they assimilate the experience with other experiences in which they observed that upper management only looks out for itself and its friends. They manage their uncertainty by concluding, "It's who you know and not what you do that matters, just like everywhere else I've been." Those who cannot reduce their uncertainty about the exchange of resources may seek information. However, TMU would suggest that competing motives involved, such as fear of negative outcomes, may cause them to use indirect approaches to gain information to understand how politics works in the organization. Since they may fear that asking the person in power about inequities might make them a target for reprisals because they are not being a team player, individuals may seek information about politics and power in less obtrusive manners.

This brief section on power suggests ways that TMU can be used to examine how members gain an understanding of power and politics in their organizations. Due to scripts and schemas, they may experience little uncertainty about power in the organization, especially deep-level power. When they do experience uncertainty, they may manage it through cognitive processes by associating it with similar experiences in their past. While they may seek information to manage their uncertainty, they may rely on indirect methods due to concerns about negative outcomes if they question those in power.

Summary

Many traditional lines of organizational research are concerned with managing uncertainties (McPhee & Zaug, 2001). This section has briefly explored some of ways that TMU could be used to examine some of these traditional areas of research. The topics examined—role negotiation (including clarity and evaluation), culture (including emotion management, work-family policies, and diversity), communication networks, and power and influence—are provided to illustrate the flexibility of TMU for exploring many areas of organizational uncertainty managed through communication. However, these are not meant to be an exhaustive discussion of those topics or an exhaustive list of topics either. TMU could be used to explore these areas and other areas in more depth.

ON MANIPULATING UNCERTAINTY

Some scholars have argued that messages can be designed to increase, decrease, or maintain levels of uncertainty (Ford et al., 1996). By arguing this, they are asserting that uncertainty is a message characteristic under the control of the sender. TMU proposes that uncertainty is a receiver phenomenon instead. Most definitions of uncertainty seem consistent with this idea. The lack of predictability that characterizes definitions of uncertainty indicates that the message receiver experiences uncertainty, and that this may be unrelated to the intended message or the actual characteristics of the situation. Similarly, the characteristics of the environment influence or moderate the experience of uncertainty, but cannot determine whether organizational decision makers feel that they are in a certain or uncertain environment (Downey & Slocum, 1975). Evidence that uncertainty is a receiver phenomenon was apparent in the way that car salespeople responded the customers who said, "I'm just looking." Whereas customers expect that such as statement reduces uncertainty due to its clarity, car salespeople perceived this quite differently and frequently made additional attempts to interact with the customer either immediately or after a short interval of time.

Defining uncertainty as a receiver phenomenon does not mean that it is impossible for message senders to influence the experience of uncertainty. Because communication influences perceptions, the language in messages can be designed to be more ambiguous with the goal of creating perceptions of uncertainty (Bradac, 2001). However, the outcome of the message is never pre-determined. Certain messages are more likely to be associated with increase or decreases in uncertainty, but the results can be quite different than anticipated. For example, a supervisor may want to maintain uncertainty about the nature of future layoffs in a department. The vaguely worded statement the supervisor gives may be designed to maintain uncertainty so that employees will continue to be productive. However, the vagueness of the statement may have a quite different effect. The employees may conclude that the vagueness is a clear sign that layoffs are imminent; they assume that a clearer statement would be made if there were not going to be layoffs and as a result, productivity may still fall. So, even though it may be appropriate to say that messages can be designed with the intent of manipulating uncertainty, it seems inappropriate to claim that they actually control the receiver's experience of uncertainty.

RESEARCH METHODS

Too often, concepts or theories become associated with a particular research method in the social sciences. For example, job satisfaction is almost always studied from a functional perspective using quantitative measures. Organizational culture has been strongly associated with an interpretive perspective and qualitative research methods, although there have been some attempts to measure it quantitatively. Critical perspectives are typically associated with textual and rhetorical analyses.

As presented, TMU can be examined from a variety of methods and from a variety of perspectives. Three different methods were used in the studies reported here. The qualitative study of interviews with car salespeople provided insight into the cognitive processes that can be used to manage uncertainty apart from information seeking. Based on an interpretive perspective that focused on understanding the individuals' experiences, the qualitative study examined how car salespeople understand their interaction with customers. This approach helped delineate the difference between content and process uncertainty. The quantitative study of individuals' responses to uncertainty in scenarios provided insight into how competing motives influence information seeking. Using quantitative measures consistent with a functional perspective, the results demonstrated that certain motives were stronger in specific situations and suggested the need for further study of the importance of inquisitiveness as a motive for seeking information. The textual analysis of the Lucille Burger story emphasized that different participants in the same event experience uncertainty differently. The analysis also demonstrated the importance of examining context to understand how people respond to uncertainty. Taken together, this suggests that researchers from a variety of methodologies and perspectives should be encouraged to continue to explore and test TMU.

POSITIVE OUTCOMES FROM UNCERTAINTY

Although never explicitly stated in definitions or discussions of uncertainty in this volume or in the research reported elsewhere, an implicit assumption in the uncertainty research seems to be that uncertainty is a negative experience. For example, organizational newcomers must reduce their uncertainty in order to adapt and be satisfied in their jobs. Organizational decision makers must try to gain control of the uncertainty of their environment in order to maintain organizational viability. Due the negative nature of uncertainty, people are motivated to reduce it to make their situations more positive. Only a few scholars have explicitly stated that uncertainty is neither negative nor positive (e.g., Babrow, 2001b; Brashers et al., 2000). Knobloch and Solomon (2002a) note that uncertainty in romantic relationships can be exciting during relationship development and that maintaining uncertainty can be a more positive alternative than reducing uncertainty. In conditions of chronically ill patients, uncertainty can have a positive impact on individuals by leading to personal growth as individuals learn new roles and gain an appreciation for life situations and the complexity of life (Mishel, 1999). For those with critical illnesses, being uncertain about their situation and their options can actually increase hope for patients (Mishel, 1988).

It would be consistent with TMU to argue that uncertainty itself is neither positive nor negative. Situations that are perceived as uncertain may be perceived as positive or negative depending on the individual or group. It is the positive or negative evaluation of the uncertainty in the situation that frequently determines how the uncertainty will be managed (Bradac, 2001). Because many of the possible negative outcomes of uncertainty are already implicitly stated, a number of positive outcomes of uncertainty are mentioned next.

At the individual level, uncertainty may allow for relationship continuation or innovative thinking. Remaining uncertain (or perhaps in the dark as it may be) about a coworker's activities may make it easier to continue working together, whereas becoming certain might make the situation intolerable if those activities are illegal or personally repulsive. Research by Van Maanen and Schein (1979) suggests that new employees who are given institutionalized socialization often assume custodial roles where they continue to do things the way the organization has always done them, whereas those who are given more individualized socialization assume more innovative roles. This suggests that the certainty of the institutionalized training reduces originality, whereas the uncertainty of individualized training promotes innovation.

Similar positive results may occur at the group or organizational level. Being uncertain about the competitive nature of the relationship between two groups or organizations may allow them to continue to work cooperatively. A group of employees uncertain about the requirements of a new product they are to create may develop an innovative new product that they would never have considered if they were aware of constraints imposed on them. The uncertainty of the situation would have allowed them to think outside the box, whereas certainty might have promoted narrow thinking.

In addition to allowing for relationships to continue and for innovative ideas, uncertainty can simply be a positive motivator for a variety of outcomes. Even though some of the great discoveries of the past were accidental, others were the result of individuals actively reducing their uncertainty or attempting to prove that what they thought was certain actually was so.

CONCLUSION

In the introductory chapter, I argued that uncertainty reduction theory was unable to explain the different responses that people had to the changing of the millennium. Faced with the uncertainty of possible computer problems and shortages of supplies, some people hoarded food and developed a bunker mentality so that they could survive the end of life as we know it, whereas many took a few steps to prepare, and others did nothing. TMU provides an explanation for these different reactions to the uncertainty. Those who developed a bunker mentality apparently thought the future was so uncertain that they sought out information that confirmed their beliefs and took action to protect themselves against the uncertainty of limited supplies of essentials. The majority who did a little apparently experienced some uncertainty about what to expect based on the information they were receiving from friends and through the media. They gathered enough information to feel that if they put in a fix on their computers and took a few other minor precautionary steps, they would be unaffected. Those who did nothing apparently did not experience uncertainty. Either they denied that any events that would occur would affect them or based on the information gathering that they did, felt that there was no uncertainty in the situation. All three of these are possible responses to uncertainty based on TMU. People manage their uncertainty through a combination of cognitive processes and information seeking. Through this they develop a personal perception of the uncertainty in the situation and act accordingly.

Uncertainty may be the great commonality among social sciences (Driskill & Goldstein, 1986). "Uncertainty is the most recognizable of our common interests" and "should be a foundational universal focus of communication theory" (Babrow, 2001a, p. 453). This makes it appropriate that scholars continue to examine how people manage their uncertainty in their daily lives as they address their individual and collective uncertainties. A theory of managing uncertainty offers an approach for examining these issues. As we deepen our understanding of how people manage their uncertainty, we will know more about the human condition.

References

Acharya, L. (1983). Practitioner representations of environmental uncertainty: An application of discriminant analysis. *Public Relations Review, 9,* 53.

Acredolo, C., & O'Connor, J. (1991). On the difficulty of detecting cognitive uncertainty. *Human Development, 34,* 204–223.

Afifi, W. A., & Burgoon, J. K. (2000). The impact of violations on uncertainty and the consequences for attractiveness. *Human Communication Research, 26,* 203–233.

Afifi, W. A., & Reichert, T. (1996). Understanding the role of uncertainty in jealousy experience and expression. *Communication Research, 9,* 93–103.

Albrecht, T. L., & Hall, B. (1991). Relational and content differences between elites and outsiders in innovation networks. *Human Communication Research, 17,* 535–561.

Alder, G. S. (1997). Managing environmental uncertainty with legitimate authority: A comparative analysis of the Mann Gulch and Storm King Mountain fires. *Journal of Applied Communication Research, 25,* 98–114.

Altman, I., & Taylor, D. (1973). *Social penetration: The development of interpersonal relationships.* New York: Holt.

Ancona, D. G., & Caldwell, D. F. (1992). Bridging the boundary: External activity and performance in organizational teams. *Administrative Science Quarterly, 37,* 634–665.

Anderson, J. A. (1996). *Communication theory: Epistemological foundations.* New York: Guilford Press.

Andrews, P. (2000). Part A: Inside Microsoft. In G. L. Peterson (Ed.), *Communicating in organizations: A casebook* (pp. 17–24). Boston, MA: Allyn and Bacon.

Ashford, S. J. (1986). Feedback-seeking in individual adaptation: A resource perspective. *Academy of Management Journal, 29,* 465–487.

Ashford, S. J., & Black, J. S. (1996). Proactivity during organizational entry: The role of desire for control. *Journal of Applied Psychology, 81,* 199–214.

Ashford, S. J., & Northcraft, G. B. (1992). Conveying more (or less) than we realize: The role of impression-management in feedback seeking. *Organizational Behavior and Human Decision Processes, 53,* 310–334.

Ashforth, B. E., & Humphrey, R. H. (1995). Emotion in the workplace: A reappraisal. *Human Relations, 48,* 97–125.

Ayres, J. (1979). Uncertainty and social penetration theory expectations about relationship communication: A comparative test. *Western Journal of Speech Communication, 43,* 192–200.

Babrow, A. S. (2001a). Guest editor's introduction to the special issue on uncertainty, evaluation, and communication. *Journal of Communication, 51,* 453–455.

Babrow, A. S. (2001b). Uncertainty, value, communication, and problematic integration. *Journal of Communication, 51,* 553–573.

Babrow, A. S., Kasch, C. R., & Ford, L. A. (1998). The many meanings of *uncertainty* in illness: Toward a systematic accounting. *Health Communication, 10,* 1–23.

Baldwin, J. R., & Hunt, S. K. (2002). Information seeking-behavior in intercultural and intergroup communication. *Human Communication Research, 28,* 272–286.

Barnett, G. A. (1988). Communication and organizational culture. In G. M. Goldhaber & G. A. Barnett (Eds.), *Handbook of organizational communication* (pp. 101–130). Norwood, NJ: Ablex.

Bastien, D. T. (1987). Common patterns of behavior and communication in corporate mergers and acquisitions. *Human Resource Management, 26,* 17–33.

Bastien, D. T. (1992). Change in organizational culture: The use of linguistic methods in a corporate acquisition. *Management Communication Quarterly, 5,* 403–442.

Baxter, L. A., & Montgomery, B. M. (1996). *Relating: Dialogues and dialectics.* New York: Guilford Press.

Baxter, L. A., & Wilmot, W. W. (1984). "Secret tests": Social strategies for acquiring information about the state of the relationship. *Human Communication Research, 11,* 171–201.

Beam, R. A. (1996). How perceived environmental uncertainty influences the marketing orientation of U.S. daily newspapers. *Journalism and Mass Communication Quarterly, 73,* 285–303.

Berger, C. R. (1975). Proactive and retroactive attribution processes in interpersonal communication. *Human Communication Research, 2,* 33–50.

Berger, C. R. (1979). Beyond initial interactions: Uncertainty, understanding, and the development of interpersonal relationships. In H. Giles & R. N. St. Clair (Eds.), *Language and social psychology* (pp. 122–144). Baltimore: University Park Press.

Berger, C. R. (1986). Uncertain outcome values in predicted relationship: Uncertainty reduction theory then and now. *Human Communication Research, 13,* 34–38.

Berger, C. R. (1987). Communication under uncertainty. In M. E. Roloff & G. R. Miller (Eds.), *Interpersonal processes: New directions in communication research* (pp. 38–62). Newbury Park, CA: Sage.

Berger, C. R. (1993). Uncertainty and social interaction. In S. A. Deetz (Ed.), *Communication yearbook 16* (pp. 491–502). Newbury Park, CA: Sage.

Berger, C. R. (2000). Goal detection and efficiency: Neglected aspects of message production. *Communication Theory, 10,* 156–166.

Berger, C. R. (2002). Strategic and nonstrategic information acquisition. *Human Communication Research, 28,* 287–297.

Berger, C. R., & Bradac, J. J. (1982). *Language and social knowledge: Uncertainty in interpersonal relations.* London: Edward Arnold.

Berger, C. R., & Calabrese, R. J. (1975). Some explorations in initial interaction and beyond: Toward a developmental theory of interpersonal communication. *Human Communication Research, 1,* 99–112.

Berger, C. R., & Douglas, W. (1981). Studies in interpersonal epistemology: III. Anticipated interaction, self-monitoring and observational context selection. *Communication Monographs, 48,* 183–196.

Berger, C. R., & Kellerman, K. A. (1983). To ask or not to ask: Is that a question? In R. N. Bostrom (Ed.), *Communication yearbook 7* (pp. 342–368). Beverly Hills, CA: Sage.

Bingham, S. G., & Burleson, B. R. (1989). Multiple effects of messages with multiple goals: Some perceived outcomes of responses to sexual harassment. *Human Communication Research, 16,* 184–216.

Booth-Butterfield, M., Booth-Butterfield, S., & Koester, J. (1988). The function of uncertainty reduction in alleviating primary tension in small groups. *Communication Research Reports, 5,* 146–153.

Bradac, J. J. (2001). Theory comparison: uncertainty reduction, problematic integration, uncertainty management, and other curious constructs. *Journal of Communication, 51,* 456–476.

Brainard, J. (2001, January 12). Panel proposes new guidelines from research with human subjects. *The Chronicle of Higher Education*, p. A24.

Brashers, D. E. (2001). Communication and uncertainty management. *Journal of Communication, 51*, 477–497.

Brashers, D. E., Goldsmith, D. J., & Hsieh, E. (2002). Information seeking and avoiding in health contexts. *Human Communication Research, 28*, 258–271.

Brashers, D. E., Neidig, J. L., Haas, S. M., Dobbs, L. K., Cardsillo, L. W., & Russell, J. A. (2000). Communication in the management of uncertainty: The case of persons living with HIV or AIDS. *Communication Monographs, 67*, 63–84.

Browning, L. D., Sitkim, S. B., & Sutcliffe, K. M. (1999, May). *Communication strategies for managing uncertainty: A comparison of science and impression management.* Paper presented at the meeting of the International Communication Association, San Francisco.

Budner, S. (1962). Intolerance of ambiguity as a personality variable. *Journal of Personality, 30*, 29–50.

Buono, A. F., Bowditch, J. L., & Lewis, J. W. (1985). When cultures collide: The anatomy of a merger. *Human Relations, 38*, 477–500.

Bus driver gets credit for saving passengers. (2001, October 4). *Columbia Daily Tribune*, p. 10A.

Buzzanell, P. M. (1995). Reframing the glass ceiling as socially constructed process: Implications for understanding and change. *Communication Monographs, 62*, 327–354.

Callister, R. R., Kramer, M. W., & Turban, D. B. (1999). Feedback seeking following job transitions. *Academy of Management Journal, 42*, 429–438.

Cannon, A., & Cohen, W. (1999, December 27). Not many Americans are fearing Y2-chaos. *U.S. News and World Report*, p. 29.

Cantor, N., Mischel, W., & Schwartz, J. (1982). Social knowledge: Structure, content, use and abuse. In A. H. Hastrof & A. M. Isen (Eds.), *Cognitive social psychology* (pp. 33–72). New York: Elsevier-North Holland.

Carpenter, M. A., & Fredrickson, J. W. (2001). Top management teams, global strategic posture, and the moderating role of uncertainty. *Academy of Management Journal, 44*, 533–546.

Casey, M. K., Miller, V. D., & Johnson, J. R. (1997). Survivors' information seeking following a reduction in workforce. *Communication Research, 24*, 755–781.

Child, J. (1972). Organizational structure, environment and performance: The role of strategic choice. *Sociology, 6*, 2–22.

Clatterbuck, G. W. (1979). Attributional confidence and uncertainty in initial in interaction. *Human Communication Research, 5*, 147–157.

Clapham, S. E., & Schwenk, C. R. (1991). Self-serving attributions, managerial cognition, and company performance. *Strategic Management Journal, 12*, 219–229.

Cohen, M. D., March, J. G., & Olsen, J. P. (1972). A garbage can model of organizational choice. *Administrative Science Quarterly, 17*, 1–25.

Connolly, T. (1980). Uncertainty, action and competence: Some alternative to omniscience in complex problem-solving. In S. Fiddle (Ed.), *Uncertainty: Behavioral and social dimensions* (pp. 69–91). New York: Praeger.

Conrad, C., & Poole, M. S. (1998). *Strategic organizational communication: Into the twenty-first century.* Fort Worth, TX: Harcourt Brace.

Conrath, D. W. (1967). Organizational decision making behavior under varying conditions of uncertainty. *Management Science, 13*, B487–500.

Cornett-DeVito, M. M., & Friedman, P. G. (1995). Communication processes and merger success: An exploratory study of four financial institution mergers. *Management Communication Quarterly, 9*, 46–77.

Cragan, J. F., & Shields, D. C. (1998). *Understanding communication theory: The communicative forces for human action.* Boston, Allyn and Bacon.

Dewey, J. (1910). *How we think.* Boston, MA: D.C. Heath.

Dewey, J. (1933). *How we think: A restatement of the relation of reflective thinking to the education process*. Boston, MA: D.C. Heath and Company.

DiFonzo, N., & Bordia, P. (1998). A tale of two corporations: Managing uncertainty during organizational change. *Human Resource Management, 37*, 295–303.

Douglas, W. (1984). Initial interaction scripts: When knowing is behaving. *Human Communication Research, 11*, 203–219.

Douglas, W. (1988). Question-asking in same- and opposite-sex initial interactions: The effects of anticipated future interactions. *Human Communication Research, 14*, 230–245.

Douglas, W. (1990). Uncertainty, information-seeking, and liking during initial interaction. *Western Journal of Speech Communication, 54*, 66–81.

Douglas, W. (1991). Expectations about initial interactions: An examination of the effects of global uncertainty. *Human Communication Research, 17*, 355–384.

Douglas, W. (1994). The acquaintanceship process: An examination of uncertainty, information seeking, and social attraction during initial conversations. *Communication Research, 21*, 154–176.

Downey, H. K., & Slocum, J. W. (1975). Uncertainty: Measures, research, and sources of variation. *Academy of Management Journal, 18*, 562–578.

Downs, C. W., Johnson, K. M., & Barge, J. K. (1984). Communication feedback and task performance in organizations: A review of the literature. In H. H. Greenbaum, R. I. Falcione, & S. A. Hellweg (Eds.), *Organizational communication*. (Vol. 9, pp. 13–47). Beverly Hills, CA: Sage.

Driskill, L. P., & Goldstein, J. R. (1986). Uncertainty: Theory and practice in organizational communication. *Journal of Business Communication, 23*, 41–56.

Duncan, R. B. (1972). Characteristics of organizational environments and perceived environmental uncertainty. *Administrative Science Quarterly, 17*, 313–327.

Duncan, R. B. (1973). Multiple decision-making structures in adapting to environmental uncertainty: The impact on organizational effectiveness. *Human Relations, 26*, 273–291.

Duncan R. B. (1974). Modifications in decision structure in adapting to the environment: Some implication for organizational learning. *Decision Sciences, 5*, 705–725.

Eisenberg, E. M. (1984). Ambiguity as strategy in organizational communication. *Communication Monographs, 51*, 227–242.

Eisenberg, E. M. (2001). Building a mystery: Toward a new theory of communication and identity. *Journal of Communication, 51*, 534–552.

Elliott, G. C. (1979). Some effects of deception and level of self-monitoring on planning and reacting to self-presentation. *Journal of Personality and Social Psychology, 37*, 1282–1292.

Ellis, B. H. (1992). The effects of uncertainty and source credibility on attitudes about organizational change. *Management Communication Quarterly, 6*, 34–57.

Emery, F. E. (1967). The next thirty years: Concepts, methods, and anticipations. *Human Relations, 20*, 199–238.

Emmers, T. M., & Canary, D. J. (1996). The effects of uncertainty reducing strategies on young couples' relation repair and intimacy. *Communication Quarterly, 44*, 166–182.

Farace, R. V., Taylor, J. A., & Stewart, J. P. (1978). Criteria for evaluation of organizational communication effectiveness: Review and synthesis. In B. D. Ruben (Ed.), *Communication yearbook 2* (pp. 271–292). New Brunswick, NJ: Transaction Books.

Festinger, L. (1957). *A theory of cognitive dissonance*. Palo Alto, CA: Stanford University Press.

Fisher, B. A. (1978). *Perspectives on human communication*. New York: Macmillan.

Fisher, B. A. (1980). *Small group decision making* (2nd Edition). New York: McGraw-Hill.

Foa, E. B., & Foa, U. G. (1980). Resource theory: Interpersonal behavior as exchange. In K. J. Gergen, M. S. Greenberg, & R. H. Willis (Eds.), *Social exchange: Advances in theory and research* (pp. 77–94). New York: Plenum Press.

Ford, L. A., Babrow, A. S., & Stohl, C. (1996). Social support messages and the management of uncertainty in the experience of breast cancer: An application of problematic integration theory. *Communication Monographs, 63*, 189–207.

Forward, G. L. (1997, November). *Encountering the nonprofit organization: Clergy uncertainty and information-seeking during organizational entry.* Paper presented at the meeting of the National Communication Association, Chicago, IL.

Fox, R. C. (1959). *Experiment perilous: Physicians and patients facing the unknown.* Glencoe, IL: The Free Press.

Fox, R. C. (2000). Medical uncertainty revisited. In G. L. Albrecht, R. Fitzpatrick, & S. C. Scrimshaw (Eds.), *Handbook of social studies in health and medicine* (pp. 409–425). Thousand Oaks, CA: Sage.

Frone, M. R., Russell, M., & Couper, M. L. (1992). Antecedents and outcomes of work-family conflict: Testing a model of the work-family interface. *Journal of Applied Psychology, 77,* 65–78.

Frost, P. J. (1987). Power, politics, and influence. In F. M. Jablin, L. L. Putnam, K. H. Roberts, & L. W. Porter (Eds.), *Handbook of organizational communication: An interdisciplinary perspective* (pp. 503–548). Newbury Park, CA: Sage.

Fung, A. Y. H., & Lee, C. (1994). Hong Kong's changing media ownership: Uncertainty and dilemma. *Gazette, 53,* 123–133.

Glaser, B., & Strauss, A. (1967). *The discovery of grounded theory: Strategies for qualitative research.* Chicago, IL: Aldine.

Goldsmith, D. J. (2001). A normative approach to the study of uncertainty and communication. *Journal of Communication, 51,* 514–533.

Graves, D. (1981). Individual reactions to a merger of two small firms of brokers in the re-insurance industry: A total population survey. *Journal of Management Studies, 18,* 89–113.

Grove, T. G., & Werkman, D. L. (1991). Conversations with able-bodied and visibly disabled strangers: An adversarial test of predicted outcome value and uncertainty reduction theories. *Human Communication Research, 17,* 507–534.

Gudykunst, W. B. (1983). Uncertainty reduction and predictability of behavior in low- and high-context cultures. *Communication Quarterly, 31,* 49–55.

Gudykunst, W. B. (1985). The influence of cultural similarity, type of relationship, and self-monitoring on uncertainty reduction processes. *Communication Monographs, 52,* 203–215.

Gudykunst, W. B. (1995). Anxiety/uncertainty management (AUM) theory. In R. L. Wiseman (Ed.), *Intercultural communication theory* (pp. 8–58). Thousand Oaks, CA: Sage.

Gudykunst, W. B., Chua, E., & Gray, A. J. (1987). Cultural dissimilarities and uncertainty reduction processes. In M. L. McLaughlin (Ed.), *Communication yearbook 10* (pp. 456–469). Newbury Park, CA: Sage.

Gudykunst, W. B., & Hammer, M. R. (1988). The influence of social identity and intimacy of interethnic relationships on uncertainty reduction processes. *Human Communication Research, 14,* 569–601.

Gudykunst, W. B., & Nishida, T. (1984). Individual and cultural influences on uncertainty reduction. *Communication Monographs, 84,* 23–36.

Gudykunst, W. B., Nishida, T., Koike, H., & Shiino, N. (1986). The influence of language on uncertainty reduction: An exploratory study of Japanese-Japanese and Japanese-North American interactions. In M. L. McLaughlin (Ed.), *Communication yearbook 9* (pp. 555–575). Beverly Hills, CA: Sage.

Gudykunst, W. B., Nishida, T., & Schmidt, K. L. (1989). The influence of cultural, relational, and personality factors on uncertainty reduction processes. *Western Journal of Speech Communication, 53,* 13–29.

Gudykunst, W. B., Sodetani, L. L., & Sonoda, K. T. (1987). Uncertainty reduction in Japanese-American/ Caucasian relationships in Hawaii. *Western Journal of Speech Communication, 51,* 256–279.

Gudykunst, W. B., Yang, S., & Nishida, T. (1985). A cross-cultural test of uncertainty reduction theory. *Human Communication Research, 11,* 407–454.

Haleta, L. L. (1996). Student perceptions of teachers' use of language: The effects of powerful and powerless language on impression formation and uncertainty. *Communication Education, 45,* 16–28.

Heath, R. L., & Gay, C. D. (1997). Risk communication: Involvement, uncertainty, and control's effect on information scanning and monitoring by expert stakeholders. *Management Communication Quarterly, 10,* 342–372.

Heath, R. L., Seshadri, S., & Lee, J. (1998). Risk communication: A two-community analysis of proximity, dread, trust, involvement, uncertainty, openness/accessibility, and knowledge on support/opposition toward chemical companies. *Journal of Public Relations Research, 10,* 35–56.

Hewes, D. E., Graham, M. L., Doelger, J., & Pavitt, C. (1985). "Second-guessing": Message interpretation in social networks. *Human Communication Research, 11,* 299–334.

Hines, S. C. (2001). Coping with uncertainties in advance care planning. *Journal of Communication, 51,* 498–513.

Hines, S. C., Badzek, L., Leslie, N., & Glover, J. (1998). Managing uncertainty in conversations about treatment preferences: A study of home health care nurses. *Communication Research Reports, 15,* 331–339.

Hirokawa, R. Y., Gouran, D. S., & Martz, A. E. (1988). Understanding the sources of faulty decision making: A lesson from the Challenger disaster. *Small Group Research, 19,* 411–433.

Hirokawa, R. Y., & Rost, K. M. (1992). Effective group, decision making in organizations: Field test of the vigilant interaction theory. *Management Communication Quarterly, 5,* 267–288.

Hochschild, A. R. (1983). *The managed heart.* Berkeley: University of California Press.

Holder, T. (1996). Women in nontraditional occupations: Information-seeking during organizational entry. *Journal of Business Communication, 33,* 9–26.

Hollingshead, A. B. (2001). Cognitive interdependence and convergent expectations in transactive memory. *Journal of Personality and Social Psychology, 81,* 1080–1089.

Honeycutt, J. M. (1993). Components and functions of communication during initial interaction, with extrapolations to beyond. In S. A. Deetz (Ed.), *Communication yearbook 16* (pp. 461–490). Newbury Park, CA: Sage.

Huber, G. P., & Daft, R. L. (1987). The information environments in organizations. In F. M. Jablin, L. L. Putnam, K. H. Roberts, & L. W. Porter (Eds.), *Handbook of organizational communication: An interdisciplinary perspective* (pp. 130–164). Newbury Park, CA: Sage.

Huber, G. P., O'Connell, M. J., & Cummings, L. I. (1975). Perceived environmental uncertainty: Effects of information and structure. *Academy of Management Journal, 18,* 725–740.

Hylmo, A., & Buzzanell, P. M. (2002). Telecommuting as viewed through cultural lenses: An empirical investigation of the discourses of utopia, identity, and mystery. *Communication Monographs, 69,* 329–356.

Ickes, W., & Barnes, R. D. (1977). The role of sex and self-monitoring in unstructured dyadic interactions. *Journal of Personality and Social Psychology, 35,* 315–330.

Jablin, F. M. (1987). Organizational entry, assimilation, and exit. In F. M. Jablin, L. L. Putnam, K. H. Roberts, & L. W. Porter (Eds.), *Handbook of organizational communication: An interdisciplinary perspective* (pp. 679–740). Newbury Park, CA: Sage.

Jablin, F. M. (2001). Organizational entry, assimilation, and disengagement/exit. In F. M. Jablin & L. L. Putnam (Eds.), *The new handbook of organizational communication: Advances in theory, research, and methods* (pp. 732–818). Thousand Oaks, CA: Sage.

Jablin, F. M., & Kramer, M. W. (1998). Communication-related sense-making and adjustment during job transfers. *Management Communication Quarterly, 12,* 155–182.

Janis, I. L. (1972). *Victims of groupthink.* Boston: Houghton Mifflin.

Johnson, J. R., Bernhagen, M. J., Miller, V., & Allen, M. (1996). The role of communication in managing reductions in work force. *Journal of Applied Communication Research, 24,* 139–164.

Jones, G. R. (1986). Socialization tactics, self-efficacy and newcomers' adjustment to organizations. *Academy of Management Journal, 29,* 262–279.

Jorgensen, J. D., & Petelle, J. L. (1992). Measuring uncertainty within organizational relationships: An analysis of the CLUES instrument. *Management Communication Quarterly, 6,* 180–203.

Kellerman, K. (1986). Anticipation of future interaction and information exchange in initial interactions. *Human Communication Research, 13,* 41–75.

Kellerman, K. (1991). The conversation MOP II. Progression through scenes in discourse. *Human Communication Research, 17,* 385–414.

Kellerman, K. (1993). Extrapolating beyond: Processes of uncertainty reduction. In S. A. Deetz (Ed.), *Communication yearbook 16* (pp. 503–514). Newbury Park, CA: Sage.

Kellerman, K., & Berger, C. R. (1984). Affect and social information acquisition: Sit back, relax, and tell me about yourself. In R. N. Bostrom (Ed.), *Communication yearbook 8* (pp. 412–445). Beverly Hills, CA: Sage.

Kellerman, K., & Reynolds, R. (1990). When ignorance is bliss: The role of motivation to reduce uncertainty in uncertainty reduction theory. *Human Communication Research, 17,* 5–75.

Kennamer, J. D., & Chaffee, S. H. (1982). Communication of political information during early presidential primaries: Cognition, affect, and uncertainty. In M. Burgoon (Ed.), *Communication yearbook 5* (pp. 627–650). New Brunswick, NJ: Transactional Book.

Keyton, J. (1999). *Group communication: Process and analysis.* Mountain View, CA: Mayfield.

Kiesler, C. A., Kiesler, S. B., & Pallak, M. S. (1967). The effect of commitment to future interaction on reactions to norm violations. *Journal of Personality, 55,* 585–599.

Knobloch, L. K., & Solomon, D. H. (2002a). Information seeking beyond initial interactions: Negotiating relational uncertainty within close relationships. *Human Communication Research, 28,* 243–257.

Knobloch, L. K., & Solomon, D. H. (2002b). Intimacy and the magnitude and experience of episodic relational uncertainty within romantic relationships. *Personal Relationships, 9,* 457–478.

Knobloch, L. K., Solomon, D. H., & Cruz, M. G. (2001). The role of relationship development and attachment in the experience of romantic jealousy. *Personal Relationships, 8,* 205–224.

Kramer, M. W. (1989). Communication during intraorganization job transfers. *Management Communication Quarterly, 3,* 219–248.

Kramer, M. W. (1993). Communication and uncertainty reduction during job transfers: Leaving and joining processes. *Communication Monographs, 60,* 178–198.

Kramer, M. W. (1994). Uncertainty reduction during job transitions: An exploratory study of the communication experiences of newcomers and transferees. *Management Communication Quarterly, 7,* 384–412.

Kramer, M. W. (1995). A longitudinal study of superior–subordinate communication during job transfers. *Human Communication Research, 22,* 39–64.

Kramer, M. W. (1996). A longitudinal study of peer communication during job transfers: The impact of frequency, quality, and network multiplexity on adjustment. *Human Communication Research, 23,* 59–86.

Kramer, M. W. (1999). Motivation to reduce uncertainty: Reconceptualizing uncertainty reduction theory. *Management Communication Quarterly, 13,* 305–316.

Kramer, M. W., & Berman, J. E. (2001). Making sense of a university's culture: An examination of undergraduate students' stories. *Southern Communication Journal, 66,* 297–311.

Kramer, M. W., Callister, R. R., & Turban, D. B. (1995). Information-giving and information-receiving during job transitions. *Western Journal of Communication, 59,* 151–170.

Kramer, M. W., Dougherty, D. S., & Pierce, T. A. (in press). Managing uncertainty during a corporate acquisition: A longitudinal study of communication during an airline acquisition. *Human Communication Research.*

Kramer, M. W., & Hess, J. A. (2002). Communication rules for the display of emotions in organizational settings. *Management Communication Quarterly, 16,* 66–80.

Kramer, M. W., & Noland, T. L. (1999). Communication during job promotions: A case of ongoing assimilation. *Journal of Applied Communication Research, 27,* 335–355.

Krone, K. J., Jablin, F. M., & Putnam, L. L. (1987). Communication theory and organizational communication: Multiple perspectives. In F. M. Jablin, L. L. Putnam, K. H. Roberts, & L. W. Porter (Eds.), *Handbook of organizational communication: An interdisciplinary perspective* (pp. 18–40). Beverly Hills, CA: Sage.

Lalljee, M., & Cook, M. (1973). Uncertainty in first encounters. *Journal of Personality and Social Psychology, 26,* 137–141.

Langer, E. J. (1978). Rethinking the role of thought in social interaction. In J. H. Harvey, W. Ickes, & R. F. Kidd (Eds.), *New directions in attribution research 2* (pp. 35–58). Hillsdale, NJ: Lawrence Erlbaum Associates.

Larkey, L. K. (1996). Toward a theory of communicative interactions in culturally diverse workgroups. *Academy of Management Review, 21,* 463–491.

Lawrence, P. R., & Lorsch, J. W. (1967). Differentiation and integration in complex organizations. *Administrative Science Quarterly, 12,* 1–47.

Leblebici, H., & Salancik, G. R. (1981). Effects of environmental uncertainty on information and decision processes in banks. *Administrative Science Quarterly, 26,* 578–596.

Lester, R. E. (1987). Organizational culture, uncertainty reductions, and the socialization of new organizational members. In S. Thomas (Ed.), *Culture and communication: Methodology, behavior, artifacts, and institutions* (pp. 105–113). Norword, NJ: Ablex.

Li, J., Karakowsky, L., & Siegel, J. P. (1999). The effects of proportional representation on intragroup behavior in mixed-race decision-making groups. *Small Group Research, 30,* 259–279.

Lindlof, T. R. (1995). *Qualitative communication research methods.* Thousand Oaks, CA: Sage.

Louis, M. R. (1980). Surprise and sense making: What newcomers experience in entering unfamiliar organizational settings. *Administrative Science Quarterly, 25,* 226–251.

Louis, M. R. (1982). Managing career transitions: A missing link in career development. *Organizational Dynamics, 10,* 68–77.

Louis, M. R., Posner, B. Z., & Powell, G. N. (1983). The availability and helpfulness of socialization practices. *Personnel Psychology, 36,* 857–866.

Martin, J. (1992). *Cultures in organization: Three perspectives.* New York: Oxford University Press.

Martin, J., Feldman, M., Hatch, M. J., & Sitkin, S. B. (1983). The uniqueness paradox in organizational stories. *Administrative Science Quarterly, 28,* 438–453.

McPhee, R. D., & Zaug, P. (2001). Organizational theory, organizational communication, organizational knowledge, and problematic integration. *Journal of Communication, 51,* 574–591.

Merry, U. (1995). *Coping with uncertainty: Insights from the new sciences of chaos, self-organization and complexity.* Westport, CT: Praeger.

Meyerson, D., & Martin, J. (1987). Cultural change: An integration of three different views. *Journal of Management Studies, 24,* 623–647.

Middleton, D. (1997). Conversation remembering and uncertainty: Interdependencies of experience as individual and collective concerns in teamwork. *Journal of Language and Social Psychology, 16,* 389–410.

Mignerey, J. T., Rubin, R. B., & Gorden, W. I. (1995). Organizational entry: An investigation of newcomer communication behavior and uncertainty. *Communication Research, 22,* 54–85.

Miles, R. E., Snow, C. C., Meyer, A. D., & Coleman, H. J. (1978). Organizational strategy, structure, and process. *Academy of Management Review, 3,* 546–562.

Miller, K. I., & Monge, P. R. (1985). Social information and employee anxiety about organizational change. *Human Communication Research, 11,* 365–386.

Miller, V. D., & Jablin, F. M. (1991). Information seeking during organization entry: Influences, tactics, and a model of the process. *Academy of Management Review, 16,* 92–120.

Miller, V. D., Jablin, F. M., Casey, M. K., Lamphear-Van Horn, M., & Ethington, C. (1996). The maternity leave as role negotiation process. *Journal of Managerial Issues, 8,* 286–309.

Milliken, F. J. (1987). Three types of perceived uncertainty about the environment: State, effect, and response uncertainty. *Academy of Management Review, 12,* 133–143.

Mishel, M. H. (1988). Uncertainty in illness. *Image: Journal of Nursing Scholarship, 20,* 225–232.

Mishel, M. H. (1990). Reconceptualization of uncertainty in illness theory. *Image: Journal of Nursing Scholarship, 22,* 256–262.

Mishel, M. H. (1997). Uncertainty in acute illness. In J. J. Fitzpatrick & J. Norbeck (Eds.), *Annual review of nursing research* (Vol.15, pp. 57–80). New York: Springer.

Mishel, M. H. (1999). Uncertainty in chronic illness. In J. J. Fitzpatrick (Ed.), *Annual review of nursing research* (Vol. 17, pp. 269–294). New York: Springer.

Mokros, H. B., & Aakhus, M. (2002). From information-seeking behavior to meaning engagement practice: Implications for communication theory and research. *Human Communication Research, 28,* 298–312.

Monge, P. R., & Contractor, N. S. (2001). Emergence of communication networks. In F. M. Jablin & L. L. Putnam (Eds.), *The new handbook of organizational communication: Advances in theory, research, and methods* (pp. 440–502). Thousand Oaks, CA: Sage.

Monge, P. R., & Eisenberg, E.M. (1987). Emergent communication networks. In F. M. Jablin, L. L. Putnam, K. H. Roberts, & L. W. Porter (Eds.), *Handbook of organizational communication: An interdisciplinary perspective* (pp. 304–342). Newbury Park, CA: Sage.

Morris, J. A., & Feldman, D. C. (1996). The dimensions, antecedents, and consequences of emotional labor. *Academy of Management Review, 21,* 986–1010.

Morrison, E. W. (1993a). Longitudinal study of the effects of information seeking on newcomer socialization. *Journal of Applied Psychology, 78,* 173–183.

Morrison, E. W. (1993b). Newcomer information seeking: Exploring types, modes, sources, and outcomes. *Academy of Management Journal, 36,* 557–589.

Morrison, E. W. (1995). Information usefulness and acquisition during organizational encounter. *Management Communication Quarterly, 9,* 131–155.

Morrison, E. W. (2002). Information seeking within organizations. *Human Communication Research, 28,* 229–242.

Morrison, E. W., & Bies, R. J. (1991). Impression management in the feedback-seeking process: A literature review and research agenda. *Academy of Management Review, 16,* 522–541.

Mumby, D. K. (1987). The political function of narrative in organizations. *Communication Monographs, 54,* 113–127.

Mumby, D. K. (2001). Power and politics. In F. M. Jablin & L. L. Putnam (Eds.), *The new handbook of organizational communication: Advances in theory, research, and methods* (pp. 585–623). Thousand Oaks, CA: Sage.

Napier, N. K. (1989). Mergers and acquisitions, human resource issues and outcomes: A review and suggested typology. *Journal of Management Studies, 26,* 271–288.

Napier, N. K., Simmons, G., & Stratton, K. (1989). Communication during a merger: The experience of two banks. *Human Resource Planning, 12,* 105–122.

Nathan, K., Heath, R. L., & Douglas, W. (1992). Tolerance for potential environmental health risks: The influence of knowledge, benefits, control, involvement, and uncertainty. *Journal of Public Relations Research, 4,* 235–258.

Nelson, D. L., & Quick, J. C. (1991). Social support and newcomer adjustment in organizations: Attachment theory at work. *Journal of Organizational Behavior, 12,* 543–554.

Nicotera, A. M. (1993). Beyond two dimensions: A grounded theory model of conflict-handling behavior. *Management Communication Quarterly, 6,* 282–306.

Nigg, J. M. (1982). Communication under conditions of uncertainty: Understanding earthquake forecasting. *Journal of Communication, 32,* 27–36.

O'Keefe, B. J. (1991). Message design logic and the management of multiple goals. In K. Tracy (Ed.), *Understanding face to face communication: Issues linking goals and discourse* (pp. 131–150). Hillsdale, NJ: Lawrence Erlbaum Associates.

O'Keefe, B. J., & Sheperd, G. J. (1987). The pursuit of multiple objectives in face to face persuasive interactions: Effects of construct differentiation on message organization. *Communication Monographs, 54,* 396–419.

O'Reilly, C. A., & Roberts, K. H. (1977). Task group structure, communication, and effectiveness in three organizations. *Journal of Applied Psychology, 78,* 674–681.

Ostroff, C., & Kozlowski, S. W. J. (1992). Organizational socialization as a learning process: The role of information acquisition. *Personnel Psychology, 45,* 849–874.

Pacanowsky, M. E., & O'Donnell-Truijillo, N. (1983). Organizational communication as cultural performance. *Communication Monographs, 50,* 126–147.

Parks, M. R., & Adelman, M. B. (1983). Communication networks and the development of romantic relationships: An expansion of uncertainty reduction theory. *Human Communication Research, 10,* 55–79.

Pavitt, C. (1982). A test of six models of coorientation: The effect of task and disagreement level on judgments of uncertainty, utility, and desired communication behavior. In M. Burgoon (Ed.), *Communication yearbook 5* (pp. 303–330). New Brunswick, NJ: Transaction Books.

Petty, R. E., & Cacioppo, J. T. (1981). *Attitudes and persuasion: Classic and contemporary approaches.* Dubuque, IA: Wm. C. Brown.

Planalp, S., & Honeycutt, J. M. (1985). Events that increase uncertainty in personal relationships. *Human Communication Research, 11,* 593–604.

Planalp, S., Rutherford, D. K., & Honeycutt, J. M. (1988). Events that increase uncertainty in personal relationships II: Replication and extension. *Human Communication Research, 14,* 516–547.

Poggie, G. (1965). A main theme of contemporary sociological analysis: Its achievements and limitation. *British Journal of Sociology, 16,* 283–294.

Poole, M. S. (1978). An information-task approach to organizational communication. *Academy of Management Review, 3,* 493–504.

Poole, M. S., Seibold, D. R., & McPhee, R. D. (1985). Group decision-making as a structurational process. *Quarterly Journal of Speech, 71,* 74–102.

Pratt, L., Wiseman, R. L., Cody, M. J., & Wendt, P. F. (1999). Interrogative strategies and information exchange in computer-mediated communication. *Communication Quarterly, 47,* 46–66.

Prisbell, M., & Andersen, J. F. (1980). The importance of perceived homophily, level of uncertainty, feeling good, safety, and self-disclosure interpersonal relationships. *Communication Quarterly, 28,* 22–33.

Putnam, L. L. (1983). Paradigms for organizational communication research: An overview and synthesis. *The Western Journal of Speech Communication, 46,* 192–206.

Rafaeli, A. (1989). When clerks meet customers: A test of variables related to emotional expression on the job. *Journal of Applied Psychology, 74,* 385–393.

Ramirez, A., Jr., Walther, J. B., Burgoon, J. K., & Sunnafrank, M. (2002). Information-seeking strategies, uncertainty, and computer-mediated communication: Toward a conceptual model. *Human Communication Research, 28,* 213–228.

Reichers, A. E. (1987). An interactionist perspective on newcomer socialization rates. *Academy of Management Review, 12,* 278–287.

Rodgers, W. (1969). *Think: A biography of the Watsons and IBM.* New York: Stern & Day.

Roloff, M. E. (1981). *Interpersonal communication: The social exchange approach.* Beverly Hills, CA: Sage.

Rousseau, D. M. (1978). Relationship of work to nonwork. *Journal of Applied Psychology, 63,* 513–517.

Rubin, R. B. (1977). The role of context in information seeking and impression formation. *Communication Monographs, 44,* 81–90.

Rubin, R. B. (1979). The effect of context on information seeking across the span of initial interactions. *Communication Quarterly, 27,* 13–20.

Salancik, G. R., & Pfeffer, J. (1978). A social information processing approach to job attitudes and task design. *Administrative Science Quarterly, 23*, 244–253.

Salem, P., & Williams, M. L. (1984). Uncertainty and satisfaction: The importance of information in hospital communication. *Journal of Applied Communication Research, 12*, 75–89.

Sanders, J. A., Wiseman, R. L., & Matz, S. I. (1990). The influence of gender on reported disclosure, interrogation, and nonverbal immediacy in same-sex dyads: An empirical study of uncertainty reduction theory. *Women's Studies in Communication, 13*, 85–108.

Sathe, B. (1983). Implications of corporate culture: A manager's guide to action. *Organizational Dynamics, 12*, 5–23.

Schlossberg, N. K. (1981). A model for analyzing human adaptation to transition. *The Counseling Psychologist, 9*, 2–18.

Schumacher, B. K., & Wheeless, L. R. (1997). Relationships of continuing uncertainty and state-receiver apprehension to information-seeking and predictions in dyadic interactions. *Communication Quarterly, 45*, 427–445.

Schweiger, D. M., & DeNisi, A. S. (1991). Communication with employees following a merger: A longitudinal field experiment. *Academy of Management Journal, 34*, 110–135.

Shannon, C. E., & Weaver, W. (1949). *The mathematical theory of communication*. Urbana, IL: University of Illinois Press.

Shaw, M. E. (1981). *Group dynamics: The psychology of small group behavior*. New York: McGraw-Hill.

Sheer, V. C., & Cline, R. J. (1995). Testing a model of perceived information adequacy and uncertainty reduction in physician-patient interactions. *Journal of Applied Communication Research, 23*, 44–59.

Sherblom, J., & Van Rheenen, D. D. (1984). Spoken language indices of uncertainty. *Human Communication Research, 11*, 221–230.

Shimanoff, S. B. (1980). *Communication rules: Theory and research*. Beverly Hills, CA: Sage.

Sias, P. M., Kramer, M. W., & Jenkins, E. (1997). A comparison of the communication behaviors of temporary employees and new hires. *Communication Research, 24*, 731–754.

Slovic, P., Fishoff, B., & Lichtenstein, S. (1982). Facts versus fears: Understanding perceived risk. In D. Kahneman, P. Slovic, & A. Tversky (Eds.), *Judgment under uncertainty: Heuristics and biases* (pp. 463–489). Cambridge: Cambridge University Press.

Smircich, L., & Calas, M. B. (1987). Organizational culture: A critical assessment. In F. M. Jablin, L. L. Putnam, K. H. Roberts, & L. W. Porter (Eds.), *Handbook of organizational communication: An interdisciplinary perspective* (pp. 228–263). Newbury Park, CA: Sage.

Smith, R. C., & Eisenberg, E. M. (1987). Conflict at Disneyland: A root-metaphor analysis. *Communication Monographs, 54*, 367–380.

Snyder, M. (1974). Self-monitoring of expressive behavior. *Journal of Personality and Social Psychology, 30*, 526–537.

Solomon, D. H., & Knobloch, L. K. (2001). Relationship uncertainty, partner interference, and intimacy within dating relationships. *Journal of Social and Personal Relationships, 18*, 804–820.

Staines, G. L. (1980). Spillover versus compensation: A review of the literature on the relationship between work and nonwork. *Human Relations, 33*, 111–129.

Sunnafrank, M. (1986a). Predicted outcome value during initial interactions: A reformulation of uncertainty reduction theory. *Human Communication Research, 13*, 3–33.

Sunnafrank, M. (1986b). Predicted outcome values: Just now and then? *Human Communication Research, 13*, 39–40.

Sunnafrank, M. (1989). Uncertainty in interpersonal relationships: A predicted outcome value interpretation of Gudykunst's research program. In J. A. Anderson (Ed.), *Communication yearbook 12* (pp. 355–370). Newbury Park, CA: Sage.

Sunnafrank, M. (1990). Predicted outcome value and uncertainty reduction theories: A test of competing perspectives. *Human Communication Research, 17*, 76–103.

Sutton, R. I. (1991). Maintaining norms about expressed emotions: The case of bill collectors. *Administrative Science Quarterly, 36*, 245–268.

Swann, W. B., & Ely, R. J. (1984). A battle of wills: Self-verification versus behavioral confirmation. *Journal of Personality and Social Psychology, 46,* 1287–1302.

Teboul, J. C. B. (1994). Facing and coping with uncertainty during organizational encounters. *Management Communication Quarterly, 8,* 190–224.

Teboul, J. C. B. (1995). Determinants of new hire information-seeking during organizational encounter. *Western Journal of Communication, 59,* 305–325.

Teboul, J. C. B. (1997, November). *Racial/ethnic "encounter" in the workplace: Uncertainty, information-seeking and learning patterns among racial/ethnic majority and minority new hires.* Paper presented at the meeting of the National Communication Association, Chicago, IL.

Thibaut, J. W., & Kelley, H. H. (1959). *The social psychology of groups.* New York: John Wiley.

Tichy, N. M. (1981). Networks in organizations. In P. Nystrom & W. Starbuck (Eds.), *Handbook of organizational design* (pp. 225–249). Oxford: Oxford University Press.

Tidwell, L. C., & Walther, J. B. (2002). Computer-mediated communication effects on disclosure, impressions, and interpersonal evaluations: Getting to know one another a bit at a time. *Human Communication Research, 28,* 317–348.

Turner, L. H. (1990). The relationship between communication and marital uncertainty: Is "her" marriage different from "his" marriage? *Women's Studies in Communication, 13,* 57–83.

Tushman, M. L. (1977a). A political approach to organizations: A review and rationale. *Academy of Management Review, 2,* 206–216.

Tushman, M. L. (1977b). Special boundary roles in the innovation process. *Administrative Science Quarterly, 22,* 587–605.

Tversky, A., & Kahneman, D. (1974). Judgment under uncertainty: Heuristics and biases. *Science, 185,* 1124–1131.

Van Maanen, J., & Kunda, G. (1989). "Real feelings": Emotional expression and organizational culture. *Research in Organizational Behaviors, 11,* 43–103.

Van Maanen, J., & Schein, E.G. (1979). Toward a theory of organizational socialization. In B. M. Staw (Ed.), *Research in organizational behavior* (pp. 209–264). Greenwich, CT: JAI Press.

Waldron, V. R. (1994). Once more, with feeling: Reconsidering the role of emotion in work. In S. A. Deetz (Ed.), *Communication yearbook, 17* (pp. 388–416). Thousand Oaks, CA: Sage.

Walther, J. B. (1994). Anticipated ongoing interaction versus channel effects on relational communication in computer-mediated interaction. *Human Communication Research, 20,* 473–501.

Wanous, J. P., Poland, T. D., Premack, S. L., & Davis, K. S. (1992). The effects of met expectations on newcomer attitudes and behaviors: A review and meta-analysis. *Journal of Applied Psychology, 77,* 288–297.

Watson, W. E., Kumar, K., & Michaelsen, L. K. (1993). Cultural diversity's impact on interaction process and performance: Comparing homogeneous and diverse task groups. *Academy of Management Journal, 36,* 590–602.

Weick, K. E. (1993). The collapse of sensemaking in organizations: The Mann Gulch disaster. *Administrative Science Quarterly, 38,* 628–652.

Weick, K. E. (1995). *Sensemaking in organizations.* Thousand Oaks, CA: Sage.

Weick, K. E. (2001). *Making sense of the organization.* Malden, MA: Blackwell Publications.

Weick, K. E., & Sutcliffe, K. M. (2001). *Managing the unexpected: Assuring high performance in an age of complexity.* San Francisco, CA: Jossey-Bass.

Wheeless, L. R., & Williamson, A. M. (1992). State-communication apprehension and uncertainty in continuing initial interactions. *Southern Journal of Communication, 44,* 249–259.

Williams, K. J., & Alliger, G. M. (1994). Role stressors, mood spillover, and perceptions of work-family conflict in employed parents. *Academy of Management Journal, 37,* 837–868.

Williams, M. L., & Meredith, V. (1984). Physician-expectant mother communication: An analysis of information uncertainty. *Communication Research Reports, 1,* 110–116.

Zey, M. (1992). Criticisms of rational choice models. In M. Zey (Ed.), *Decision making: Alternatives to rational choice models* (pp. 9–31). Newbury Park, CA: Sage.

Appendix: Car Salesperson Interview Schedule

1. When a new customer you've never seen before enters your store or lot and you're not busy with another customer, do you always approach them? Why or why not?
2. What do you look for to make the decision to approach them or not?
3. What are some of the main types of customers that you deal with on a regular basis at your job (for example, the just-looking customer, bargain hunter, the eager-to-buy customer, etc.)?
   a. How would you describe each type?
   b. Are there any other common types? What are they like?
   c. How do you decide what type of customer a person is?
4. Are there any customers, new or previous, that you do not bother approaching?
   a. How do you make that decision?
   b. What do you think they would say if you would approach them?
   c. Does it ever bother you that you might have missed a sale?
5. On the opposite side, are there any types of new or previous customers that you almost always try to approach?
   a. How do you make that decision?
   b. What do you want to find out about them?
   c. How do you go about getting that information?
6. When you approach a new customer, do you always use the same strategy?
   a. How do you go about determining what type of sales strategy to use?
   b. What information do you use to make that decision?
   c. Do customers tell you things you don't need to know or care to know? What kinds of things don't interest you?
7. When you are trying a certain strategy with a customer, how do you know if it is working or not?
   a. When it's not working, what do you do?
   b. How do you select a new strategy?
   c. When do you stop trying to sell to a customer?

8. Do you ever get stuck in a conversation with a customer for longer than you would like?
   a. Why do you wish you could get out of the conversation?
   b. Why don't you get out of the conversation sooner?
   c. How do you get out of the conversation?
9. In my experience, sales people sometimes do a follow-up phone call when they don't make a sale on the initial contact. Do you ever do a follow-up call?
   a. What do you base that decision to call or not to call on?
   b. What do you hope to find out about the customer from the call?
   c. How do you decide to quit calling them back?
10. That was my last question. Is there anything else you might add that might help me understand how you or other sales people go about their initial interactions with customers?

Author Index

Subject Index